THE SECRET KINGDOM

THE SECRET KINGDOM

Pat Robertson

Your path to peace, love and financial security

WORD PUBLISHING

Word (UK) Ltd
Milton Keynes, England

WORD AUSTRALIA
Kilsyth, Victoria, Australia

WORD COMMUNICATIONS LTD
Vancouver, B.C., Canada

STRUIK CHRISTIAN BOOKS (PTY) LTD
Maitland, South Africa

CHRISTIAN MARKETING NEW ZEALAND LTD
Havelock North, New Zealand

JENSCO LTD
Hong Kong

JOINT DISTRIBUTORS SINGAPORE –
ALBY COMMERCIAL ENTERPRISES PTE LTD
and
CAMPUS CRUSADE

SALVATION BOOK CENTRE
Malaysia

THE SECRET KINGDOM

ISBN 0-85009-589-1 (Australia ISBN 1-86258-247-5)

Reproduced, printed and bound in Great Britain for Word (UK) Ltd., by Cox and Wyman Ltd., Reading.

93 94 95 96 / 10 9 8 7 6 5 4 3 2 1

Then He said to them, "These are the words which I spoke to you while I was still with you, that all things must be fulfilled which were written in the Law of Moses and the Prophets and the Psalms concerning Me." And He opened their understanding, that they might comprehend the Scriptures.

Luke 24:44–45 NKJV

Contents

Preface

During the steamy hot first days of August 1992, I found myself in an airport lounge at the British Airways terminal at Kennedy Airport in New York preparing to board a flight to London. I would make a connection there to my destination, Lusaka, Zambia, which is located at the center of one of the most savage droughts in the history of southern Africa. Hundreds of thousands of people in that troubled land have been experiencing dire poverty and possible starvation.

The scene at the airport was much as it was ten years ago when *The Secret Kingdom* was first published. Businessmen were intent on making deals in Europe. Families were ready for the vacation of a lifetime. Students were on their way to school. Tourists—replete with cameras, dark glasses, and polyester pants—were getting ready for the sights and sounds of the Old World.

Then I glanced at the front-page headlines of the day's *New York Times*. From left to right here were the day's headlines: SHELLING BY SERBS POUNDS SARAJEVO . . . TERRORIST BOMBS STRIP LIMA OF UTILITIES . . . 200 KILLED IN ASIA IN TWO PLANE CRASHES . . . LATIN DEBT LOAD KEEPS CLIMBING . . . DRUG RESISTANT TB IS SEEN SPREADING WITHIN HOSPITALS.

I asked myself, had the world improved in the ten years since *The Secret Kingdom* first appeared? The answer is both yes and no.

On the one hand, Communism has collapsed. The Berlin Wall has fallen. On the surface it appears that a superpower nuclear confrontation is no longer a threat to mankind.

Yet the world seems no better. Active, small-scale wars now total forty or more around the world. The debt load of the United States and its Western Allies has not abated, but accelerated wildly. From Somalia to Afghanistan, from Burma to Brazil, from Moscow to the Cape of Good Hope, there is crushing debt, unemployment, poverty, disease, political unrest, crime, ethnic tension, war, and now there has arisen a plague virtually unknown in 1982, the greatest killer since the Black Death, AIDS.

AIDS is a disease transmitted primarily by homosexual relations, extramarital heterosexual relations, and intravenous drug use. A shocking study printed in the July 27, 1992, issue of *U.S. News & World Report* indicated the potential by the year 2000 for 100 million deaths from AIDS, an annual cost for AIDS treatment between $81 to $107 billion in the United States, with that figure leaping to $356 to $514 billion worldwide.

Not only will all of the material progress of the developing countries during the past twenty years be drained by the AIDS epidemic, but a significant percentage of their key middle-level technicians and executives will be dead. In Zambia, for instance, where AIDS infection has touched 30 percent of the population, I was told by a high-ranking government official that Barclay's Bank is losing so many middle managers to AIDS that they are forced to hire two people for every job. Despite a veneer of extraordinary wealth in the United States, Western Europe, and Asia, there is an underlying fear that things are not right in our world. We see the meltdown of the enormously inflated Japanese stock market and the companion Japanese real estate market, and we realize that the accumulation of the wealth of a lifetime can vanish in a few months or even a few days of market panic.

We are in the most sexually liberated generation in modern history, yet this liberty has brought with it tragically shattered marriages and a holocaust of abortion which exceeds the worst barbarities of recorded history. The generation of children who remain—those we have permitted to live—are permanently scarred by divorce, neglect, and abandonment; by physical, mental, and sexual abuse; and by a pandemic rise in sexually transmitted diseases of all sorts.

In the United States, our elites have replaced God's clear moral law with their version of what is "politically correct." Situational ethics have replaced God's absolutes. The courts have so restricted religious instruction in the public schools of the United States that a legal challenge has been mounted against a family life sexual education curriculum in Jacksonville, Florida, by Planned Parenthood, on the grounds that teaching premarital sexual abstinence to young teenagers is a "religious doctrine" which violates the "separation of church and state."

It is now asserted that the practice of homosexuality is not the sinful abomination which the Bible declares it to be, but a protected civil right. Fornication and adultery are not only condoned but encouraged by countless subtle media messages. The message reaching most Americans in the 1990s is that nothing is morally wrong except lying to the press or the government, failing to pay income taxes, making racial slurs, or denigrating the open expression of homosexuality and lesbianism.

We do this in the name of pluralism, yet men's hearts cry out for *values* to give stability to their lives and conduct. Someone has defined pluralism as the name we give the transition from one orthodoxy to another. Without clearly defined values, people are confused, restless, and fearful. They lose hope, for to them the events of their lives and those around them seem to have lost their meaning.

To quote columnist Erma Bombeck from the August 12, 1992, edition of *USA Today,* "People are going crazy because there's no stability here anymore in our lives. There's no anchor. No center. People don't seem to have something they can hang onto and believe in anymore. People are really confused and they've lost their way."

But there is hope. God has given us a clear framework for our lives. His kingdom is not diminished by men's mistakes. In fact, it

11

glows brighter in the darkness. In the first edition of *The Secret Kingdom* I laid out a set of principles given by Jesus Christ which hold the answer to success in international relations, in national government, in business, in families, in personal life, and in the church. Now *The Secret Kingdom* has been revised to show how the timeless principles of God's eternal kingdom can dramatically touch the lives of those who face the problems of the 1990s. In addition I have added and illustrated two more key laws of the kingdom, the Law of Fidelity and the Law of Change.

In the words of Jesus Christ, "The time is fulfilled, and the kingdom of God is at hand. Have a change of mind and believe in the good news" (Mark 1:15, literal translation). Indeed at this very moment "the kingdom of God is at hand!" May its principles revolutionize your life as they have mine.

Introduction
to the First Edition

The yellow moon hung low over the Atlantic. Two hundred feet from the narrow beach the surf boomed and crashed, streaking white in the crystal moonlight. Beyond the breakers a hundred sea gulls settled for the night, rising and falling in the dark swells.

I turned and looked north. Cape Henry, shadowy under the soft sky, stretched before me, a gathering of sand dunes named after the eldest son of King James I of England. It was utterly peaceful, clutching to itself a history little noticed as the noisy twentieth century raced toward conclusion. For that gentle corner of the Chesapeake Bay's great mouth had been the stage for a small drama of unusual significance to America.

On April 26, 1607, a small band of settlers arrived from England to lay claim to a new world, stepping from their boats into the fine sands of the cape, anxious and weary. Three days later, amazed by this big fresh land, they carefully carried ashore a rough, seven-foot oak cross and plunged it into the sand. As they knelt around it, their spiritual leader, an Anglican clergyman named Robert Hunt, reminded them of the admonition of the British Royal Council, derived from the words of the Holy Scripture: "Every plant, which my heavenly Father hath not planted, shall be rooted up."[1]

With face turned toward heaven, the priest then dedicated the vast new land and their future in it to the glory of Almighty God.

Revived, eager, and joyful, these brave pioneers reboarded their tiny ships and sailed around Cape Henry and into the mouth of a river they named in honor of their monarch, James. Before long they sighted an outcropping along the banks that seemed entirely suitable to their immediate needs and on May 3 founded Jamestown, the first permanent English settlement on the North American continent.

Their "plantation" was indeed not "rooted up." From it and later settlements in Massachusetts, Rhode Island, Pennsylvania, New York, and Maryland grew the most prosperous nation in humanity's history. Unparalleled freedom and creativity burst upon the earth.

As I surveyed that historical site and looked eastward at the Atlantic beneath that dazzling moon, I was gripped by the renewed realization that a dread disease had fastened itself upon the lands sending forth our forefathers. As I turned westward toward my car, my mind's eye swept across the huge country that lay before me. And I mourned more deeply because the same sickness was fastening itself upon my land, the New World so sincerely dedicated to God 375 years ago.

Yes, the disease seemed epidemic throughout the earth. Could it be fatal? Was an "uprooting" to come?

So great are our problems that to think of them as incurable is not unreasonable. Thoughtful men frequently compare the recent course of Western civilization with the collapse of the ancient Roman Empire. Everywhere scholars, politicians, industrialists, financiers, sociologists, and futurists see grave trouble ahead. Yearningly, they look back to the optimistic beginnings of our country and the whispers seep from their pursed lips, "What went wrong?" "What happened to the hopes and aspirations of the pioneers?" "Were their brave struggles in vain?"

The thoughts accruing from many months of reading and meditation poured in upon me that night when I looked upon the Atlantic where the American dream had begun. I, like other concerned persons, seemed to have nothing but questions. Is our nation—our world—faced with collapse? Can we survive? Is our only choice between anarchy and dictatorship? Or is there an alternative?

More than any time in my life, I knew that night that we must urgently seek a third choice. I knew we would have to reach into the invisible world that has been there all along, a world far truer than any civilization in history. We have wasted too much time, decades of delay and doubt.

The challenges of my contemporaries rang in my ear: Is there truly an invisible world of the spirit? Is it possible to draw help from that invisible world? Can there be, as Presidents Carter and Bush have promised, a new world order?

Yes. It will not be a secular order but a divine one, ordained by God and conforming to the timeless principles of His kingdom.

This book comes from convictions about these questions. Its purpose is to foster understanding of the invisible world, better described as an invisible kingdom, the kingdom of God. It has principles. They can be learned.

My recognition of this has come slowly, spanning several years, and is still expanding. First was a prayer for wisdom, spoken quite naively, perhaps in the manner of King David's son Solomon. I desperately wanted to understand—God, the world, the present, the future, the working of things.

Oddly, or so it might seem, my first awareness of the possible answer to that prayer dawned as my interest became fixed on the words of John the Baptist in the early pages of the New Testament: "Repent, for the kingdom of heaven is at hand."[2]

I was struck by the words "at hand." What did they mean? Eventually my mind recalled similar words of Jesus, spoken the night of His betrayal as Judas approached with his rowdy gang: "the one who betrays Me is at hand!"[3]

In this case, the meaning was obvious. Judas had arrived; he was there. John the Baptist, using the same words, had obviously meant the same thing. The kingdom had arrived; it was there, at hand.

This was revolutionary understanding, as simple as it may seem these six or seven years later. I had been instructed to regard our time as the age of the church, and it is that in a very real sense, but John the Baptist and later the Lord Jesus Christ declared the arrival of the kingdom of God. Somehow I had failed to take seriously the fact that the kingdom of God is the central teaching of Jesus. He began His earthly ministry by declaring the arrival of the kingdom,[4] and He ended it when "he spoke to them about the kingdom of God."[5] Indeed He described such teaching as His ultimate purpose: "I must preach about God's kingdom to other towns, too. *This is why I was sent.*"[6]

That the kingdom of God was at the heart of the Lord's work is obvious, and furthermore He spoke of it as existing then and now, not to arrive at some far-distant time and place. The kingdom of God is in our midst.[7]

My constant prayers for wisdom brought additional insight over the weeks, months, and years, and I gradually perceived that Jesus had spoken quite precisely about how this kingdom worked. He was far from theoretical. He actually laid down specific principles, so sweeping that they might be better considered as laws, even at the risk of offending those who cringe at the merest hint of legalism. Jesus quite bluntly said, "If you do this, then this will happen." When He added no restrictions as to time, place, nationality, and the like, then they were laws, in the same sense as the natural laws established by God—those governing motion, gravity, sound, and such. They simply work.

Sitting in a big stuffed chair morning after morning in my living room, poring over the Scriptures, praying, thinking, making notes on a yellow legal pad, I uncovered one, then two, and three, and more of these major principles. But, equally important, I put them to work in my life, my family's life, and the life of the Christian Broadcasting Network. I wasn't interested in abstraction. I wanted to determine if they worked.

They did. And they do. They, and they alone, can alter the world's slide into anarchy or dictatorship. They offer a third choice.

Part 1

Two Domains

1

The Visible World

*T*he modern world is in crisis. Many people have the feeling that unless drastic changes are made quickly in the way this country is being run, the United States may not last out the century as the number-one superpower. We are moving rapidly into a state of social, intellectual, economic, and moral decline. Anywhere you look today you can see the evidence of looming disaster; you can hear urgent cries for change. Where can we turn for stability in our life? Is there anything or anyone to help us? The world as we know it is in chaos.

It is clearer each day that the world is hurtling toward some type of catastrophe. The upheavals in Eastern Europe and problems with the political process in the United States are ongoing concerns. The federal budget deficit is out of control, and the worldwide debate over ecology and the environment is escalating as never before. Anyone can see that our problems are only getting worse, and the people of America and the entire world are reaching the point of desperation. Some people are apparently willing to try solutions that are not well thought out or well reasoned, just to make a change.

Recently we saw what could happen when, in similar circumstances, a new president came into power virtually overnight in Peru and took drastic measures to restore order and balance in his country. The reformer, President Alberto Fujimori, effectively abandoned the democratic process. He could see that the system had grown corrupt, crime was out of control, and the entire nation was seemingly in peril, so he simply took matters into his own hands and the people went along with it. That is a potentially dangerous precedent. Yet, despite his dramatic action, months later terrorists were bombing the utilities of Lima, the capital city of Peru.

In this country we need only pause to consider what happened in the spring of 1992 in South Central Los Angeles. As a result of the unpopular jury decision in the Rodney King case, angry protesters took part in riots that cost more than forty lives and more than $1.5 billion in property damages. There is unrest and bitterness in the black community and a splintering of society. There is a deepening decline in moral values. What have we left to build upon? Everywhere people are crying out for something better.

In my book, *The New World Order*, I surveyed the conditions driving the world toward chaos. We don't hear as much about the government's world order agenda these days, but the conditions are still there, and, if anything, they are intensifying. Looking at the economic trends of the 1990s, it is clear that the exponential compounding of debt has taken us to the brink of economic collapse. Today there is a very real possibility of a money crisis to be followed by ruinous inflation.

During 1991 and '92 I was invited to go to Zaire and develop agricultural and economic programs to help aid that faltering economy. Zaire is an example of a rich, productive economy that collapsed under decades of mismanagement. Today anyone can see the results of the breakdown there. The currency has inflated from one zaire-to-three dollars to eight hundred thousand zaires-to-one dollar.

Nothing works properly. Airlines fly erratically; telephone service is not available; the roads are impassable; the hospitals have no medicine. Once an exporter of food, there is now not enough food for the people. Seventy percent of the people are unemployed. Forty percent of them have AIDS. There is catastrophe everywhere. Conditions for Zaire and other nations of Africa have plunged precipitously in the ten years since I first wrote down the principles of the secret kingdom.

Rich and Poor

In many parts of the world there is a heightened sense of uncertainty amid what seems to be incredible prosperity. The wealthy are very wealthy; those with access to capital have never had it so good. The wealth available to them is simply staggering. The statistics in various news magazines indicate that the percentage of wealth controlled by the top 1 percent of the population continues to grow while the bottom 63 percent of wage earners have experienced only marginal growth in income over the past decade.

Of course the economic structure is not totally frozen: Some people have been able to move from middle-income levels into the upper-income brackets—there is still some economic mobility—but there is no question that the total share of wealth to those in the upper-income categories has grown more rapidly than the other segments of society.

Over the past ten years CBN News has tracked the social and moral conditions of this nation, and the reports I have seen are shocking. The educational crisis is appalling. This country is becoming a nation of illiterates. We have also done story after story on crime, addiction, divorce, the collapse of the family, and other issues, and the situation is not getting any better. We don't see any signs in this country that things are improving.

Ironically, in the former Soviet Union moral conditions are no worse and potentially much better than here. At least there is a genuine hunger for moral and spiritual values, and that is the absolutely essential first step to recovery. It is ironic that while America is moving away from the heritage which made us great, the former Communist nations are seeking after God.

The key words in any description of our plight are economy, energy, crime, poverty, morality, education, hunger, and pollution. Volumes are written on each. And each carries the same deterioration theme—deterioration and danger. The great cosmic clock appears to be winding down.

All about us we see "fear in a handful of dust," in Eliot's words, as man stares horror-stricken at,

> A heap of broken images, where the sun beats,
> And the dead tree gives no shelter, the cricket no
> relief,
> And the dry stone no sound of water.[1]

Even starker are the images from the Book of Isaiah in which the Old Testament prophet speaks of the darkness that descends upon a people when they have been disobedient to the will of God. Isaiah writes:

> We grope for the wall like the blind,
> And we grope as if we had no eyes;
> We stumble at noonday as at twilight;
> We are as dead men in desolate places.
> We all growl like bears,
> And moan sadly like doves;
> We look for justice, but there is none;
> For salvation, but it is far from us.
> For our transgressions are multiplied before You,
> And our sins testify against us;
> For our transgressions are with us,
> And as for our iniquities, we know them.[2]

Just as Isaiah predicted, the world is crying out for solutions to problems that are too big for us. Our governments are on the verge of collapse; our finances are in desperate condition; the environment is polluted; millions die of starvation in Third World nations where the population is skyrocketing and industry is collapsing. Underlying fear is covered by a thin veneer of affluence. "'There is no peace,' / Says my God, 'for the wicked.'"[3]

Our condition is not difficult to understand. And the purpose of this book is not to dwell on that condition, but rather to explore reliable remedies. Nonetheless, to understand the encompassing nature of those remedies, we should take a few moments to set the stage of the visible world. We need only trace a few strands of the hangman's noose that seems poised over our heads, beginning with the most immediately destructive, the threat of nuclear holocaust.

The Age of Terror

Let us go back to 1940. Three physicists—Enrico Fermi, Leo Szilard, and Eugene Wigner—working in a makeshift laboratory in a handball court under the grandstand at the University of Chicago, split the atom and thereby confirmed the theoretical formula of Albert Einstein: $E=mc^2$. The split, or fission, caused a multiplication of energy in the order of 6 million-to-one.

At last man had found a source of cheap and abundant energy for the world forever. A new industrial revolution was at hand. Age-old territorial disputes would end. Wars would cease. The poor could be warmed, sheltered, fed. No nation need be without.

History records a different outcome. The work of those three deeply religious men evolved into an age of terror, not an age of abundance. There was Hiroshima. Then Nagasaki.

That was only the beginning. Physicists quickly perfected nuclear fusion and a release of energy of 50 million-to-one. Utilizing hydrogen, a fuel as abundant as the waters of the seas, this process held promise as the energy source of the millennium. There need be no fossil fuel shortage, no air pollution, no fabulously wealthy OPEC oil cartel, and no desperately poor Third World.

The utopia did not come. Instead we have hydrogen bombs rated in millions of tons of TNT. The superpower nations, during the fifties and sixties, built arsenals capable of destroying all life on earth. A balance of terror developed between the United States and the Soviet Union bearing the terrifying acronym MAD—Mutual Assured Destruction.

Then came the seventies. The United States, wearied by its struggle in Southeast Asia, gradually dismantled its military capability, delaying the start of weapons systems commensurate with advanced technology. The Soviet Union, meanwhile, pushed its flagging economy to the breaking point to build the most awesome array of weapons ever assembled by a nation in peacetime.

Instead of balance, the world of the 1980s was faced with an imbalance of terror in favor of a malevolent dictatorship bent on world domination. Ultimately it was the inherent weaknesses of the Soviet system which brought that giant colossus to its knees. Its economy was in such terrible decay after years of godless socialism, collapse was inevitable. Even though I had predicted the collapse of the Soviet Union as early as 1969, it was stunning to see that event fulfilled in 1989 and 1990.

Today it is clear that Marxism was a failure from the very beginning. Its leadership was corrupt. The people lacked incentive to work; moral decay destroyed the sanctity of the family. Faith in God was prohibited, thus the souls of the people grew pale and desperate. Some kind of change had to come about.

Today Russia and the Commonwealth of Independent States (CIS) are looking to the West for help. Having endured a long string of upsets, complicated by hunger, a shocking coup attempt, and general disarray, the leaders of these fifteen former Communist nations are more open-minded now than ever. But we should never forget that the majority of the former Soviet nuclear capability is still intact, and the possibility of a hardline pro-Communist coup is very real indeed.

And nuclear weapons have found their way to Iraq and Iran. Nuclear and chemical technology rests with the madman Saddam Hussein. Mohamar Qaddafi of Libya and Syrian President Hafez al Assad are still very real threats to peace. The nations controlling Middle East oil are often ruthless, as we witnessed in the Iraqi invasion of Kuwait and the events of Operation Desert Storm in the spring of 1991. Despite the apparent peace in the Middle East, our age still retains the potential to touch off World War III. "Age of terror" is an apt description. But there is a solution, as we will see.

The Struggle for Energy

Intertwined with the age of terror is the concern for sufficient energy to satisfy the mushrooming demands of our planet. Scientists believe the demand for energy may be as ominous as the nuclear threat, despite the deceptive ebb and flow in short-range supply and demand.

In 1950 there were 2.51 billion people in the world. By 1980 the figure soared to 4.41 billion. The demand for everything from food to factories skyrocketed. Today we have a worldwide population of nearly 6 billion people, and unless interrupted by drastic changes or some terrible catastrophe, by 2010 the population will exceed 8 billion men, women, and children. With a birthrate of 100 million per year and a death rate of 50 million, the population of the world is growing with unbelievable speed.

But nothing exploded like the demand for energy. In 1950 the world used the equivalent of 2.66 billion metric tons of coal. In 1980 consumption was 9.5 billion metric tons. Today the world consumes the equivalent of 14.5 billion metric tons of coal, and the demand continues to grow.

In thirty years the population had not quite doubled; yet energy use had more than tripled. We were running wild with everything that required fuel.

This massive growth presented a simple truth as the decade of the eighties got under way: The planet does not contain enough nonrenewable and renewable sources of energy to supply indefinitely the basic needs and growing aspirations of a world population that continues to explode.

It seems clear that if some sort of solution is not forthcoming, we face the following perilous prospects:

• Those possessing dwindling energy sources will extract ever-increasing prices. This trend will hold true in the long run, even when temporary conditions cause occasional price drops that give the world a false sense of security. If recent patterns continue, the cost of energy will place such insupportable burdens on worldwide industry and financial markets that money supplies will be imprudently increased. This could set off hyperinflation and lead to worldwide financial collapse.

• To prolong high-energy lifestyles, the developed nations may use military force to seize dwindling resources. The war in the Persian Gulf was after all not so much an exercise to support the rights of the oppressed as it was a move to protect our continued access to Middle East oil.

• As oil import costs continue to mount, industrially developed nations will show more and more strain as they try to maintain a balance of trade. Aggressive financial actions, including punitive trade measures, seem certain and will heighten world tension.

• The prognosis is even worse for the weaker nations. They simply do not have the money to buy oil and pay interest on their huge debts at the same time. Many face bankruptcy already. Such default by any of several nations can cause suffering internally and global economic confusion externally. It could trigger a worldwide bank collapse, for example, unless the United States is willing to bail out the country in trouble.

• America's cities pose a unique danger that has wide-ranging potential, traceable in large part to energy consumption and high costs. The mammoth office buildings, shopping centers, and apartment houses of New York, Detroit, Chicago, Cleveland, Boston, Philadelphia, and other cities are energy gluttons. The rising operating costs have been staggering. Compounding this financial burden is the fact that the physical plants of these cities—the sewers, water lines, and other underground support utilities, plus the roads, bridges, and other systems above ground—have far exceeded their life expectancies. The cities don't have the money for proper maintenance and replacement. Time bombs are ticking away both above and below ground. Should they begin to explode, the cities will be brought to their knees. The social and economic consequences nationally and globally will be staggering.

• Imprudent substitution of hazardous, untested energy sources in the face of diminishing traditional sources could present the world with intolerable environmental problems affecting all of life. Yet rigid regulation could inhibit exploration, discovery, and creativity needed to overcome shortages. The dilemma breeds deep strife.

• The reluctance and/or inability of car manufacturers to respond to worldwide energy problems threw a major portion of American industry into a tailspin that threatened the wider economy. By the early eighties, foreign car manufacturers, led by the Japanese, had seized 28 percent of U.S. domestic auto business. Today, including foreign transplant operations, that figure has grown to 30 percent. Many major American industries, in fact, have been badly hurt in recent years by foreign competition and trade practices. Anger and discontent are mounting, with a crescendo of protectionist threats all around us.

The struggle for energy and the manifold ramifications of that struggle have propelled the world to the brink of upheaval. Even the tiniest of international movements has the potential for escalation. We will see, however, that there are alternatives.

Economic Disaster

Picking up another related thread, we learned that the lesser-developed nations of the world owed more than $500 billion to banks and wealthier nations early in 1981. Annual interest on those loans approached $100 billion, which was $35 billion more than the total debt of those nations only eight years earlier. Now, by 1992, just the Latin American nations have a combined debt of $442.7 billion. Tragically, they are being forced to borrow simply to pay their interest charges. A number of loans are being refinanced so the nations do not appear to be in default.

During this period, Poland was in the news as its people suffered the penalty of reaching for freedom from Soviet-led repression. That country's disastrous financial condition is typical of many other countries of the world. In 1982 it owed $24 billion of the total $89 billion owed to the West by Russia and the Eastern Bloc countries. By 1987, Poland's debt had soared to more than $40 billion. An agreement by foreign creditors arranged by the Paris Club in 1991 to write off nearly half that amount has given them some leverage, but current debt remains at more than $25 billion, and today the hopes of the Polish people for democracy and privatization remain in doubt.

It seems certain, with so many countries in a condition like Poland's, that one day a scene similar to the following will be played out.

A sweaty-palmed finance minister from Russia or Brazil or Poland will sit in a room in Switzerland or Germany or France and be told by several dignified bankers that his country's loans are in default. No more money is available. When word leaks out, the canny finance minister from oil-rich Kuwait, Abu Dhabi, Saudi Arabia, Iraq, or Libya could quietly withdraw his country's deposits from the banks in question. When word of this withdrawal is circulated, a wild scramble to get cash out of weakening banks could result.

Major institutions could fall like dominoes overnight. Eurodollar certificates of deposit could be wiped out, along with other large domestic certificates. Broad-based money market funds could lose virtually all their bank assets. There would very possibly have to be a nationwide freeze on bank withdrawals in this country to prevent a collapse of the banking system. Bonds, stocks, gold, silver, and jewels would fall like stones. Trade and commerce could be brought to a standstill.

Only a multinational effort to print a trillion or more dollars could stave off fiscal disaster. And this rescue would merely accelerate post-World War I, German-style hyperinflation, followed eventually by a worse crash.

In 1974–75 the world economy lurched, and several big banks and real estate operations failed, but the system held together. In 1980 it lurched again. That time silver crashed and the bond market lost $300 billion. Many financial institutions became technically insolvent as the market value of their bond and mortgage portfolios plunged in the wake of a 21 percent prime interest rate. One major bank failed and Chrysler became a government ward, but the system survived.

It lurched again with the savings and loan collapse, but was saved by a $500 billion federal bailout. Despite high profits, banks and insurance companies have neither restored liquidity as they did after the mid-seventies problem, nor have their portfolios improved as much as desired. Nonbank businesses are still illiquid and over-extended despite recent dramatic drops in short-term interest rates.

Furthermore, the U.S. government continues to borrow to cover budget deficits. The federal deficit is a record $400 billion and the direct debt is a mind-boggling $4 trillion. Inflation, although dipping at least temporarily, can still come alive quickly. It seems built into the system at every level. Prices do not actually fall; their rate of increase merely slows.

Questions are inevitable. Are major business and financial institutions, as well as individuals, bound for bankruptcy? Will this trigger the sort of doomsday scenario described above?

There are options, as we will see.

A Tailspin in Morality

As the nineties unfold, nothing portrays our world crisis more clearly than man's internal and moral condition. The unmistakable scent of what the Bible calls the antichrist spirit is in the air. It was present at the tower of Babel and at Sodom and Gomorrah. It was present in the French Revolution and in Nazi Germany. And it is present in Europe and the United States today. The signs of this spirit are clear. They emerge in this fashion: A significant minority, then an actual majority, of the people in a society begin to throw off the restraints of history, then the restraints of written law, then accepted standards of morality, then established religion, and, finally, God Himself.

As the rebellion gains momentum, the participants grow bolder. Those practices that once were considered shameful and unlawful move into the open. Soon the practitioners are aggressive, militant. As each societal standard falls, another comes under attack. The pressure is relentless. Established institutions crumble. Ultimately the struggle that began as a cry for freedom of expression grows into an all-out war against the rights of advocates of traditional morality. The latter are hated, reviled, isolated, and then persecuted.

Honor, decency, honesty, self-control, sexual restraint, family values, and sacrifice are replaced by gluttony, sensuality, bizarre sexual practices, cruelty, profligacy, dishonesty, delinquency, drunkenness, drug-induced euphoria, fraud, waste, debauched currency, and rampant inflation,

The people then search for a deity that will both permit and personify their basest desires. At Babel it was a tower—man's attempt to glorify himself. In ancient Mediterranean cultures, like those of Sodom and Gomorrah, it was a god or goddess of sex. In France, it was the goddess of reason; in Germany, Hitler and the Nazi party; in Europe and especially in the United States, the god of central government under the religion of secular humanism.

The pattern is always the same. So is the result. No society falling under the grip of the Antichrist spirit has survived. First comes a period of lawlessness and virtual anarchy, then an economic collapse followed by a reign of terror. Then comes a strong dictator who plunders society for his personal aggrandizement; he dreams of a worldwide empire and storms into war. Eventually come defeat and collapse.

In some cases God intervenes directly to destroy the Antichrist society before it reaches full flower. In others, the society destroys itself. Sometimes a righteous nation takes action; in others the task is performed by stronger barbarians. But always there is destruction.

In the United States, trends, also reflected in other countries, are well defined:

• Organized crime is the largest industry in the land. With gross revenues of $150 billion, the profits of crime eclipse the profits of the American oil or auto industries, producing power and influence that compromise and corrupt the fabric of society. The impact of illegal drug use, as only one example, is staggering. In

1981 cocaine grossed $35 billion and marijuana $24 billion, establishing that Americans spent more on those two illegal drugs than they contributed to all charities, education, and religion combined. By 1991, there were 6.3 million users of cocaine in the United States and 19.5 million users of marijuana, and national spending on drugs continues to climb.

• The sexual revolution has snaked its way into the schools, the homes, and virtually all of society. Traditional standards regarding nudity, fornication, adultery, homosexuality, incest, and sadomasochism have been under fierce attack and many are crumbling. Educators deluded by humanism are offering sex education without moral standards to children; some courses appear to advocate masturbation, premarital sex, and homosexuality. Motion pictures, television, and the publishing industry pour the excesses of unbridled gratification into communities and homes.

• From this rampant hedonism has emerged permission to minimize the inconvenient side effects of sexual pleasure. The Supreme Court ruled that the thing conceived through sexual relations between two humans is not itself a human and therefore may be destroyed prior to the fourth month of pregnancy. The killing of unborn infants through abortion has thus proceeded at the rate of 1.5 million a year.

• At the same time, family life has been battered. In the decade of the seventies, the number of couples living together outside of marriage doubled, and divorce reached a rate of one for every two marriages. But data were not crystallized for the marred lives of children caught in the breakup of families, for the suicides of young and old unable to survive the trauma of sudden rootlessness, for the wasted lives of despair.

Financial morality has been corrupted as the government, exalted by humanist philosophy, has become god and provider. In 1941 the population of the United States was 133.7 million; government spending was $13.6 billion. Forty years later the population had grown by 72 percent, to 229.3 million; federal spending had grown by 4,762 percent, to $661.2 billion. By 1992 the population had grown to 250 million, an increase of 92 percent over 1940, yet the spending of the federal government had grown an astounding $1.5 trillion, an increase of 10,929 percent over 1940. We have already touched on the result: federal debt nearing $4 trillion, ever-increasing inflation, and domestic and world economies in danger of collapse.

• As self-restraint and regard for God rapidly diminish under the assault of secular humanism, a new rule of law has been emerging. Judges are less inclined to make decisions based on the Bible, the Constitution, natural laws, or precedent. Instead, they often impose as a rule of law whatever seems sociologically expedient or whatever reflects the prevailing sentiment of the ruling elite. As Justice Charles Evans Hughes declared early in the century, "The Constitution is what the judges say it is," pointing to a trend in which a government based on men's opinions would supersede a government based on laws. Lawlessness has thus come a long way.

But we will see that there is a remedy.

Revolt Against God

Underlying all the threads we have examined as integral to the deepening crisis coming upon the world—and we have examined only a fraction of them—is one that transcends all others. It is the increased disregard for the Creator of the world.

Shortly after the turn of the century, a false view of reality began to take hold in America. Although its name did not become well known immediately, humanism spread into all aspects of life and became the dominant philosophical view about the time of World War II. Today millions of people openly embrace it, and many millions more follow along under its influence.

Francis A. Schaeffer, the Christian philosopher-theologian, described humanism's influence this way:

> . . . the humanist world view includes many thousands of adherents and today controls the consensus in society, much

of the media, much of what is taught in our schools, and much of the arbitrary law being produced by the various departments of government.

The term humanism used in this wider, more prevalent way means Man beginning from himself, with no knowledge except what he himself can discover and no standards outside of himself. In this view Man is the measure of all things, as the Enlightenment expressed it. . . .

Since [the humanists'] concept of Man is mistaken, their concept of society and of law is mistaken, and they have no sufficient base for either society or law. They have reduced Man to even less than his natural finiteness by seeing him only as a complex arrangement of molecules, made complex by blind chance. Instead of seeing him as something great who is significant even in his sinning, they see Man in his essence only as an intrinsically competitive animal, that has no other basic operating principle than natural selection brought about by the strongest, the fittest, ending on top. And they see Man as acting in this way both individually and collectively as society.[4]

Thus, for a vast number of people, God has been removed from the center of things, and man has taken His place. All things exist for man and his pleasure.

In a church-state dialogue sponsored in 1981 by the Virginia Council of Churches, a professor of humanistic studies summed up the direction of American leadership most clearly: "We must throw off the tyranny of the concept that the Bible is the Word of God. We must be freed from the tyranny of thought that comes from Martin Luther, John Calvin, [Ulrich] Zwingli, and John Knox."

He discarded the Bible as the authoritative guide for faith and conduct, casting with it such long-accepted truths as the doctrine of man's sinfulness, the doctrine of eternal reward and eternal punishment, the necessity for repentance and justification by faith in Jesus Christ, and the necessity for holy living to please God. Such astounding recommendations can only be grasped when one recalls the words of *Humanist Manifesto I* and *II* (produced in 1933 and 1973), which denied the "existence of a supernatural God who hears and answers prayer."

With all standards and yardsticks removed, society first eased, then rushed toward the extremes of hedonism and nihilism, with increasing numbers finding fulfillment in "doing their own thing."

"If it feels good, do it," comes the advice of everyone from parents to psychologists. This, they say, is freedom. Meanwhile, as we noted earlier, nothing works. Bodies wear out early as sickness and disease soar. Never has there been so much cancer, so much heart disease. Brains, too, wear out. Never have emotional and mental breakdowns run so high; never have suicides reached such levels. Schools fail; businesses fail; governments fail.

Yes, humanism and its society are failing, although seemingly few have perceived the depth of that failure. Most see only symptoms, not the underlying sickness.

Perhaps the bright spot for those of faith is that the collapse of the Soviet Union showed the world the stark and terrible failure of a social and political system founded on humanism. Despite its seemingly unassailable grip on the power centers of Western society, humanism has clearly been exposed as a failed system that cannot withstand the assault of resolute faith. In the 1990s and beyond, the battle is not going to be fought much longer between Christianity and atheistic humanism, but between Christianity and satanic-inspired Eastern religions. In truth the collapse of Communism has opened up for the Soviet Union, the Eastern Bloc countries, and the so-called Third World the greatest religious revival in the history of mankind.

Inevitable Conclusions

The fear has become widespread that our society—and the world's—is beyond repair. There is confusion everywhere. At times the confusion approaches chaos. It seems clear that we will slide further into chaos, the jungle of anarchy: "I've got mine; to heck with you"—"do unto others before they can do unto you"—"every man for himself," or in desperation we will yield to dictatorship. Which will it be?

It matters not that both of the prevailing philosophies of materialism have been proven corrupt and ineffective. Communism said materialism is the goal but the state should control it. Now Communism has fallen. Emerging democracy and capitalism go hand in hand. But unbridled capitalism strives for materialism and the strong control of it. Both systems without a biblical balance will move toward dictatorship, either oligarchical or individual.

Eventually a strong man will be chosen if secular, capitalist materialism fails—unless we turn to the third choice that is available to us.

What will we do?

2

The Invisible World

*T*hroughout His earthly ministry, Jesus Christ preached the good news of the kingdom. He said, "The time is fulfilled, and the kingdom of God is at hand. Repent, and believe in the gospel."[1] That was His central message. He instructed His followers to go out and teach the people and to tell them that "The kingdom of heaven is at hand."[2] For when Christ came as Messiah, He was the fulfillment of Old Testament prophecy and the realization of the promises of God toward His people. That is the central truth of Christianity.

Jesus brought the kingdom with Him, and He left tangible and very real evidence of the kingdom in our hands when He was taken up into heaven. When Christ went ahead to prepare a place for us, He fully expected us to claim the rights and privileges of our citizenship from that moment on.

Jesus taught that the kingdom has two dimensions: the immediate and visible, which we see, and the invisible kingdom, which we do not see now but which will be fully revealed at the close of this age. From beginning to end, the Bible teaches that these two dimensions are real and very powerful.

True enough, the people of His own day wanted tangible evidence of God's power. They wanted to see signs and miracles; they wanted physical bread and wine; and they wanted assurances that their king would be either a great conqueror or a great provider. In teachings such as the Sermon on the Mount and the Beatitudes, Jesus made many promises about the kingdom to come, but He also taught them to live in the kingdom of God's present revelation. He told them to trust in God not only for their spiritual food, but for their earthly needs as well. He said:

> Therefore do not worry, saying, "What shall we eat?" or "What shall we drink?" or "What shall we wear?" For after all these things the Gentiles seek. For your heavenly Father knows that you need all these things. But seek first the kingdom of God and His righteousness, and all these things shall be added to you. Therefore do not worry about tomorrow, for tomorrow will worry about its own things. Sufficient for the day is its own trouble.[3]

The truths of Christ's teachings were not merely comforting ideas, pious meditations, or convenient philosophies. Jesus taught that these principles were to be understood in all their reality by anyone who would truly listen to what He was saying. "For there is nothing hidden which will not be revealed, nor has anything been kept secret but that it should come to light. If anyone has ears to hear, let him hear."[4]

The principles of the invisible kingdom in our midst do not change. They apply to all people in all situations, everywhere, equally. I have seen rapt attention to them recently in Zaire among those looking to become successful leaders. I've seen families that give them the same kind of attention. These principles have applications in every situation. And even while the world seems to be in constant change around us, the principles are faithful and true.

I firmly believe that the principles of the kingdom are God's answer for the world in which we live in the 1990s and the coming new millennium. Their insights into the workings of the kingdom can offer powerful solutions to the problems of this or any other time.

Calm Amid the Storm

Fortunately, a Voice speaks steadily and clearly into the turmoil and dread of the day, a Voice that contradicts our finitude and limitation and restriction. It says, "But seek first His kingdom and His righteousness; and all these things shall be added to you."[5]

Obviously the words are those of Jesus, climaxing a teaching about food, clothing, shelter, and all the "things" needed for life. God, His heavenly Father, was able and eager to provide the necessities for happy, successful living on Earth if the people merely turned to the right place—His kingdom.

His point immediately established a fact that the world has in large measure refused to consider—the fact that an invisible world undergirds, surrounds, and interpenetrates the visible world in which we live. Indeed, it controls the visible world, for it is unrestricted, unlimited, infinite.

The problem of the world, and of many Christians, has not been simply refusing to acknowledge the possibility of such a kingdom, but failing to perceive that it exists right now, not in some far-off time or far-off place called heaven. This is so strange because Jesus spent virtually all of His earthly ministry telling people that the kingdom of God had come and then explaining its workings.

For reasons that are beyond our comprehension, even we Christians missed it as we soaked up the good news of salvation, the fullness of the Holy Spirit, the fellowship of the church, and the future millennium. In fact, it is embarrassing today, as we begin to glimpse the core of what Jesus was doing, to note that practically everything He said pertained to the "kingdom." For example, His first utterance in His public ministry, according to Matthew, was: "Repent, for the kingdom of heaven is at hand."[6]

Each of the Gospel writers said it similarly. "The time has come," Jesus declared, in essence. "The kingdom is here, and I've come to open it to you and to show you how it works."

His pattern recalls the days following the anointing of Saul as Israel's first king when it became necessary for the prophet Samuel to teach how things should work: "Then Samuel told the people the manner of the kingdom, and wrote it in a book, and laid it up before the LORD."[7]

Jesus did much the same, teaching His followers "the manner of the kingdom," but leaving it to others to put it in writing.

Many of us are now discovering this central purpose of our Lord, perceiving that the kingdom of God, though invisible, is right now nonetheless real, nonetheless powerful. We are much like the servant of Elisha who went outside the tent one morning and saw Syrian troops ready to close in on them from every side.

"We're surrounded!" he yelled.

But Elisha calmly asked the Lord to open the young man's eyes. Then he saw into the invisible world. Chariots of fire, the heavenly host, were everywhere about them, protecting Elisha. As the prophet had said, "those who are with us are more than those who are with them."[8]

Things That Endure

Yes, the kingdom of God is here—now. And the message of the Bible is that we can and should look from this visible world, which is finite, into the invisible world, which is infinite. We should look from a world filled with impossibilities into one filled with possibilities.

We should do more than look, however, if we believe the Scriptures. We should enter. We should reach from the visible into the invisible and bring that secret kingdom into the visible through its principles—principles that can be adopted at this moment.

"The kingdom of God is like this . . . ," Jesus said, in effect. "It operates this way . . ." "If you want this, then do this . . ." Over and over.

So real is this invisible world, that when Jesus comes to Earth the second time, things will be turned inside out, through a sort of skinning process, you might say—and the invisible will become visible. The kingdom of God and its subjects will be manifested—unveiled. In the language of Paul's letter to the Romans: "The creation waits eagerly for the revealing of the sons of God."[9] It "groans and suffers"—"standing on tiptoe," according to J. B. Phillips's translation—as it yearns for that unveiling.

The apostles had a foretaste of the inside-out effect during their days with Jesus. First came a statement by the Lord that has puzzled many Bible readers through the centuries: "Truly I say to you, there are some of those who are standing here who shall not taste death until they see the Son of Man coming in His kingdom."[10]

A most marvelous event occurred six days later. We refer to it as the Transfiguration. Taking Peter, James, and John with Him, Jesus went to a high mountain.

> And He was transfigured before them; and His face shone like the sun, and His garments became as white as light. And behold, Moses and Elijah appeared to them, talking with Him. And Peter answered and said to Jesus, "Lord, it is good for us to be here; if You wish, I will make three tabernacles here, one for You, and one for Moses, and one for Elijah." While he was still speaking, behold, a bright cloud overshadowed them; and behold, a voice out of the cloud, saying, "This is My beloved Son, with whom I am well-pleased; hear Him!" And when the disciples heard this, they fell on their faces and were much afraid. . . . And lifting up their eyes, they saw no one, except Jesus Himself alone.[11]

The Lord became like lightning, shining white, and what had been invisible within Him became visible. The inside became the outside. The Law (Moses) and the prophets (Elijah) were fulfilled, and the Son of Man (Jesus) came visibly in His kingdom, in power and glory.

The disciples had a taste of what the kingdom will be at its manifestation. But what they saw at that moment had been resident in Jesus all the time. It had merely been invisible, but no less real and powerful. And that is what the Lord was telling His followers to lay hold of when He instructed them to seek the kingdom first so that all of their needs would be met.

"Reach into the invisible and apply it to the visible," He said, in effect. "For all things are possible with God."[12]

The Unlimited World of Jesus

Almighty God has been warning for thousands of years that because of our foolishness we will face crises. We are face to face with nuclear terror, a massive energy shortage, an insoluble economic crisis, debilitating moral bankruptcy, and other impossible difficulties. But Jesus explained that we are limited in our ability to cope with such problems only because we insist on living according to the ways of a world that is limited.

In effect he has said, "That need not remain so. An unlimited world surrounds you.

"You are finite; it is infinite.

"You are mortal; it is immortal.

"You are filled with impossibilities; it is filled with possibilities."

That was the world of Jesus, even when He came as a man to live on this finite earth. He was careful to say, "the Son can do nothing of Himself, unless it is something He sees the Father doing; for whatever the Father does, these things the Son also does in like manner."[13]

The invisible world of His Father was Jesus' world throughout His incarnation. It was a world where everything was beautiful. And He became upset when His disciples failed to follow His example.

Once, when they were in the middle of the Sea of Galilee on a boat journey Jesus had instructed them to make, a storm arose and their mission was near failure as their little vessel was swamped and showed signs of sinking. They rushed to wake Him from a much-needed nap. He was visibly perplexed. Why hadn't they been able to cope with the situation? They had failed to see into the invisible world where there were no impediments to the Lord's mission, and they had allowed themselves to be limited by world conditions.

So Jesus Himself arose and spoke to the storm, calming it. He then asked a rather humbling question: "Why are you timid, you men of little faith?"[14]

They had refused to reach into the world of the possible. And Jesus was angry, frustrated by the unwillingness of those He loved to accept the truth of what He had told them. One cannot help but wonder about His frustration as His followers seem so impotent to overcome the visible world today.

A Major Lesson

The Gospel according to Mark contains one of the Lord's most compact, yet most comprehensive, teachings about how to manifest the power of the invisible world in the visible today. Although we will be exploring the passage in more detail later, it is so significant for our initial understanding of the kingdom that we need to look at it in part now.

Jesus set the stage for the teaching when, on the way with His disciples to the temple to deal with the mockery practiced there under the guise of worship, He walked up to a fig tree in leaf, examined it for fruit, found none, and said: "May no one ever eat fruit from you again."[15]

We must understand immediately that Jesus was not being capricious or petulant. He didn't simply lose His temper. The fig tree, as is so often the case in Scripture, symbolized Israel in biblical times. When He cursed it, He was symbolically addressing a religious system that was often outwardly showy and inwardly fruitless. It was a system that practiced money changing and the selling of doves for sacrifice within the temple walls but gave the people little to feed their souls. He cursed that practice, too, as the Scripture goes on to report, and drove the money changers from the premises: "It is written in the Scriptures, 'My Temple will be called a house for prayer for people from all nations.' But you are changing God's house into a 'hideout for robbers.'"[16]

No, He was not showing off. As with everything in His brief time on earth, the Lord made a point of tremendous significance. The next morning it came to light.

Jesus and His disciples passed the fig tree on the way back into Jerusalem and it had died, withered under His curse. Still failing to perceive the invisible world but yet observing its effects, Peter blurted out, "Look, the fig tree you cursed is all dried up!"

Then came the simplest insight into the deepest phenomenon: "Jesus answered, 'Have faith in God.'"[17]

Those four words burst through the frontiers of heaven, laying bare the invisible kingdom. *Have faith in God.* We must totally believe in and trust Almighty God. We must know that One sits on the throne of the universe, as John saw in his great vision in the Book of the Revelation.[18] He controls everything to the uttermost. He is without peer. He is omnipotent, omniscient, and omnipresent—the only free, unrestricted being in the universe.

Kathryn Kuhlman often said during her powerful ministry, "I sometimes think we're too familiar with God." She was right. Many times it seems we are trying to make Him into a toy that we can wind up and get to do our bidding. We sing Him little songs and utter all manner of things that threaten to demean His utter sovereignty. Kathryn's point was that God is God Almighty, the Great I AM. He created the sun and the moon and the earth and the solar system. It is staggering! He merely said, "Let there be light,"[19] and the power of a billion hydrogen bombs began to move, rolling from one end of the solar system to the other. The distances and the energy are awesome. And they clearly illustrate the truth that a power exists in the universe transcending anything finite man's tiny mind can imagine. Paul the apostle put it into words, but even they are inadequate: "Now to Him who is able to do exceeding abundantly beyond all that we ask or think . . ."[20]

That is God. And Jesus said, "Have faith in Him." Touch Him, He said, and anything is possible.

The Living Presence

The Lord wants us in league with His Father. His teachings make it plain that total faith and trust in God—for every breath and every second—are to produce a oneness with Him. We are to see with Him, think with Him, as Jesus did, so that we can say along with Jesus that we do only what we see the Father doing.

That way, we will reach into the invisible world even though living in the visible.

In the fig tree episode, Jesus went on to explain another point that will be dealt with fully in another chapter, but for now we will simply reflect on it:

> Truly I say to you, whosoever says to this mountain, "Be taken up and cast into the sea," and does not doubt in his heart, but believes that what he says is going to happen, it shall be *granted* him. Therefore I say to you, all things for which you pray and ask, believe that you have received them, and they shall be granted you.[21]

In short, Jesus told His disciples that if they truly had faith in God, believed in His absolute sovereignty and mighty power, and entered into league with Him, they would become participants in the same energy and power that prevailed at the Creation. They would work as God works, be fellow workers with Him, in the words of Paul.[22]

Yes, Jesus said, there is an invisible world, but we can see into it and touch it—here, now. God works; He wants us to work.

The great book of the Bible dealing with the early church, the Book of Acts, doesn't have a conclusion. It just stops with the apostle Paul in his own rented house, receiving all who came to see him in Rome. That was the end of the account. Some of the Gospels indicate that they are the good news of what Jesus began to do and to teach. Jesus told His disciples that they would do the things that He did and greater things because He was going to be with His Father and would send the Holy Spirit to guide them.

There has never been any thought in the Christian church until very recently that the miracles of Jesus stopped. In fact, in the Third World in particular, we are seeing an explosion of miraculous activity. We are receiving astonishing reports from Africa where there are healings of every known malady. People who were dead are actually being raised again. There are miraculous provisions of food. There have been storms that have been stilled, and large rain clouds have been dispersed over the open-air evangelistic meetings.

It just seems that in the world today the fastest growing segment of Christianity is what is called the charismatic group. Those numbers have been estimated at anywhere between 160 million and 360 million people. Now, for these believers, miracles are an article of faith: They are taken as part of what they receive when they become Christians.

At CBN we have seen tens of thousands of answers to prayer. I recall one dramatic instance that occurred when I was campaigning for the presidency of the United States in 1987. I had addressed a Republican party luncheon in Huntington, West Virginia, accompanied by a reporter for the *New York Times.* As I was leaving the luncheon, a young man came up to me and said, "Mr. Robertson, I've got to talk to you." So I listened. He said, "I was blind, and I was watching 'The 700 Club,' and after prayer I began to see." I said, "Well, thank you very much." But he stopped me again and said, "But you don't understand. I was blind and now I can see!" He wasn't exaggerating; he was thrilled because God had performed a miracle in his life, and he was changed.

This kind of thing has been repeated over and over again. I meet people who were dying of cancer, and they say that because of prayer they were completely restored to health. On many occasions women with little children in their arms have come up to me and said, "My husband and I were barren; we couldn't have children. After prayer with the people on your program, we conceived a child."

I will never forget the Jewish man who lived in Nazareth, the hometown of Jesus. He was paralyzed from the waist down, and was watching from a wheelchair our "700 Club" program being broadcast through our station in Lebanon called Middle East Television. On that broadcast, our co-hostess, Danuta Soderman, during a time of prayer received a word from God that someone in the audience who was paralyzed was being healed. She spoke this word, the program was recorded, and the Israeli man in Nazareth watched the tape replay. He went to bed totally paralyzed, but when he woke up the next morning there was feeling in his feet and legs.

For the first time in years he stood up without a brace and walked. When our film crew recorded him some months later, he was jogging around the streets of Nazareth. He now has a vibrant testimony of his faith in Jesus as his Messiah. That is just one of the tens of thousands of miracles that have been reported to us concerning prayer offered on our program.

George Gallup told me several years ago of his findings that at least 7.5 million Americans have reported some kind of miraculous answer to prayer, primarily in relation to physical healing.

Principles of the Kingdom

Having been trained and surrounded by Christians who did not concern themselves especially with the Lord's teachings on the reality of the kingdom here and now, I didn't begin to catch glimpses of this reality in any meaningful way until the mid-seventies. I, too, had dwelt pretty much on the good news of salvation and the work of the Holy Spirit in believers' lives, and that truly is good news. But there is much more.

By mid-decade, I was wrestling with John the Baptist's insistence that "the kingdom of heaven is at hand."[23] As I have said, I soon saw he was reporting that the kingdom was here—here on earth—obviously because Jesus Christ was here.

I mused over this for many weeks and months, tracking through the Scriptures, praying for wisdom, and talking with one or two friends. As I badgered the Lord for wisdom, I began to realize that there are principles in the kingdom as enunciated by Jesus Christ and that they are as valid for our lives as the laws of thermodynamics or the law of gravity. The physical laws are immutable, and I soon saw that the kingdom laws are equally so.

How can we determine those principles? They are found in the Bible. When we see a statement of Jesus that is not qualified as to time or recipient, then we have uncovered a universal truth. If He uses the terms "whosoever" or "whatsoever" or some other sweeping generalization, we should be especially alert. He is probably declaring a truth that will apply in every situation, in every part of the world, in every time.

It sounds so simple, and it is. Not every word spoken by the Lord had direct application for everyone; some were restricted. But others were without restriction—a "house divided against itself shall not stand,"[24] for example.

Once we perceive this secret, we realize anew that the Bible is not an impractical book of theology, but rather a practical book of life containing a system of thought and conduct that will guarantee success. And it will be true success, true happiness, true prosperity, not the fleeting, flashy, inconsistent success the world usually settles for.

The Bible, quite bluntly, is a workable guidebook for politics, government, business, families, and all the affairs of mankind.

There are dozens of these principles sprinkled throughout, and they are all marvelous. But there are several broad, overriding ones that I like to think of as "laws" of the kingdom. They span all of life, often overlapping and supplementing one another, but never contradicting. We will be probing into those major ones that hold special potential for revolutionizing our time and world.

They give us an alternative in our current world dilemma.

Now Is the Time

Think for a moment about those strange words of Jesus, "seek first His kingdom and His righteousness; and all these things shall be added to you."[25]

So many of us see the words and are conscience-stricken. But for the wrong reasons.

We say, "Oh, if I could only bring myself to pray a lot and read the Bible and go to church every day, then God would like me and I would be His, and He would send His blessing to me."

We are not even certain we understand what we mean when we say "blessing."

Jesus was much more concrete than that. He was saying, "The kingdom of God rules in the affairs of men. It has principles for living, and they will bring success." Indeed, they will bring forth the kinds of things the world needs so desperately—the food, the shelter, the clothing, the fuel, the happiness, the health, the peace.

"But you shouldn't spend all your time and concentration seeking those things," He said in effect. "Seek the kingdom, understand the way it works, and then, as day follows night and as spring follows winter, the evidences of earthly success will follow you."

If we press this through to its logical conclusion, possibilities for life will rise up that we long ago relegated to the musty, unused portions of our Bibles, thinking of them as those promises made for a future time referred to as "the millennium." We will see that many of those conditions—those blessings we feared might turn out to be lofty Bible language that would pass us by—can be experienced in large measure right now. For they exist in the kingdom now. And we are speaking of reaching into that kingdom and letting its principles govern us right now.

Only God will inaugurate the visible reign on earth of His Son and those who will rule with Him,[26] but His word for the last two thousand years has been to "prepare the way."[27] His purpose is that His people know Him and learn how His secret kingdom functions. For the most part, we have fallen far short. But the word persists, and we can readily expect the willing fulfillment of some of the millennium blessings, like those foreseen by the prophet Isaiah, if we will follow His instructions:

> They will not hurt or destroy in all My holy
>   mountain,
> For the earth will be full of the knowledge of the
>   LORD
> As the waters cover the sea.[28]

> . . . they will hammer their swords into
> plowshares, and their spears into pruning
> hooks.

Nation will not lift up sword against nation,
And never again will they learn war.[29]

There *can* be peace; there *can* be plenty; there *can* be freedom. They will come the minute human beings accept the principles of the invisible world and begin to live by them in the visible world.

Can mankind do that? We will see how.

3

Seeing and Entering

*W*hy is there so much controversy about the divinity of Jesus Christ? If Jesus were only a historical figure with no importance in this modern world, why is He constantly in the news? Why is He the subject of books, films, speeches, debates, sermons, plays, documentaries, television specials, court cases, public hearings, and articles of every kind? If Jesus were only a good man, why is He still a figure of such heated debate?

During the past several months, the Dead Sea Scrolls have been in the news a great deal. Even though the scrolls were discovered by a group of Arab shepherds in a Jordanian cave in 1947, it was not until late 1991 that authenticated photographs of the ancient texts were circulated among scholars and researchers. That event precipitated another round of conjecture and debate.

Doubtless there were many reasons for keeping these important documents under wraps. Harvard University Professor John Strugnell, an Oxford-trained specialist in ancient Semitic texts and a renowned Bible scholar, told reporters he had hoped to produce an exact and reliable translation before releasing any preliminary fragments of the scrolls. After all, there are dozens (actually hundreds) of scrolls and fragments to be reviewed. However, by 1991, portions of the scrolls were made public, and eventually a series of photographs prepared for the Huntington Library was distributed covertly to archaeologists and scholars.

Why did Strugnell and his colleagues keep such secrecy? One answer is that the editors felt that the degree to which the texts verified the Holy Scriptures and confirmed the reality of Jesus Christ as the Jewish Messiah could be controversial and inflammatory. Indeed, Strugnell's candid comment to a *New York Times* reporter that the scrolls proved modern Judaism to be a Christian heresy sent shock waves through the religious community. Strugnell was excoriated by the media, by the Jewish community, and by the liberal church, and he was summarily fired from his post.

But this is only the latest flareup. Throughout history the deity of Jesus Christ has been a matter of intense debate. True believers openly declare their faith in Christ as the Son of God and the only hope for a fallen world. While there are cults and religious groups claiming to be Christian which deny the divinity of Christ—and churches which deny the significance of the redemption He offered through His death on the cross—it is impossible to be a follower of Christ unless one believes His essential teaching; namely, that Jesus Christ is the only begotten Son of God who came to save the lost and to usher in the kingdom of heaven.

A Ruler of the Jews

In New Testament times, there was a man who perceived there was more to Jesus than met the eye. He may have heard John the Baptist refer to Him as one who "existed before me."[1] The strange prophet, who lived alone in the desert, had even called Him "the Son of God."[2] Jesus of Nazareth was real and down-to-earth. Yet there was something otherworldly about Him. He spoke with authority, like the authority of Jehovah written about in the scrolls.[3] He must have been sent from heaven.[4]

One night this man, Nicodemus,[5] a ruler of the Jews, found Jesus alone and managed to talk with Him, which was hard to do because of the crowds. He may have been glad no one would see him.

He fumbled a bit for something to say and then blurted out: "Rabbi, we know You've come from God as a teacher, for no one can do the signs You do unless God is with him."

It was an awkward start, but it summarized what he was feeling. Nicodemus wanted to know God, and he instinctively realized that Jesus could give him teaching that would lead directly to God.

The Lord skipped small talk and went to the heart of Nicodemus' concern, preserving for all generations an understanding of the indispensable initial step toward life in an invisible world that governs all else. The kingdom of God is not really a place—at least not yet—but rather a state of being in which men, women, and children have yielded all sovereignty to the one and only true sovereign, Almighty God. It is the rule of God in the hearts, minds, and wills of people—the state in which the unlimited power and blessing of the unlimited Lord are forthcoming.

The natural eye cannot see this domain, and Jesus quickly explained that. He probably spoke softly, but distinctly. "Unless one is born again, he cannot *see* the kingdom of God."[6]

Nicodemus was startled. What kind of a remark was that? So, getting bolder, he answered back more directly than he had begun: "How can a man be born when he is old? He cannot enter a second time into his mother's womb and be born, can he?"[7]

The poor man had wanted to glimpse the invisible world and had been told how, but it went right by him, as it probably would have most of us. But Jesus really had told him how to peer into the throne room of God, from which the universe is directed. It should be noted, however, that He referred first to "seeing" the kingdom. Next, He took it a step further: "Unless one is born of water and the Spirit, he cannot *enter* into the kingdom of God."[8]

Jesus knew His man. Nicodemus wanted it all. He had suspected this very special rabbi, although visibly a flesh-and-blood man, was somehow living at that moment in contact with God. So Jesus laid it out for him.

God is spirit. Those who would know Him—who would worship Him—must do so in spirit.[9] Since the Fall left man spiritually dead,[10] we must be reborn. Flesh begets flesh and spirit begets spirit,[11] so this rebirth must be accomplished by God the Holy Spirit. After that, being children of God,[12] we are able to engage in communion and fellowship with Him, as Adam did in the original kingdom in the Garden of Eden.[13]

You Must Be Born Again

Nicodemus' amazement soared, so Jesus pressed on with many deep things of the spirit—the things that men and women everywhere must make a part of themselves if they are to begin to deal successfully with our world in crisis:

> "Do not marvel that I said to you, 'You must be born again.' The wind blows where it wishes and you hear the sound of it, but do not know where it comes from and where it is going; so is every one who is born of the Spirit." Nicodemus answered and said to him, "How can these things be?" Jesus answered and said to him, "Are you the teacher of Israel, and do not understand these things? Truly, truly, I say to you, we speak that which we know, and bear witness of that which we have seen; and you do not receive our witness. If I told you earthly things and you do not believe, how shall you believe if I tell you heavenly things? And no one has ascended into heaven, but He who descended from heaven, even the Son of Man. And as Moses lifted up the serpent in the wilderness, even so must the Son of Man be lifted up; that whoever believes may in Him have eternal life. For God so loved the world, that He gave His only begotten Son, that whoever believes in Him should not perish, but have eternal life."[14]

The New Testament evidence is that Nicodemus did eventually believe,[15] accepting entry into the secret kingdom even while coping with the trials of the visible one.

Like millions and millions of others, this once-timid man received Jesus into his life, accepting Him for who He was—God incarnate, the Word become flesh, Savior of the world, Lord of all.

Forgiven for his sins, he was reconciled to God Almighty and enabled to perceive the "heavenly things" Jesus had spoken of, to gain access to the kingdom of God.

He was, in short, born again—born from above, as some translators prefer, born of the Spirit. He could say with Paul the apostle who later wrote:

> Now we have received, not the spirit of the world, but the Spirit who is from God, that we might *know the things freely given to us by God,* which things we also speak, not in words taught by human wisdom, but in those taught by the Spirit, combining spiritual thoughts with spiritual words.[16]

Both Nicodemus and Paul discovered that the kingdom of heaven is based on an invisible, spiritual reality, capable of visible, physical effects.

This is the reality that the world craves so badly.

A Matter of Authority

Unhappily, evangelical Christians have for too long reduced the born-again experience to the issue of being "saved." Salvation is an important issue, obviously, and must never be deemphasized. But rebirth must be seen as a beginning, not an arrival. It provides access to the invisible world, the kingdom of God, of which we are to learn and experience and then share with others. Jesus Himself said it clearly before His ascension:

> All authority has been given to Me in heaven and on earth. Go therefore and *make disciples* of all the nations, baptizing them in the name of the Father and the Son and the Holy Spirit, *teaching them to observe all that I commanded you;* and lo, I am with you always, even to the end of the age.[17]

The commission was to make followers and learners—converts—and to *teach* them the principles of the kingdom. Entry into the body of believers was not enough. They were to learn how to live in this world, although their residence was in the kingdom. The invisible was to rule the visible. Christ has authority over both.

We have fallen short. Occasionally we have perceived God's hand at work in the world. But we have not striven to understand how the kingdom functions nor have we fully participated in its manifestation on earth.

We *must* hear this before it is too late: Jesus has opened to us the truths of the secret world of God! He has given us entrance into a world of indescribable power.

The atom gives us a clue as to what we're dealing with. We can't see an atom—solid matter looks like solid matter. But atomic theory convinces us the atoms are there, pressed together into material substance at some point in time. And with Einstein's $E=mc^2$, we have discovered that this means matter is energy—sheer power capable of blowing up the world. Yet all we see is the matter, even though the energy controls the matter.

Now this terribly great power is a tiny fraction of what we touch when we touch God's power. And it, too, is unseen—totally undiscerned—by one who has not been born again. The unspiritual man or woman regards such possibilities as foolishness.[18] And even many who have been born anew by the Spirit, though possessing the internal eyesight to see and believe in the invisible realm, refrain from appropriating its power for their daily lives. Having "seen" the kingdom, but not having fully "entered" in, they allow the conditions of the world to dominate them, contrary to the instructions of the Lord. The rebirth should give us the power to prevail over circumstances surrounding us.

Jesus gave us an additional piece of insight on this score. If we are to enter into the kingdom, taking full hold of that which is available, then we must "become like children," He said.[19] That is hard for our sophisticated generation, for it requires simple trust. A child is willing to leap ahead and seize any opportunity his father lays before him. So it must be with Christians and their heavenly Father, who gladly offers them the inexhaustible riches and power of His kingdom.[20] Indeed, He is pressing them upon us, if we will only respond confidently, joyfully, exuberantly—like little children.

You Shall Know the Truth

In light of the critical condition of the world, we need to examine even more philosophically why we are falling short in the matter of entering into the kingdom after rebirth. For if Christians miss the mark, how will the *world* learn?

Let's look at the logic of the problem. It leads us right into the issue of truth, and if there is anything the people of the world are looking for, it's truth.

First, we should recall the teachings of the Lord delivered through His encounter with a woman of Samaria. It is remarkable that this discourse, containing spiritual instruction with practical physical effects, involved one from the despised Samaritans, a people of mixed Assyrian and Jewish blood resulting from the Assyrian invasion of the Israelites' land centuries earlier. The Lord, a Jew, obviously wanted to show that His message extended to all people. We pick up the conversation in the middle of profound insights into the Holy Spirit, eternal life, adultery, worship, and ministry to the world, with Jesus speaking:

> An hour is coming, and now is, when the true worshipers shall worship the Father in spirit and *truth;* for such people the Father seeks to be His worshipers. God is spirit; and those who worship Him must worship in spirit and *truth*.[21]

That alone sounds right and good, but how does one practically do it?

Fortunately Jesus also said the following in a discussion with His disciples: "I am the way, and the *truth,* and the life."[22]

Putting those two revelations together, we see that we are to bring ourselves into line with a standard that is true. Jesus is the *truth,* so, being born of His Spirit, we are to conform to Him. We are to walk in His will. Only then can we worship God in spirit and truth. Only then can we move in truth. Note how essential He said this was: "Not every one who says to Me, 'Lord, Lord,' will enter the kingdom of heaven; but *he who does the will of My Father* who is in heaven."[23]

We need to be clear on this. Truth is the very centerpiece of the kingdom and its principles. We must be certain of the essential rightness of the principles, as opposed to other views. They lead to a new system of life that is better than any other system, the most practical possible, providing peace of mind, health, happiness, abundance, joy, and life everlasting. But we believe them because they are *true*.

Consider the following dialogue between Jesus and Pontius Pilate, the Roman governor at the time of the Lord's arrest and crucifixion:

> Then Pilate went back into the palace and called for Jesus to be brought to him. "Are you the King of the Jews?" he asked him. "'King' as *you* use the word or as the *Jews* use it?" Jesus asked. "Am I a Jew?" Pilate retorted. "Your own people and their chief priests brought you here. Why? What have you done?" Then Jesus answered, "I am not an earthly king. If I were, my followers would have fought when I was arrested by the Jewish leaders. But my Kingdom is not of the world." Pilate replied, "But you are a king then?" "Yes," Jesus said. "I was born for that purpose. *And I came to bring truth to the world. All who love the truth are my followers.*"[24]

The Kingdom of His Truth

Yes, there is a kingdom. Jesus said it is founded on truth. He, the Truth, is king of it. Everyone who loves the Truth—Him—and wants to follow the Truth is a member of that kingdom.

> He who sent Me is true; and the things which I heard from Him, these I speak to the world. . . . If you abide in My word, then you are truly disciples of Mine; and you shall know *the truth,* and *the truth shall make you free.*[25]

Not only is He true, the Lord said, but the things He teaches are true. And if we accept and practice these truths, we will be free, another condition the people of the world so desperately seek. I want to emphasize what it is that makes us free. It is not merely the acceptance of Jesus and His atonement, but *the doing of the truth*—putting into practice the principles of the kingdom.

As I said, we too often stop short. We must start with the crucifixion and the resurrection, but we must follow through with the practice of the principles, the laws of life. For God said thousands of years ago:

> I will give you a new heart and put a new spirit within you; and I will remove the heart of stone from your flesh and give you a heart of flesh. And I will put My Spirit within you *and cause you to walk in My statutes, and you will be careful to observe My ordinances.*[26]

He has gone to great lengths over many centuries to plant within our hearts His ways, His truth, His principles. What He has done surpasses the old covenant of law and regulation handed down to the people of Israel at Mount Sinai. Jesus has fulfilled the written law, placing it within His subjects, but they must live out the principles.

Applying this to our personal conduct, we see that speaking the truth is central. Its importance must never be minimized. Just as Jesus is the King of truth, the Holy Spirit (the Lord and giver of life) is called "the Spirit of truth."[27] Where He abides there is truth. At the same time, Satan (the adversary) is described as "the father of lies"[28]

Although true speech is only a part of ultimate truth, it is no mere coincidence that the apostle John tells us God's final heaven will exclude anyone who "maketh a lie."[29] "All liars," he declares, "shall have their part in the lake which burns with fire and brimstone."[30] Telling the truth is a serious matter! In the world we see conduct that flies flagrantly in the face of these warnings. The now defunct Soviet Union was an atheistic society which traded in and survived by "disinformation"—that is, the systematic spreading of lies through the free press of its adversaries. While communism and Soviet tactics have been discredited in the eyes of the world, many of their practices survive in the United States today, in some cases turning our institutions of higher learning into socialist disinformation factories.

Big Brother Returns

The "big lie" has become so frequent, and perhaps even so necessary, in dictatorial societies that George Orwell, in his book *1984*, portrayed the ultimate dictatorship as one in which there was no truth, only a reordering of facts. History books were burned and the facts were rewritten to suit the lie. The people learned to use "truth" selectively, in a language of convenient lies called "newspeak."

Ironically, this is precisely what is happening in our colleges and universities. Campus gurus and thought police have attempted to strip from our society all references to our Christian heritage, to the faith of our fathers, to the artistic and literary achievements of Western Christian civilization. They have discarded the venerable political thought of great thinkers such as Hugo Grotius, John Locke, and Thomas Hobbes, who wrote the political treatises from which our forefathers learned.

Many of those pioneers, if not all of them, were profoundly Christian in orientation. But the revisionists have ignored the truth; they are rewriting history as fast as they can to favor the plight of the so-called oppressed classes in a struggle for minority rights, women's rights, and others such as homosexual and lesbian rights, which have never been tolerated in civilized societies throughout recorded history.

I can't help but recall Prime Minister Lloyd George's remark when asked if he would like the British government to recognize the Bolsheviks in Russia. He said they might as well legalize sodomy as recognize Communists. Both were anathema to civilized peoples just seventy years ago. And now, at the end of the century, we are seeing sodomy go from a crime to a protected right! Homosexuals have proclaimed themselves a protected class, and they are staging marches outside of Christian churches protesting Christianity as being a religion of bigots and "homophobes."

Even worse, in the spring of 1992 we saw militant lesbians and gays desecrating churches and violating the freedom of religion, which is protected by the Constitution. I believe such people have proved why the Bible calls their practices "abominations." When homosexuals invade churches and cathedrals, as they have done in this country, screaming blasphemies at priests, pastors, and worshipers, defiling the very house of God, they have reached the depths of depravity.

A group of homosexuals from the organization called Queer Nation picketed the Founder's Inn Hotel and Conference Center at our CBN headquarters in Virginia Beach in early 1992. I publicly said that I felt that homosexuals are "hurting" and that they are "sinners." They said such statements were examples of "hate crimes." They and their allies are asking the government to track similar "hate crimes," and then establish a procedure like the one in Canada to punish free expression. Needless to say, the is beyond belief; even Big Brother in Orwell's epic might have been shocked by such behavior.

Even more shocking, however, is the news that parts of the government, the media, and the liberal establishment are very supportive of homosexuality. Recently CBS broadcast a prime-time documentary about homosexuals and lesbians adopting children. The only editorial comment was that this is a growing new trend.

There was not one word of criticism; not one indication of the sin such practices represent in the eyes of a righteous God. No one pointed out that every healthy society has always, from the beginning of time, condemned such practices. We can only wonder what judgment God will visit upon a nation that would tolerate, and even praise, such behavior.

Newspeak All Over Again

Now that the Soviet Union has come unraveled, we can see the hypocrisy and the absurdity of Communism for what it was. We see the sham and the fraud that was partially hidden by lies. Yet in the past few years we have begun to see Orwell's dire prophecies matched and even exceeded by the promoters of the socialist agenda in this country. Consider, for example, the ongoing controversy over "politically correct thinking."

The biggest upset for liberal faculty members and the new generation of would-be revolutionaries on America's college and university campuses in recent months has not been the collapse of Communism, the attempted Soviet coup, or the Iraqi invasion of Kuwait, but the news that responsible Americans are offended by the foolishness of "political correctness" ("PC"). Like a new wave of Leninists or Nazi secret police marching against Western Christian values, the campus liberals have tried to rewrite the dictionary and redefine what is acceptable and unacceptable speech.

But the American people are upset for very good reason, since "PC thinking" sets out to reinterpret history and ideas through the vocabulary of radical feminism, virulent racism, belligerent homosexuality, and bizarre social ideals that are flagrantly anti-democratic.

Dinesh DeSouza's bestselling book, *Illiberal Education: The Politics of Race and Sex on Campus*, helped to bring this phenomenon to light. The book generated heated debate on and off campus and generally helped to discredit the types of mind control advocated by the latent Marxists and sociophobes who dominate higher education in the 1990s. DeSouza points out that the term "politically correct" was first used by Marxists in the early part of this century to classify ideas which aided their socialist and deconstructionist agenda. The term disappeared for a while but, predictably, reappeared on campuses in the 1960s, associated with feminism, racism, environmentalism, and other politicized issues. By and large, the leaders of the movement are activists, abetted by junior faculty members and compliant administrators, who have a sinister social agenda. "Like the Stalinists and

Trotskyists of an earlier day," says DeSouza, "contemporary campus activists maintain that 'everything is political' and thus it seems quite proper to insist that classroom lectures, the use of language, and even styles of dress and demeanor reflect the P.C. stance of the new generation of professors and administrators—products of the counterculture of the 1960s—who are coming to power in American universities."

Newsweek's cover story on the thought police helped alert the general public to PC thinking. Major articles in the *New York Times, New York* magazine, and other publications also helped demonstrate the absurdity of PC logic. Suddenly we became aware of such neologism as "multiethnic," "multicultural," "developmentally challenged," and even the ludicrous description of short people as "vertically challenged."

Dangerous Illusions

The real irony is that a movement which marches under the name of "diversity" and "pluralism" is actually one of the most closed-minded, judgmental, condemning, and potentially dangerous -isms since the rise of Nazi Germany. Politically correct thinking denies the value of a canon of great literature because it reflects the biases of "dead white European males." History, too, is colored by imperialism, greed, and racism. The recent attacks on Christopher Columbus and the founding fathers of the United States reveal the types of hostility and divisiveness that underlies such views.

In a July 1991 article in the *Reporter Dispatch,* Louis Rukeyser spoke out against the radicals who claim that America's place in history is tarnished by a heritage of bigotry and greed. Their charges are absurd at best and anti-American at worst, he said, "Yet that is the message behind the current nonsense that holds that celebration of America's place in history is nothing more than a paean to racist, sexist, dead white European males."

"Spare me," says Rukeyser. "Those who pursue this sort of demagoguery are cheaply inflaming group bigotry. Worse, they are endangering this nation's ability to compete and flourish in the 21st century."

As a respected broadcaster, author, and Wall Street analyst, Rukeyser recognizes the liberals' appeal for "diversity" as a thinly disguised attempt to split America into radical factions and, thus, to destroy the unity and the spirit of cooperation upon which this nation was founded. "In fact," he says, "it is tribalism—one of the planet's oldest and most destructive tendencies. Human progress in general and the American experience in particular have sought assiduously to overcome it."

The fact that there are still social and racial problems in this nation, the writer argues, "is scarcely reason to abdicate to the apostles of division. On the contrary, it is reason to rededicate ourselves to making the American dream a reality for all our citizens."

Clearly Rukeyser is right and perhaps most perceptive in his observation that, "Exclusionist, paranoid ethnicity is alien to American instincts." From the very beginning, this was a country of widely different peoples assimilated as a nation by a unique experiment in cooperation. The radicals who espouse "diversity" and politically correct thinking are, once again, trying their hardest to split us apart. Their objective is insidious and dangerous; ultimately it is the work of the deceiver.

But Dinesh DeSouza points out another dangerous trend in the PC movement; namely, the growing backlash among those groups who resent and resist the labels being put on them by advocates of PC. In reaction to Black Studies, Women's Studies, and Gay and Lesbian Studies programs on some campuses, there is an outcry for White Studies, Men's Studies, and the like. PC thinking has, in fact, reawakened a warfare between the races, encouraged a degree of hostility between the sexes, and incited deeper resentment between all classes of people by virtue of its twisted judgments and perverse logic. It has awakened angers and resentments that are unprecedented in this culture. People who have never held racist or sexist emotions of any kind are suddenly enraged because they have been condemned and discredited for simply being born.

The Fifth Column

The vocabulary of the activists condemns traditional or historical orthodoxy in favor of an untested and potentially dangerous new orthodoxy. I call these revisionists the fifth column, for like the saboteurs and collaborators of wartime, their very purpose is to destabilize and undermine American society from within and ultimately to destroy our Western heritage from the ground up. They will use any means, employ any weapons, and assault any sacred traditions that suit them in order to accomplish their goals.

If the problems on the university campus were not enough, an article in *The New Republic* by Kay Sunstein Hymowitz tells about the PC invasion of kindergarten. For example, a new handbook for teachers, entitled the *Anti-Bias Curriculum,* alerts teachers to the dangers of such classic stories as Hansel and Gretel, Cinderella, Babar, and others.

Among the dangers noted by the PC adviser is the negative stereotyping of the witch in Hansel and Gretel, identified as an old hag, when in fact witches are "actually good women who used herbal remedies to help people." Elsewhere, the director of a politically correct child studies center in South Hadley, Massachusetts, claims that Babar (including all the books in this famous series) is unacceptable for children since it "extols the virtues of a European middle-class life-style and disparages the animals and people who have remained in the jungle."

I have heard that there are councils and companies that do nothing but rate books for children on the basis of racism, sexism, ageism, handicapism, and other "anti-human values." Children are thus taught from infancy to distrust their culture, to repudiate traditional values, to disavow the role of father as principal provider and mother as homemaker and nurturer of children. In one series of books being promoted by women's studies programs, the little girl who is the main character of the stories finally achieves ultimate maturity and wisdom when she grows up to disavow motherhood and childbearing.

What troubles me most of all in this movement is that the freedom of childhood fantasy has been politicized and violated to such an extent through overt demagoguery and socialist ideologies. What will become of such children? What happiness can they look forward to? What hope is there for a nation whose children (at least those who manage to survive the legal assault on pregnancy and childbearing) are routinely subjected to this kind of relentless and hostile programming in the nursery?

Where will it end? Dinesh DeSouza observes wisely, "The current revolution of minority victims threatens to destroy the highest ideals of liberal education," and he adds that "liberal education is too important to entrust to these self-styled revolutionaries." He is absolutely right.

What an obvious tragedy exists when those who lead our society first repudiate the One who is the way, the truth, and the life, then turn their backs on the Spirit of truth, and finally set out to destroy the historical record of truth which underlies our entire society. However, in the United States, regard for truth still exists in some quarters, although it is clearly diminishing along with regard for absolute values. Perjury—the willful telling of a lie while under lawful oath—is a felony and stands as a secular affirmation of the kingdom's demand for truth. One wonders when a liberal group will bring a suit against perjury laws as an "establishment of religion" because they reflect the ninth commandment, "Thou shalt not bear false witness against thy neighbor."

His Way Is True

Since the kingdom of God is the kingdom of truth, how sad that in some instances we find people in the church who believe they can further God's kingdom by the use of falsehoods and building up with one hand but tearing down with the other. Exaggeration, embellishment, and even fabrications have become instruments of evangelism in some quarters. Christians must understand that the Lord does not need our embellishment to accomplish His purpose or to glorify His name. We do Him and ourselves a disservice when we depart from the truth.

Jesus and His Ways are true. As the One by whom and for whom all things were created,[31] He understands precisely how the world works. His teachings, which so many in the world have tried to relegate to the categories of goody-goody daydreaming or pietistic navel-gazing, are functional.

The world yearns for peace; He can provide it. The world wants love; He has the formula. The world wants riches, honor, and full life; He promises them all.

But there are requisites. One must be born again by accepting the free gift of salvation that He alone provides, learn from Him, and put His principles into practice.

What are the key laws or principles that govern the deepest desires and needs of mankind? They embody the truths that we will be examining and illustrating in detail in the following chapters, along with the virtues and subprinciples flowing through them.

We will see that the truths of Jesus have the characteristic of the "truths" of the American Declaration of Independence—they are "self-evident." We will begin to understand why a society that abandons these laws, which are self-evident, will collapse. And equally evident will be the reasons why a society that voluntarily adheres to such laws can be expected to prosper.

Do not forget: The One proclaiming the laws created and controls both the visible world and the invisible kingdom. He knows how they both work!

4

How God's Kingdom Works

To understand how the kingdom of heaven works and how it holds sway over the visible world, we must place two facts in the brightest light.

First, there is absolute abundance in the kingdom of God.

Second, it is possible to have total favor with the ruler of that abundance.

On the first point, Jesus, telling His disciples that they were being permitted to know the secrets of the kingdom,[1] set forth the truth of abundance with a parable about a sower.[2] The seed that fell on good ground, He said, yielded crops of thirtyfold, sixtyfold, and a hundredfold. *That* is abundance—returns of 3,000, 6,000, and 10,000 percent. You see, there is no economic recession, no shortage, in the kingdom of God.

Throughout our forests, we see this truth touching the physical world. Consider the profusion of seed that comes from a maple tree. Look at the multiplicity of colors in a sunset; there are more hues than we can name. Plant life, marine life, bird life—there is no end, almost as though God had sent abundance into the universe as testimony to His own infinitude.

Because He is the only truly free being in the universe, His kingdom is a sphere of total possibility. Jesus emphasized this when He multiplied the loaves and fishes, taking a little boy's lunch and feeding more than five thousand hungry people.³ God is never diminished by circumstances.

Neither is He limited by His own universe or the natural laws He Himself established. Some of the new environmentalists, who are actually New Age pantheists, attempt to convince us that God is merely *in* nature. But were that true, He would be limited. No, He is above the laws of nature and any restrictions that those laws might try to impose. He can create from nothing, or He can take existing matter and transform it. His is a total world—total health, total life, total energy, total strength, total provision.

In the matter of favor, Jesus, of course, was our perfect illustration of God's provision: "And Jesus kept increasing in wisdom and stature, and in *favor* with God and men."⁴

Within a few short years, God presented the supreme token of this grace at the time of the baptism of Jesus in the River Jordan: "And immediately, coming up from the water, He saw the heavens parting and the Spirit descending upon Him like a dove. Then a voice came from heaven, 'You are My beloved Son, in whom I am well pleased.'"⁵

This, God the Father was saying, was the One He had spoken of and promised for centuries. He was going to pour out His grace and blessing on His only begotten Son and on those who belong to Him.

First, we need to recognize that when the Bible speaks of God's "grace," it is speaking of His "favor." In the New Testament, the Greek word for grace is *charis,* perhaps best defined as "the unmerited favor of God."

Before His Throne

This favor, the apostle Paul said, allows us to stand before God Himself.⁶ It is our sole means of access to the throne of the kingdom.⁷ Think of it: If we have access to the Father, standing before Him in His favor, then we have the prospect of continuous blessing. Indeed, Paul wrote that the prospect was for *increasing* blessing:

But God, being rich in mercy, because of His great love with which He loved us, even when we were dead in our transgressions, made us alive together with Christ (by grace you have been saved), and raised us up with Him, and seated us with Him in the heavenly places, in Christ Jesus, in order that *in the ages to come He might show the surpassing riches of His grace* in kindness toward us in Christ Jesus.[8]

Now when God blesses us and keeps us, and lets His face shine upon us, and is gracious to us,[9] then before men we appear in a light that far transcends any of our natural abilities. He can cause our plans to succeed. He can cause people to like us. He can cause us to be preferred and chosen above others of equal talent. He can protect our children. He can guard our property. He can cause His angels to aid us.

How well I remember the day in the late sixties when God showed forth this favor in my life in a practical, workaday manner. CBN was in urgent need of $2.3 million worth of modern equipment that would allow us to broadcast with the power and quality needed if we were to do what the Lord had called us to do. With absolutely no worldly credentials or the support that would normally be required to do business at this level, I began negotiations with one of the world's leading electronics manufacturers. There was no reason to expect a successful outcome.

But God had other plans. In the most remarkable, yet smooth and calm manner, I received total favor from this giant company and arranged for our equipment needs to be met for a period of years at the finest terms imaginable. Others in the industry were envious, for I had received every concession in price, down payment, and credit terms that it was possible to get.

You see, God had let His face shine upon us and was gracious to us. We had favor with Him in the invisible world, and since He ruled even the visible world that tried to ignore Him, He gave us favor there as well.

With those two truths of abundance and favor established, we are ready for the fact that God has entered into a partnership with redeemed man. He has given us the potential of cooperating with His Spirit in the whole work of the kingdom.

Prayer is the link between finite man and the infinite purposes of God. In its ultimate sense, prayer consists of determining God's will and then doing it on earth. It does *not* consist merely of asking for what *we* want. To pray in the truest sense means to put our lives into total conformity with what God desires. We make ourselves available to God.

We begin this process by dropping our own preconceived ideas and entering His presence by grace to wait upon Him. Our thought should be: "Lord, what do *You* want? What are *You* doing?" As George Mueller, the great British man of faith, said, "Have no mind of your own in the matter."

The Power of Speech

The Lord's chastisement of the false prophets, recorded in the Book of Jeremiah, illustrates the importance of this. Warning the people against those prophets who were speaking visions of their own imaginations and not from the mouth of God, He asked: "But who has stood in the council of the LORD, / That he should see and hear His word? / Who has given heed to His word and listened?"[10] They were to be alone with the Lord, to see and to hear what He was doing. They were not to put their own ideas first.

So it should be with us when we pray. We should stand in the Spirit in the invisible kingdom; there we will see and hear, and our role in the partnership can become active.

If we turn again to the account of Jesus and the fig tree as recorded in Mark's Gospel, which we touched on in chapter 2, this becomes clear. We should recall that Jesus, discussing the power that withered the tree, said that the first thing required was "faith in God," absolute trust and confidence that He is God Almighty, unlimited and infinite. Implied was the fact that He speaks to His people, revealing what He is doing. Then Jesus said this:

For assuredly, I say to you, whoever says to this mountain, "Be removed and be cast into the sea," and does not doubt in his heart, but believes that those things he says will come to pass, he will have whatever he says. Therefore I say to you, whatever things you ask when you pray, believe that you receive them, and you will have them.[11]

If we fully believe God and have discerned His will, Christ said that we may translate that will from the invisible world to the visible by the spoken word. In short, God uses the spoken word to translate spiritual energy—sheer power—into the material.

The most vivid illustration, of course, was the creation of the world. God spoke to the void and said, "Let there be light,"[12] and there was light. The same with the firmament and the waters and the dry land; the same with everything that was created.[13] All things were made by the Word.[14] And that which was spoken was energized by the Spirit, moving upon the face of the waters,[15] shaping matter, which is itself energy, into God's predetermined patterns.

In like manner, our partnership with God is fulfilled when we speak His word in the power of the Holy Spirit. As Jesus taught: "So I tell you to believe that you have received the things you ask for in prayer, and God will give them to you."[16] Thus He took us right back to where He began. Have faith in God, know who He is, know what He is doing, trust His favor upon us, participate with Him. What we say in His name should then come to pass.

The Missing Link

For the vast majority of Christians throughout history, the "speaking" has been the missing link between what we believe and what we do. We have lost the understanding of how God Almighty works, how His Son works, and how we are to work once we enter into the unobstructed view of God that Jesus provides in the kingdom.

The thing that clouds our view is sin. But once the sin is forgiven, we are to enter bodily into the throne room of grace and commune with God by His Spirit, who communicates with our spirit. It's a bit like tuning in to a radio or television station. You get on the right frequency and you pick up a program. So it is with listening to the Lord. He is speaking constantly, but we are often on the wrong frequency.

Once He has spoken to us, we are to speak after Him. If we do, miracles occur. If we don't, usually nothing will happen. For, in the material world, God has chosen to enter into partnership with us, his co-laborers, whom He is grooming for the perfect, visible establishment of His kingdom on earth.

Right now, in this life, He would have us stop cajoling and begging. He would have us live in the kingdom, in harmony with Him, receiving His thoughts by the Spirit. As the apostle Paul said, "We have the mind of Christ."[17] So speak that mind, Jesus was saying in the fig tree episode. Speak His thoughts. Don't be afraid. Don't doubt. "For God has not given us a spirit of timidity, but of power and love and discipline."[18]

We must see that, by living in the kingdom now, we enter back into what man lost in the Garden of Eden. We return to the authority God gave us at the creation. Like Adam, we hear the Lord's voice revealing the secrets of the world. And, as He speaks, we speak after Him in the manner of Ezekiel in his vision in the valley of dry bones.

> Again He said to me, "Prophesy over the bones, and say to them, 'O dry bones, hear the word of the LORD.'"[19]

The prophet listened as the Lord said He intended to give the bones life, sinews, flesh, skin, and breath. Then it was Ezekiel's turn.

> So I *prophesied* as I was commanded; and as I *prophesied*, there was a noise, and behold, a rattling; and the bones came together, bone to its bone. And I looked, and behold, sinews were on them, and flesh grew, and skin covered them; but there was no breath in them. Then He said to me, "Prophesy

to the breath, prophesy, son of man, and say to the breath, 'Thus says the Lord GOD, "Come from the four winds, O breath, and breathe on these slain, that they come to life."'" So I *prophesied* as He commanded me, and the breath came into them, and they came to life, and stood on their feet, an exceedingly great army.[20]

In this Old Testament episode, Ezekiel learned what I call the word of faith, which didn't receive full development until the New Testament was written. The lesson was this: Through our words, we translate the will of God in the invisible kingdom to the visible situation that confronts us. We speak to storms, and they cease. We speak to money, and it comes. We speak to crops, and they flourish.

Although I will discuss this miraculous phenomenon in detail later, the simple truth is that God's word, spoken into a situation, will perform His purpose: "So shall My word be which goes forth from My mouth; / It shall not return to Me empty, / Without accomplishing what I desire, / And without succeeding in the matter for which I sent it."[21]

The Way It Will Be

Some day, when the kingdom is fully manifested, the speaking will not be necessary. The thought will become the deed, as it is in heaven today.

On my television program, "The 700 Club," I did an interview with Dr. Richard E. Eby, a well-known California obstetrician and gynecologist, that illustrates the point vividly. In 1972, Dr. Eby said he fell from a second-story balcony and split his skull. He told me that he died (whether for minutes or hours, he doesn't know) but miraculously returned to life and at the time of the interview was perfectly healthy and normal. During the experience, Dr. Eby related, his spirit left his body and apparently went to heaven, or paradise. As one would expect, he found it to be a most beautiful place. At one stage he entered a field of flowers and as he walked along, he was overwhelmed by their beauty. "Wouldn't it be wonderful if I had a bunch and could smell them?" he thought. But as he started to bend over, he looked at his hand, and it was already full of flowers.

At another point, he was thinking how good it would be to go to a distant valley, and suddenly he was there.

As a scientific man, he naturally analyzed these experiences carefully and concluded that in heaven the mere thought produces the action. As the psalmist declared: "Delight yourself also in the LORD, / And He shall give you the desires of your heart. / Commit your way to the LORD, / Trust also in Him, / And He shall bring it to pass."[22]

In his brief visit to heaven, Dr. Eby was delighting himself in the Lord, doing His perfect will, and the yearnings of his heart were immediately fulfilled. He didn't have to speak them. On earth a translation is required, but not so in the ultimate kingdom. One day we will not need telephones, mass transit, or computers; the speed of thought exceeds the speed of light. But now we need the spoken word.

What Is Faith?

As we have emphasized several times, the covering statement for the entire matter of how the kingdom works is "Have faith in God." Faith governs all. But it is frequently misunderstood.

The Bible says bluntly:

Now faith is the substance of things hoped for, the evidence of things not seen. For by it the elders obtained a good testimony. By faith we understand that the worlds were framed by the word of God, so that the things which are seen were not made of things which are visible. . . . But without faith it is impossible to please Him, for he who comes to God must believe that He is, and that He is a rewarder of those who diligently seek Him.[23]

The Living Bible's paraphrase is helpful:

What is Faith? It is the confident assurance that something we want is going to happen. It is the certainty that what we hope for is waiting for us, even though we cannot see it up ahead.[24]

Said another way, faith is the title deed to things we can't see. When we buy property, we meet with the seller and papers are drawn up. We receive a deed, and it says we own a stated piece of property. The minute it is signed, we own the property. We don't have to go to it; we don't have to see it. It is ours. We have a title deed.

It is the same with faith. We have a title deed to what God has promised. Our role is to believe in our hearts that it has been accomplished, according to what God has given us the deed to, and then to speak it. We can't force it. We can't sit around a room with a group and work it up. We can receive it only from God. The Bible says: "So then faith cometh by hearing, and hearing by the word of God."[25]

We hear the Lord's Word; it builds in our hearts, and the light goes on. "It's mine!" Deep down inside, there will be no doubt. That is what the Lord meant in the fig tree episode when He referred to the one who speaks to the mountain and "does not doubt in his heart." The mountain will move if the Lord has spoken.

The Bible also cautions about double-mindedness:

. . . let him ask in faith without any doubting, for the one who doubts is like the surf of the sea driven and tossed by the wind. For let not that man expect that he will receive anything from the Lord, being a double-minded man, unstable in all his ways.[26]

There can be no equivocating, no going back and forth. So many of us hear something from the Lord, we believe it briefly, but the wind blows and the storm pounds and our faith in what God said vanishes like the mist. We need to counter by speaking the word God has given and then simply accepting it.

I must add a word, however, to drive home a subtle point. Our faith throughout all of this must be in the Lord—"have faith in God," Jesus said—and not in our ability, not in our stubborn strength. Our faith is not to be *in our faith:* "Trust in the LORD with all your heart, / And lean not on your own understanding; / In all your ways acknowledge Him, / And He shall direct your paths."[27]

While structuring most of His dealings with man around the point of faith, the Lord made plain that His insistence on faith was not quantitative, but qualitative. He said that we would move mountains even if our faith were no larger than a mustard seed.[28] We don't need a mountain of faith to move a mountain of dirt or even a mountain of world problems.

The object and reality of the faith are the issues. We don't need stubbornness, but confidence.

> . . . this is the confidence which we have before Him, that, if we ask anything according to His will, He hears us. And if we know that He hears us in whatever we ask, we know that we have the requests which we have asked from Him.[29]

The Importance of Right Thinking

We begin to see that in the kingdom:

- Spirit controls matter.
- Lesser authority yields to greater authority.
- The mind is the ultimate conduit of the spirit.
- Speech is the intermediate conduit between spirit and matter and between greater and lesser authority.

That which the writers of the many "success" books call "positive mental attitude," or PMA, is indeed important. Because our minds are the agents our spirits use in influencing the world around us, it is patently clear that negative attitudes can weaken our most valiant attempts. Conversely, positive thinking will more often than not lead to successful action.

Unfortunately, people such as Napoleon Hill, author of the book, *Think and Grow Rich,* attempt to trade on the truth of the kingdom principles without first obtaining their citizenship in the kingdom. Positive thinkers in the secular world, whatever their stripe, have gleaned only a few of the truths of the kingdom of God. Nevertheless, they try to gain the kingdom without submitting themselves to the King. There are inherent dangers with that approach.

Some of the metaphysical principles of the kingdom, taken by themselves, can produce fantastic temporal benefits. But without the lordship of Jesus Christ, these benefits are both transitory and harmful. In fact, many of the advocates of mind over matter ultimately end up involved in spiritism. Jesus warned, "For what will it profit a man if he gains the whole world, and loses his own soul? Or what will a man give in exchange for his soul?"[30]

Many sincere followers of Jesus destroy their effectiveness in this world because they do not understand the laws of spiritual authority and the way this authority is transmitted. They especially are not aware of the power of what they say.

Solomon wrote: "From the fruit of a man's mouth he enjoys good."[31] In other words, when you confess blessing, favor, victory, and success, those things will come to you.

But the majority of Christians ignore this truth. "How do you feel?" we ask someone.

"I feel terrible," he replies, not realizing he has commanded his body to be sick.

"Can you do it?" we ask.

"I can't do that," he replies, not knowing he has limited God and himself by his words.

"I can't get out of debt," someone says. He has just commanded his debt to continue.

We call such negative assertions "realistic appraisals" of the situation. But they aren't realistic, for they ignore the power of God, the authority of the invisible world of the spirit, and the grant of power made by God to His children.

A much more realistic assertion was made by the apostle Paul when he boldly declared: "I can do all things through Him who strengthens me."[32]

Seeing the Possible

Pettiness, overemphasis on minutiae, fear of failure, constant complaining, murmuring—all inhibit the realization of kingdom conditions. As a man thinks in his heart, so is he.[33]

Many athletes have realized this principle. Golfers, from Ben Hogan to Jack Nicklaus, have long made this technique a part of their game. As they approach each shot, in their mind's eye they see themselves swinging the club and the ball traveling in a perfect arc, landing in a particular spot. By visualizing the perfect shot, they set the pattern in the mind, and then they simply follow through with the body. Clearly, their success with this technique has been spectacular.

The same has been true with runners and jumpers. God has given us minds and bodies that work that way. Our bodies will obey our minds, for the most part. Added to that is the fact that our spirits can be in touch with God. Now if our spirits govern our minds and our minds govern our bodies, then God in the invisible world governs us in the visible world.

At the same time, the Lord has called for us to be honest and truthful in the innermost being,[34] so we are not to delude ourselves and to say something is true when it is not. We are not to engage in superstition or silliness. We merely are to have confidence that with Him all things are possible.

Perhaps the most dramatic example of proper thinking, speaking, and doing came to my attention through "The 700 Club." It involved Leslie, May, and Joe Lemke and an extraordinary true-life story of love.

The story began in 1952 when May, a nurse-governess with a reputation for unusual ability with children, was asked to take care of a six-month-old baby named Leslie who was retarded, who had cerebral palsy, and whose eyes had been removed because they were diseased. Leslie was not expected to live long.

The Lord gave May a great love for Leslie, and she began to treat him like a normal baby. She taught him to feed from a nursing bottle by making loud sucking noises against his cheek. Soon she gave up everything else to take care of the child. "I have a job to do for Jesus now," she said, "and I'm going to do it."

By the time he was ten, Leslie could move only a hand and friends advised May that she was wasting her time. But she refused to concede. "I'm doing something for an innocent boy who will be something some day," she said. "I believe in God, and He will do it."

She carried the boy around and spoke her love into his ear, holding him and squeezing him, continuing to treat him like a normal child. Eventually he learned to stand by holding onto a fence and then to walk by following it.

Throughout it all, May prayed constantly for Leslie. Before long, she added a thought to her petitions, repeating it to the Lord several times a day: "Dear Lord, the Bible says you gave each of us a talent. Please help me find the talent in this poor boy who lies there most of the day and does nothing."

May noticed that the boy seemed to respond to musical sounds like the plucking of a string or a cord. So she and her husband, Joe, bought a piano, and she played him all kinds of music, using the radio and records. Leslie listened for hours, seemingly in deep concentration.

After four years of praying for the boy's "talent" to be revealed, May and Joe were awakened at 3:00 A.M. one night by the sound of piano music. They found Leslie sitting at the piano playing beautifully, like a trained musician. He was sixteen years old.

Over the next ten years, the boy learned dozens of songs—classical, popular, jazz—and has even learned to sing with the playing. His talent was fully manifested through May's constant love and confession that nothing is impossible with God. She discerned God's purpose and spoke it into being, thoroughly rejecting negativism.

Necessary Ingredients

Perhaps history's biggest roadblock to the effective demonstration of the invisible kingdom is found in negativism. For in the final analysis, it reveals the absence of *unity*, about which I will have more to say in conjunction with the other principles. But at this point, we need to see that the kingdom of God works through the phenomenon of harmony.

To begin with, entrance into the kingdom, totally dependent upon grace and not upon any kind of status or merit, immediately establishes a basic equality among people. No one can say, "I've earned a better place than you." Growing from that, logically, is a new relationship between individuals. It is one based on the will of the Father, surpassing existing national, racial, familial, or church relationships. The Lord Jesus was precise on this: "My true brother and sister and mother are those who do what my Father in heaven wants."[35]

That statement transcended the Lord's own family relationships, and it transcends ours. The kingdom thus is a family. Jesus is our elder brother; His Father is our Father. That cuts across all lines. My mother can be a black woman who does the will of the Father. My brother can be a Chinese who does likewise, or a Jew, or an Arab.

How we need to see this! All strife and turmoil in the world can be eliminated simply by its fulfillment. The Middle East can be at peace. Latin America can be at peace. The aged and the young can be at peace.

This wholly unique concept of love and family relationships can produce that which has escaped man's grasp from the beginning. But peace will not be the only fruit of such transferal of kingdom life to this world. Paul the apostle wrote of the "fruit of the Spirit" that would grow in a climate of unity—"love, joy, peace, patience, kindness, goodness, faithfulness, gentleness, self-control."[36] Against such characteristics there is no law, Paul added. None is needed.

The Scripture's classic illustration of the transfer of kingdom power to the visible world when there is unity comes in a well-known but underutilized portion of Matthew's Gospel.

> Also, I tell you that if two of you on earth agree about something and pray for it, it will be done for you by my Father in heaven. This is true because if two or three people come together in my name, I am there with them.[37]

The full implication of the point is that when there is no unity of purpose, no crossover of barriers, then the power is not activated.

Prospects for Improvement

I am confident that we will see the kingdom of God working more in the visible world as the Lord continues to bring people to Himself. Should the world experience the great revival of faith in Jesus Christ that I am expecting, then it would be reasonable to see an increase in the exercise of these truths of the kingdom. This, I am sure, will enable the world to transcend many of the limitations we are experiencing now.

For example, it is important for us to continue to develop new sources of energy. The panic of the 1970s' "energy crisis," as it turns out, was largely false. Industry analysts have told us that the endless string of crises during the time of Jimmy Carter's administration were actually fabricated in order to justify a variety of expensive government programs and to justify increased taxes and reduced supplies. In reality, there never was an oil and gas shortage.

But even if research should prove that we can't keep burning up our energy resources forever, it is just as true that we are surrounded by oceans, and sea water contains hydrogen. Someday God may give to one or more of His people a concept for running cars on hydrogen produced from this untapped source. Perhaps He will allow some privileged man or woman a peek into the invisible world to see His purpose. Then a faithful one will speak and act according to the revelation, and the concept will take life.

I believe we can expect this in the area of building materials, perhaps to replace steel and other items in short supply. I am sure there will be foodstuffs we haven't dreamed of, perhaps new living space to accommodate vast populations. The limits are not found in what we see, feel, and taste. They are in our hearts and our willingness to stand in that place where we have an unclouded view of what the Lord is doing.

Thoughts like these invariably cause concern about whether someone who is not prospering or indeed is suffering in slums and poverty is violating the truths of the kingdom. Such questions must not be dismissed hastily. For there is suffering in the world and there are, of course, many Christians who are living short of the ideals we are discussing in this book.

So what does this mean? Are the principles in error? No, on the contrary. I am convinced that if a person is *continuously* in sickness, poverty, or other physical and mental straits, then he is missing the truths of the kingdom. He has either failed to grasp the points we have been making in this chapter about the operation of the kingdom or is not living according to the major principles we will be exploring. He has missed the prosperity I believe the Scripture promises.

Suffering and Poverty

Obviously there will be times of suffering for God's people, times that are given us by the Lord to bring us closer to Him. The apostle Peter says, "he who has suffered in the flesh has ceased from sin, that he no longer should live the rest of his time in the flesh for the lusts of men, but for the will of God."[38] So suffering, trial, and tribulation have a very real and worthwhile role in bringing us near to Jesus. But John, in his third letter to the believers, said, "I pray that you may prosper in all things and be in health, just as your soul prospers."[39]

The normal condition for God's people is spoken about in the book of the Law, in Deuteronomy, where Moses tells the people of the blessings God has ordained for them so long as they follow His commandments. He said:

And the LORD will grant you plenty of goods, in the fruit of your body, in the increase of your livestock, and in the produce of your ground, in the land of which the LORD swore to your fathers to give you. The LORD will open to you His good treasure, the heavens, to give the rain to your land in its season, and to bless all the work of your hand. You shall lend to many nations, but you shall not borrow. And the LORD will make you the head and not the tail; you shall be above only, and not be beneath, if you heed the commandments of the LORD your God, which I command you today, and are careful to observe them. So you shall not turn aside from any of the words which I command you this day, to the right or to the left, to go after other gods to serve them.[40]

Of course, we must not forget that God also gave the children of Israel a stern warning. He said that the commandments He gave through Moses were inviolable. Moses told them: "But it shall come to pass, if you do not obey the voice of the LORD your God, to observe carefully all His commandments and His statutes which I command you today, that all these curses will come upon you and overtake you."[41] The litany of curses was awful, but much of the Old Testament turns out to be a record of the ways in which the people, in fact, turned their backs upon God and how God brought destruction upon Israel, drove them out of the land, and scattered the people all over the globe.

The concept of God's people being bankrupt and always needy and begging from the world for subsistence is not a scriptural concept. There are times when God's people have to be fed by manna and go through extraordinary trials, but we have probably interlarded a medieval monasticism with Judeo-Christian thought that is not necessarily biblical.

It is more like what Paul was warning about in Colossians: "It has a show of will worshiping and neglecting the flesh," but that really isn't what God is interested in: He's interested in a pure heart.

By Dedicated Effort

On the other hand, the Name-It-and-Claim-It school that says, "I want a new Cadillac, and I think good thoughts, and I speak to get a Cadillac, and I pray . . . ," is not what we're talking about. The principles of God, if put to work, will result in prosperity. People will give money, they will save money, they will work hard, they will be sober, they will bring up families in the knowledge and admonition of the Lord, they will work heartily as unto the Lord, they will gain new skills and abilities, and if they invest their money and it builds up with compound interest, after a while they will have more. It is just that simple.

This isn't instant riches, nor is it some kind of flashy conspicuous consumption. It's just that the normal consequence of godly, frugal living and generosity is to have more. The religious hucksters of this world, like those we see in the news, are teaching some kind of miracle rabbit's foot where people send them $100 and all of a sudden begin receiving bucketloads of money. It just does not work that way.

But Jesus did say, "Give, and it will be given to you: good measure, pressed down, shaken together, and running over will be put into your bosom. For with the same measure that you use, it will be measured back to you."[42] If you give love, you will get love; if you give good service, you will get good service. If you give money to people and to the Lord, money has a way of coming back to you. That's just one of the fundamental laws of the kingdom, and we will discuss each of its facets in greater detail in subsequent chapters.

It is important, however, that we not try to equate scriptural prosperity with riches. We are speaking of the Lord's blessing, not great material wealth. Some people are not capable of handling money or other wealth. Some would be destroyed by pride. So God prospers according to His wisdom, according to the true need of those involved.

Nonetheless, I believe Christians can escape any ghetto to which they have been confined, real or imagined. God will make a way. He will provide methods with which to reverse conditions and attitudes. Shortage will turn to abundance, hostility to favor.

When I look at the problems in our inner cities and in the pernicious pockets of poverty in this country, I realize that those places are ready for the hand of God to bring change and hope and renewal. Look at the problems that surfaced in South Central Los Angeles. If we could be free from the mocking scorn of the liberals and the humanists to teach God's principles to everyone, entire communities could be changed.

By the proclamation of new life in Christ, by teaching people the principles of God and how to follow them, and by teaching the principles of marriage and the family, the explosive situation in these pockets of poverty would be eliminated.

Feeding on the Poor

The problem is that the liberals in government, the media, and the education establishment do everything they can to discredit the efforts of those who know God's solutions to social problems. Often they hinder rather than help. The people in the ghettos, in the slums, along with the disenfranchised and the unhappy people in our cities make up their power base. They have built their power on poor people, and if anyone were to come in and clean up the mess and help restore the values that lead to prosperity, contentment, and peace, the liberal bureaucrats would have lost their constituency. They would be out of a job.

In all fairness, I suppose some of them actually feel that their concepts are right. They can't see that their concepts are abysmal failures. So they demand more money to spend on more of the things that do not work.

Over the years I have tried to set a standard of at least the Old Testament concept of tithing, which to me is a triple tithe, and the Lord has honored it. And I think He will honor anybody who abides by these precepts. But the Bible also says the borrower is the servant of the lender. Yet millions of Christians are slaves to debt; facing 18 to 22 percent interest rates. "Easy credit" is literally stifling their lives.

God spoke through the prophet Hosea: "My people perish for lack of knowledge." If they were to follow the principles of the kingdom they would understand the necessity of paying off debt and then letting their savings work for them.

Debt is not only a form of slavery, it leads to poverty, as does drunkenness, dissipation, divorce, and lack of education. Some people have tragedy thrust upon them, but it is certain that a drunkard, a drug addict, a person who refuses to save or exercise self-control, or a person who refuses to study and learn is going to be poor.

That does not mean that everybody who is poor is cursed by God. It doesn't mean that being poor or having financial difficulties is a sin. But sloth, which is cursed by God, and ignorance will always lead to poverty. Virtually anyone who wants to break the cycle of debt and poverty can do so with the power and blessing of God.

As for tragedy and seemingly inevitable mishap, the Bible says:

> The steps of a good man are ordered by the LORD: and he delighteth in his way. Though he fall, *he shall not be utterly cast down:* for the LORD upholdeth him with his hand.[43]

Furthermore, it says that when the wicked will try to harm the righteous, "the LORD will not leave him in his hand."[44] There may be difficult days and even stumbling, but God's arm will be there to deliver those who faithfully obey His commandments.

5

Progressive Happiness

$\mathcal{A}$s we have seen, the kingdom of heaven exists now, here. Although it is spiritual and invisible, it governs the material and visible. It is inhabited by people who have been born again spiritually. It operates in a specified manner.

Now we see that it also has a constitution, a system of fundamental principles and virtues to determine the quality and conduct of life. That constitution is contained in what has come to be known as the Sermon on the Mount, presented by Jesus quite early in His public ministry, probably within the first year.

This constitution of the kingdom has no amendments; it was set down perfectly and with divine insight. It clearly sums up a new way of life. It demands an inner revolution of attitude and outlook. It turns ordinary ideas upside down.

In early 1991, President George Bush said that the unity of purpose demonstrated by the nations allied against Iraq in the Persian Gulf crisis set the stage for a *new world order*. The fact is, politicians and intellectuals have been formulating a secular new world order for decades. In my book on this topic I reviewed the origins of the term in great depth. However, Jesus Christ announced His program for a new world order more than nineteen hundred years ago, and His constitution and bylaws are eternal in consequence and application. This constitution has a preamble.

We label its eight points as the Beatitudes, which is fitting since they truly do guarantee "blessedness" or "happiness." Happy are those who live by them, but more importantly, those who live by them are blessed by God.

The Beatitudes also show us a lot about the nature of God, the one ruling the kingdom.

Complemented by principles and virtues set forth throughout Scripture, they provide the underpinning and framework for our lives, even during a time of transition from the old, discredited order into the emerging future.

As we explore these well-known, yet still-alien words, we should peer between and behind them to perceive the Lord Himself. For the Beatitudes demonstrate the nature of God in a sweeping foundational way.

We should start by remembering that God's name, Yahweh, is no mere label but is significant of the real personality of the One bearing it. It stems from the Hebrew word for "to be," and some authorities believe it may be the so-called *hiph'il* tense, which would mean "He who causes everything to be."

At any rate, He revealed Himself to the covenant people as "I AM."[1] It was almost like a blank check. God said, "I AM ___," and His people were to fill in the blank according to their need. If they needed peace, He was Jehovah-shalom ("I am your peace").[2] If they needed victory, He was Jehovah-nissi ("I am your banner, your victory").[3] If they needed help of any kind, as Abraham so desperately did when he was being tested regarding his son, Isaac, then He was Jehovah-jireh ("I am your provider").[4]

The point we should remember, which is the one the Beatitudes demonstrate so simply, is that God revealed Himself, His nature, His power, and His will at the point of the need. The people had to recognize and acknowledge their need.

This is an overriding lesson of the Beatitudes, which is essential to life in the kingdom. The one who feels he has need of nothing *will receive nothing*. He will never experience the full name and nature of God. He will never know His peace and comfort; he will never know His victory; he will never know His provision of every need of life. Indeed, he will never know His salvation and experience the name God gave to His Son—Jesus, which means "I Am Salvation."

No, the self-sufficient, the self-righteous will not experience the kingdom of heaven. The void within them will not be filled if they do not cry out, "God Almighty, come and meet the deepest need in my life."

Let's look at the Beatitudes themselves,[5] taking note of their progressive nature in the working of an individual's life.

Spiritual Beggars

> Blessed are the poor in spirit, for theirs is the kingdom of heaven.

As with each of the points, the Lord began with a word that is preserved for us in the New Testament as *makarios*, which we render usually as "blessed" or "happy." Therefore, each of the points contains a guideline to happiness, which our world desperately craves.

"Happy are the poor in spirit." What a contradiction this seems! But upon closer examination it becomes clear. First, we must understand that the Lord meant more than merely "poor." His words conveyed the meaning "beggarly." Happy are the beggars in spirit, the spiritual beggars, those who know they are needy and are not afraid to say so, as we noted above.

The Lord's teaching at another time made the point most dramatically. Contrasting a shame-stricken publican (or tax-gatherer) with a proud Pharisee, He revealed a man who was poor in spirit.

> And the publican, standing afar off, would not lift up so much as his eyes up to heaven, but smote upon his breast, saying, God be merciful to me a sinner. I tell you, this man went down to his house justified rather than the other: for every one that exalteth himself shall be abased; and he that humbleth himself shall be exalted.[6]

He was exalted right into the kingdom, into perfect happiness. He had been empty, but he was filled, simply because he was ready to acknowledge that he needed God and was willing to beg for help. The kingdom was his, right then—"theirs *is* the kingdom." He had taken the first step in the progression demonstrated in the Beatitudes.

The Intercessors

Blessed are those who mourn, for they shall be comforted.

This contradiction seems more extreme than the first. Happy are those who mourn. How can it be?

We find help from the writings of Paul, in which he told of a "godly sorrow" that works repentance.[7] This is what Jesus was pointing to. For "repentance" means "afterthought" or "reconsideration." A man is to be repentant, to have an afterthought, to reconsider. He is to be sorry for his sins; he is never to be self-satisfied. As the psalmist wrote:

> The sacrifices of God are a broken spirit;
> A broken and contrite heart, O God, Thou wilt
>   not despise.[8]

So the Lord's message in this second Beatitude was, in essence, "If you want the comfort of God surrounding you, you must come to a place where you mourn for your sins." But He pressed it beyond that; He wanted us to mourn for the sins of people around us, too. The world does not want to mourn; it wants to laugh all the time. But rather than thumbing our noses at the world, we are to mourn, to hurt, to cry out for the lost.

We have the biblical account of Lot in Sodom and Gomorrah, where greed, drunkenness, homosexuality, and corruption were rampant. Lot, a "righteous man," was not merely angered by the filthy deeds of the wicked; he was "vexed" and "tormented" in his soul.[9] He mourned over their deeds. And God comforted him by sending angels to preserve him when those cities were destroyed.[10]

Do you see the progression? The kingdom becomes ours; we are in it. Immediately, the magnitude of our sin falls upon us, even though the Lord has forgiven us. In quick succession, we then see the sin of others—our relatives and friends who are not saved, indeed, the whole world. We are burdened with concern for others. We mourn. We become intercessors.

A philosophy has swept the earth that says, in effect, "I'm OK; you're OK." Without Jesus' salvation there is no room in His kingdom for such thinking. Complacency is an abomination. We have only to recall the lesson He gave when speaking of His second coming. It will be just like the days of Noah, He said:

> For as in those days which were before the flood they were eating and drinking, they were marrying and giving in marriage, until the day that Noah entered the ark, and they did not understand until the flood came and took them all away; so shall the coming of the Son of Man be.[11]

He deplored the people's complacency over the condition of the world. In the kingdom, this must give way to concern and mourning. Then we can expect the fulfillment of Jeremiah's prophecy: "For I will turn their mourning into joy, / And will comfort them, and give them joy for their sorrow."[12]

A Matter of Control

Blessed are the gentle, for they shall inherit the earth.

This next step in the progression is one of the most misunderstood verses in the Bible. It has convinced many that Jesus wanted His people to be dull, obsequious, spineless, and stupid. This, of course, runs contrary to everything we find about the men and women of God in the pages of Scripture. They were strong, vocal, and often brilliant.

Our problem has been with the word *meek* in the King James Version. It *does* mean "humble" and "gentle," even "docile." But the definition cannot stop there. Biblical meekness does not call for the abject surrender of one's character or personal integrity. It calls for a total yielding of the reins of life from one's own hands to God's hands. But it doesn't stop there either. The meek exercise discipline, which results in their being kept continuously under God's control.

Thus, a meek man is a disciplined man who is under the control of God. He is like Moses, a strong, bold leader who at the same time was described as the meekest man on earth.[13] Having seen his sin and that of others, the meek person takes the next step and places himself under God's control and discipline. He serves God. But, remember, God will not seize control. He will govern a life only if it is constantly yielded to Him, and that requires constant discipline. God is not interested in building robots.

Happy is the man who is under control—of God and of himself. Earlier I mentioned Paul's reminder to his beloved Timothy that they had received a spirit of "power and love and *discipline* [or self-control]," not of "timidity."[14] This is what the Lord was talking about. One with this virtue will inherit the earth.

So often Christians have been misled into thinking that once they are born again, nothing is required. This, as we will see, is damaging. The Lord and all those who wrote of Him made clear that rebirth was only the beginning, to be followed by discipline, work, and suffering. Obviously the drunk, the drug addict, the lustful, the slothful do not have the discipline to rule the earth and to correct its evils. No, it is for the meek, the disciplined—those who are controlled by God, who follow His Son, who struggle to inherit the earth and govern it.

Remember these powerful words: "from the days of John the Baptist until now the kingdom of heaven suffers violence, and violent men take it by force."[15] Zealous men force their way in. That's what it means. Though weaklings and wimps will fall by the wayside, God's meek men and women will inherit the earth; the undisciplined and the profligate will lose it.

Hunger and Fullness

Blessed are those who hunger and thirst for righteousness, for
they shall be satisfied [filled].

God is righteousness. To be righteous is to be Godlike. Jesus
said we should hunger and thirst after righteousness. It is a free
gift,[16] but we must seek it. We should desire in every fiber to be
Christlike in nature. For such can be ours. According to the Bible,
God planted the Spirit of His Son within us when we received
Him, not being satisfied that we merely be adopted children, but
that we also have Christ's very nature *within* us.[17]

Setting our life's course in pursuit of Him, we must yearn for
this nature, this righteousness and holiness, to flood us. Having had
the righteousness of Jesus *imputed* to us, we now should desire to
have that righteousness *imparted* to us, actually living it out. If we
remain unrighteous, the Bible says, we will miss the kingdom.

> Or do you not know that the unrighteous shall not inherit
> the kingdom of God? Do not be deceived; neither fornicators,
> nor idolaters, nor adulterers, nor effeminate, nor homosexu-
> als, nor thieves, nor the covetous, nor drunkards, nor revilers,
> nor swindlers, shall inherit the kingdom of God.[18]

"I want to know more of God"—that should be our cry. "I
want His Spirit to possess more of me. I want to be more effective. I want to see His kingdom come on earth."

With that cry of hunger and thirst for God, for more of His
power, we in fact are crying out for an anointing of the Holy Spirit
for service, which the Bible calls baptism in the Holy Spirit. This
actually fulfills the next step in the progression of development
revealed in the Beatitudes, providing an empowerment for serving God.

Jesus described it this way: "You shall receive power when the
Holy Spirit has come upon you; and you shall be My witnesses
both in Jerusalem, and in all Judea and Samaria, and even to the
remotest part of the earth."[19] You will indeed be effective—being

filled with the miraculous power of God Himself—simply because you hungered and thirsted for Him.

Yes, Jesus said, you will be filled and satisfied. Interestingly, the Greek word that we translated "filled" is *chortazo*,[20] which carries the implication of "gorged." We won't merely have a little, the Lord said; we will be gorged with righteousness, power, and everything good in the kingdom.

This obviously is the perfect fulfillment of "seek, and you shall find."[21]

The Flow of Mercy

Blessed are the merciful, for they shall receive mercy.

Most of us grasp this one, but we may fall short in seeing its magnitude.

The root Greek word for mercy is *eleos*, containing the sense of compassion and tenderness, of kindness and beneficence. It flows from the greater to the lesser: God is merciful to man; a wealthy man is merciful to a poorer man.

Thus we see a further progression in the Beatitudes. We begin to think toward men as God thinks toward us, extending our work out into the world. Having received mercy from One greater than we are, we are to give mercy to those we are in a position to favor.

Although our motivation should be purer than this, the fact is that as we show compassion to someone below us, there is always someone upstream to do the same for us—either men or God Himself. Behind this is a broader law that we will examine at greater length.

Ultimate Happiness

Blessed are the pure in heart, for they shall see God.

From the Middle Ages came the idea that "the highest good," the *summum bonum*, was the "beatific vision." The ultimate happiness was to see God. There could be nothing greater. It was its own reward—an end, not a means.

In this Beatitude, Jesus showed the way for the fulfillment of that truth, elevating to its climax the progression of experience we have observed in these teachings.

If the highest good, the supreme happiness, is to see God—and it is—then purity in heart is required. Again, we grasp this simple statement rather quickly, but frequently its greatness passes over our heads.

In the Bible the word "pure" often means clean and untainted, but it is also used to describe gold that is without alloy or unadulterated. So the Lord was saying more than "blessed are those who have clean hearts." He was additionally saying "blessed are those whose hearts are single and undivided, whose devotion is without mixture."

As for the word *heart*, it means the center of our being, the core of our spirituality and deepest motivations. It is the real person.

It is not uncommon for people to want God, at least part of the time or with part of themselves, while at the same time wanting money and fame and all the world has to give. That won't do if you want to see God and receive the ultimate happiness, Jesus said.

Again, we need to see the insistence on unity and wholeness that filled the Lord's ministry. If your eye is unclear or dark, then your whole body will be full of darkness, He said, adding: "No one can serve two masters; for either he will hate the one and love the other, or he will hold to one and despise the other. You cannot serve God and mammon."[22]

We must focus on heaven or on earth. If it is the former, we will find the highest good.

Children of the King

Blessed are the peacemakers, for they shall be called sons of God.

Most of us would indeed be happy were we the children of a reigning monarch with power to act in his name and eventually to rule. Well, that can be the case, and the monarch is known as the "KING OF KINGS"[23] whose realm is all of creation.

Now a child of God is an heir of God,[24] the recipient of authority, possession, wealth, and even the kingdom itself. In short, he is the inheritor of everything that exists.

But, Jesus said, to progress to that status you must be a "peacemaker." And that is one who stops conflict and war.

The Lord Himself was the unique peacemaker, bringing peace between man and God.[25] In His name we are to do the same. We are to be going throughout the earth saying to all men, "Your sins are pardoned. You can be reconciled to God." As Paul taught:

> All this is from God. Through Christ, God made peace between us and himself, and God gave us the work of telling everyone about the peace we can have with him. God was in Christ, making peace between the world and himself. In Christ, God did not hold the world guilty of its sins. And he gave us this message of peace. So we have been sent to speak for Christ. It is as if God is calling to you through us. We speak for Christ when we beg you to be at peace with God.[26]

Indeed, we as peacemakers should be *begging* people to accept that which God has already done, since reconciliation is a two-way street requiring a response from both parties. For the world still echoes with the song of the heavenly host on a quiet night two thousand years ago: "peace, good will toward men."[27] Each Christmas Eve, even the hardest hearts quiver at the prospect. Man craves God and peace from his deepest recesses.

However, the sons of God, the peacemakers, do not stop at the point of peace with God. They work for peace between men. They themselves are not warriors, and they counsel others to stop fighting among themselves. Their goal is peace among individuals and among nations as they constantly strive to bring conflicting groups together and seek harmony and love, not at the expense of godly principle, but through godly relationships.

These will be blessed, for they do the will and the work of the Father, as sons and daughters. They will mature as heirs, and they will inherit their Father's estate, the kingdom.

Persecution Will Come

Blessed are those who have been persecuted for the sake of righteousness, for theirs is the kingdom of heaven.

Blessed are you when men cast insults at you, and persecute you, and say all kinds of evil against you falsely, on account of Me.[28]

A new world order is coming. It will not be the synthetic secular order promised by the United Nations or the Council on Foreign Relations. No, it is called the eternal kingdom of heaven, to be brought about by God Almighty. Only certain people will live in it. And it is the Lord's intention that those people practice living in it right now, doing His will and experiencing the blessings at this time.

As they do so, however—bringing every thought captive and exercising the authority of the kingdom—they will become visible for who they are, and opposition will mount. Abuse will come. It came to Jesus; it came to the early saints.

But, this Beatitude says, they will be happy as they continue in their remarkable realm. Indeed, wrote the apostle Peter, they will be experiencing genuine maturity: "If you are reviled for the name of Christ, you are blessed, because *the Spirit of glory and of God rests upon you.*"[29] The blessing can hardly be greater than that in this life.

Many people innocently ask, "But why would anyone want to persecute people if they're loving and kind?"

The answer lies deep in the innermost parts of unregenerate man. He is offended by the goodness of others, by their brightness, their happiness, their prosperity. He prefers a dark, worried countenance over a clear, carefree one. He simply loves darkness more than light, which is a specific disclosure of Scripture.[30]

The Bible says those who are following Christ bear a fragrance that is distinguishable both to the believer and the unbeliever. To one, it is the sweet aroma of life; to the other, the stench of death.[31] Such a person produces either appreciation or offense. The offense has at times turned to rage and persecution.

The Greek root behind the word we translate "persecute" means "to pursue" in the manner one would chase a fox or rabbit in a hunt, and pursuit is sometimes what results from the world's rage and persecution. "We must drive them from our midst," people roar. "We must search them out and destroy them." Before his conversion Paul the apostle did the same thing to the Christians as his offense turned to fury.[32]

But whether it be rage or merely rudeness, Jesus said we would be happy. "When men lie about you, when they curse you, when they throw you into prison because you remind them of God," He said, "be glad, rejoice, jump up and down, for the kingdom is yours. It is already yours."

But now the progression has reached fullness.

6

Upside Down

*F*rom the constitution of the kingdom of God, which so clearly reverses normal world thinking, we see that one virtue comes ahead of all others in the invisible realm. It is humility.

How can humility underlie happiness, prosperity, and fulfillment?

In my own case, the deep significance of this virtue unfolded in my constant search for wisdom from God. For, as we will see, wisdom and humility are thoroughly intertwined.

At one point, the following words sprang to life in my spirit: "God *resisteth* the proud, but giveth grace unto the humble."[1] The power of those words is devastating if you trace the logic. Not only does God help those with genuine humility, but also He actively *opposes* those who are proud.

Of course, the definition of humble that is easiest for most of us to grasp is that it is the opposite of proud. Most of us seem to know what pride is. God insists that we be the very opposite if we are to receive His favor and blessing; otherwise He is against us.

Thus it became clear to me that if we desire to live in the kingdom of God, to receive God's favor, we must make humility the number one virtue. It is foundational. Jesus, the very Son of God, existing in the form of God, took on the likeness of man without diminishing His deity and "humbled Himself by becoming obedient to the point of death, even death on a cross."[2] And His Father *favored* that humility in this manner. "Therefore also God highly *exalted* Him, and bestowed on Him the name which is above every name."[3]

The Old Testament prepares us for such a consequence with words like: "The reward of humility and the fear of the LORD / Are riches, honor and life."[4]

Those humble before God, obedient and reverent toward Him and His will, are the victorious ones, the ones elevated to the rewards that the world scrambles after—riches, honor, life. Just consider the competition, the greed, the worry, the abuse, the killing expended in the race for those benefits. People worldwide want (1) enough to live on, (2) recognition and approval of what they do, and (3) good health and long life. To the humble and obedient, these blessings come naturally.

The Path of Pride

The path of the proud is perfectly clear from Scripture, for without question pride is the greatest sin there is in the eyes of God. It thwarts His goodness toward man.

The proud man says, "I'll do it my way. I'm sufficient. I can control my destiny. I'm the captain of my soul, the master of my fate." There is nothing spiritually beggarly about him, nothing regretful about his inner condition, nothing hungering to be Godlike. In short, he lacks humility, and he receives nothing from the Lord, as we saw in discussing God's nature. His rewards, which are from men, are like vapor; they vanish suddenly, imperceptibly. For the wisdom of the Scripture says, "Pride goes before destruction, / And a haughty spirit before stumbling."[5]

Where there is pride, there will always be a fall. It is inevitable. We see it all about us, on a large scale and on small. Nations and individuals are slipping. They become arrogant; they cut off advice from old and respected friends; they go alone, and they fall.

As we strive to look into the invisible world to see God, to hear what He is saying, it is essential that we always bear in mind that our knowledge of that world comes primarily through His disclosure. *He* must reveal. Otherwise, we cannot see. Remembering that should keep us humble, even though our confidence rests in the fact that He said He would be found by those who diligently seek Him.[6] The proud, however, cannot bring themselves to seek, for that requires coming in from a lower position, and they have been conditioned otherwise.

As I said, humility is closely entwined with wisdom, which was the object of my diligent search years ago. I had been impressed with Solomon's reply to the Lord's offer one night following King David's death, "Ask what I shall give you."[7]

Can you imagine how most of us would have replied? But the Bible shows that Solomon revealed great humility in even approaching God, describing himself as a little child. "I do not know how to go out or come in," he said.[8] "Give me now wisdom and knowledge . . . for who can rule this great people of Thine?"[9] The Lord's response laid bare the pattern prevailing in the kingdom of heaven.

> Because you had this in mind, and did not ask for riches, wealth, or honor, or the life of those who hate you, nor have you even asked for long life, but you have asked for yourself wisdom and knowledge, that you may rule My people, over whom I have made you king, wisdom and knowledge have been granted to you. And I will give you riches and wealth and honor, such as none of the kings who were before you has possessed, nor those who will come after you.[10]

Echoing throughout were the words of Christ centuries later. "Seek first His kingdom and His righteousness; and all these things shall be added to you."[11]

I have become convinced that wisdom is the key to the secrets of the kingdom of God. It leads to favor. But the starting point is humility, as Solomon knew. For humility reveals fear of, or reverence for, the Lord.

The Book of Proverbs reveals the next step: "The fear of the LORD is the beginning of wisdom, / And the knowledge of the Holy One is understanding."[12]

Solomon Was Right

The cycle is complete—from humility, to fear of the Lord, to wisdom, to knowledge of the Holy One.

Wisdom, or spiritual understanding, *is* knowledge of the Holy One. And that is what we are seeking—knowledge of God, knowledge of His will and purpose, knowledge of the invisible world and how it works, knowledge of how to reach into it and bring its blessing and prosperity into our visible world.

In its ultimate sense, wisdom is understanding that an action taken today will be proven in the future to have been a correct one. And God provides that understanding.

To the people of Israel, God presented a body of Law that was to be their wisdom, an external expression of His will. If they followed those rules and principles in their society, then many years later people would look back and say that they had acted wisely. Unfortunately, they were inconsistent and often improperly motivated, and God's wisdom was not fully realized in their lives.

Through the incarnation of Christ and the coming of the Holy Spirit to dwell within believers, the wisdom of God took on an internal expression, with which we are now dealing. Obviously, like the Israelites, we have not been consistent or sincere in all of our efforts to manifest it.

But this wisdom from God is still available. Knowing that He governs all things, present and future, we can approach Him with pure hearts and say: "Show me how to run my life. Show me how the world works. Show me Your ways, Your principles, for running this enormously complex universe. I want to conform to what You do, to Your will, Your purpose, Your plan."

At that point we are seeking truth, and He will grant us wisdom for that. His entire purpose is to have us conform to truth. His wisdom will come; His principles will work. We will act, and the future will bear us out. People will say, "My, wasn't that man wise? Where did he get such wisdom?"

And all the while, it came from God.

Lesson from the Garden

It is helpful to recognize that the entire point of conflict in the Garden of Eden came from God's attempt to teach Adam and Eve wisdom. It was not that God wanted to prevent them from obtaining knowledge by forbidding them to eat from the tree of the knowledge of good and evil. His purpose was that they would gain wisdom by obeying Him. Day after day they were to pass that tree, saying, "If I eat the fruit from there, that will be evil; if I refrain from eating it, that will be good." They were to learn good and evil simply from having that tree in their midst.

We know that they ate, did evil, and failed to obtain what God intended. For good is doing what God wants; it reveals wisdom. Evil is doing what He does not want; it reveals foolishness.

God was, and still is, looking for people who will do what He wants, people with wisdom, that He may enter into their lives, their visible world, and favor them. No problem, no shortage, no crisis is beyond His ability.

But instead He encountered, and still encounters, foolishness fed by pride.

Three Cardinal Virtues

The three cardinal virtues in the kingdom of God are *faith, hope,* and *love.* We've already spoken of the centrality of faith in seeing, entering, and experiencing the kingdom, but it is also interwoven with the virtues of hope and love. Paul the apostle more than once put them together in describing the Christian life and ministry: "So these three things continue forever: faith, hope, and love. And the greatest of these is love."[13]

Faith is essential to the functioning of a civilization. We daily reveal faith in the laws of the creation. How could the world function if it didn't have faith that there would be a tomorrow? How could medical doctors and scientists function without faith in an orderly universe? How could we exist without faith, to some degree, in other people? How could we conduct business without faith in the marketplace and the rules of commerce? Nothing would work without some kind of faith.

Since we as spiritual beings are saved by the grace of God "through faith,"[14] it is obvious that faith is indispensable in any relationship with the Lord. Without it, we don't even know God exists. We are lost in our sins and are unable to see or to enter the invisible world, let alone transfer its blessings into this visible one.

As for hope, we need to make a distinction between it and faith. Hope is the ability to transfer our reliance from ourselves to God. It is founded on the sovereignty of God, His total independence of circumstances, His limitlessness.

It does not develop in us until our faith is tried, until under pressure we realize there is a Creator who will work things out for those with whom He is pleased. The apostle Paul described the progression:

> Therefore having been justified by faith, we have peace with God through our Lord Jesus Christ, through whom also we have obtained our introduction by faith into this grace in which we stand; and we exult in *hope* of the glory of God. And not only this, but we also exult in our tribulations, knowing that tribulation brings about perseverance; and perseverance, proven character; and proven character, *hope*.[15]

God's purpose is that our faith be tested, expressly to refine and strengthen it. Our endurance purifies and toughens our character; resolute hope in God and His plan results.

Note how Paul concludes the development of his thought: "and hope does not disappoint."[16]

Why is this true? Because hope shaped on the anvil rests in Him and in the moral rightness of His ultimate purpose—that the wicked will fall and the righteous will be rewarded.[17] Any expectation of the transfer of the blessings of the kingdom into our lives depends on it.

Finally, there must be love, which Paul described as the greatest of the trinity of virtues. Interestingly, it grows out of the other two. Hope grows out of faith, and love grows out of hope.

The Ability to Love

When a person has hope, when he knows that his future is assured, he stops struggling to maintain his own sphere of dominance; he stops fighting other people. He is willing to let the moral law of God work to defend his place. Then he is free to have concern for the well-being of others. He is no longer threatened and can give himself, his possessions, his life to someone else and know that God will make it right.

This process—and it usually is a process rather than an immediate change—was radical in my life. Stepping from the role of aggressive, competitive young lawyer who was just beginning the climb up the power ladder in a major international corporation, to the role of a man whose hope is secured by Almighty God completely altered my life and lifestyle. That hope released my ability to love—to love *real* people in *concrete* ways, not merely abstractly. Those in corporate halls were no longer shallow faces; folks in the hard, dirty streets of New York City were no longer the masses. They were people. I had been set free to express my concern for them, which eventually led my family and me to share our lives—our food, our clothing, our shelter—with others in one of the most wretched sections of New York. Our concern took on visible expression.

The Lord's experience with the cross was the ultimate expression of hope and love, of course. He had no visible assurance that He wouldn't be found absolutely foolish. He could have turned out to have been the most tragic figure in history, but He had hope in the rightness and goodness of His Father. He was free to love His people and to die for them. Hope and love are what we must have, Paul said, if we are to experience the power of God in the world today. Love is the strongest force possible. The reason is simple: God *is* love. No negative can overcome that positive. The perpetrators of hate and darkness have tried since the beginning but the light from Him has prevailed.[18]

Love is so overwhelming that it nullifies the physical principle under which every action produces an opposite, equal reaction. If someone pushes someone else, the latter will push hard in return, and escalation develops, usually to the point of violence. But Paul advised, "Absorb the push. Break the cycle. Overcome evil with good."[19]

We need to see that He wasn't advocating merely defense, but rather the perfect offense with the only weapon capable of absorbing and defeating evil. If someone demands you to go one mile, you can fight him; you can go sullenly and curse him all the way, feeling beaten and rejected. Or you can go on the attack and follow the charter of the kingdom: "If someone forces you to go with him one mile, go with him two miles."[20] Love will thus heap burning coals on his head, and the conviction of the Lord will work in His life for good.[21]

Yes, any of us who yearn to see our world changed and have been disappointed by the relative importance of the people of God must examine ourselves regarding the virtue of love. For the picture painted by Paul in one of his most famous discourses has to convince us that, were love to underlie all of our thoughts, words, and deeds—our use of the principles of God—then the world *would* be changed.

> Love is patient, love is kind, and is not jealous; love does not brag and is not arrogant, does not act unbecomingly; it does not seek its own, is not provoked, does not take into account a wrong suffered, does not rejoice in unrighteousness, but rejoices with the truth; bears all things, believes all things, hopes all things, endures all things. Love never fails.[22]

Eventually, Paul said, all else will pass away. The special gifts and talents, the wonderful endowments from on high—they will all run their course. But love endures forever, bridging eternity.

Holy Paradoxes

I trust it is abundantly clear that the constitution of the kingdom of God (the priorities of anyone who would experience the power and blessings of life there) is riddled with paradox. One can almost hear the Lord chuckle as the world looks in disbelief at what would appear to be anti-principles, in light of the way most people and nations conduct their affairs.

The world says hate your enemies. The kingdom says love your enemies.

The world says hit back. The kingdom says do good to those who mistreat you.

The world says hold onto your life at any cost. The kingdom says lose your life and you will find it.

The world says a young and beautiful body is essential. The kingdom says even a grain of wheat must die if it is to have life.

The world says push yourself to the top. The kingdom says serve if you want to lead.

The world says you are number one. The kingdom says many who are first will be last and the last first.

The world says acquire gold and silver. The kingdom says store up treasure in heaven if you would be rich.

The world says exploit the masses. The kingdom says do good to the poor.

Sadly, the church itself has often been a leader among those blinded to the paradoxes of the kingdom of God. So many times congregations have fled from the inner city, where they are so desperately needed, to comfortable suburbs, where they could luxuriate and not have to face the poor and their problems. Or they have served a political or social movement rather than the needy. Or they have embraced the management techniques of corporations rather than the government techniques of God. In short, they lost the sound of truth.

The temptations of worldly thinking are great, but they must be resisted even at the cost of appearing foolish by embracing truths that are paradoxical to conventional wisdom.

You see, one major paradox that we must accept as we try to change the world is this: The people of God are to live out the Beatitudes and the virtues of humility, wisdom, faith, hope, and love while at the same time becoming leaders.

"You are the light that gives light to the world," Jesus said.[23] In darkness, the man or woman who carries the light does not follow; he or she leads the way.

Yes, the humble, the disciplined, the wise, the faithful, the hopeful, the loving—they are to lead. *That* is the holy paradox.

And how will it be brought to pass? The laws of the kingdom in the following chapters will show us.

Part 2

Laws of the Kingdom

7

The Law of Reciprocity

*O*ne simple declaration by Jesus revealed a law that will change the world: "Give, and it will be given to you."[1]

Eight words. They form a spiritual principle that touches every relationship, every condition of man, whether spiritual or physical. They are pivotal in any hope we have of relieving the world's worsening crises.

Jesus expanded the universality of this theme throughout His ministry, varying subject matter and application. His point was so encompassing that it demanded many illustrations. In the discourse from which we get the eight words, we find this expansion: "just as you want people to treat you, treat them in the same way."[2] And from that, of course, came what the world describes as the Golden Rule: "Do unto others as you would have them do unto you."

Jesus went on, putting a frame around the eight key words in this manner:

> Be merciful, just as your Father is merciful. And do not pass judgment and you shall not be judged: and do not condemn, and you shall not be condemned; pardon, and you will be pardoned. Give, and it will be given to you; good measure, pressed down, shaken together, running over, they will pour into your lap. For whatever measure you deal out to others, it will be dealt to you in return.[3]

By putting this together with the world's greatest teaching on love, repeated from the Old Testament by Jesus as the heart of God's will, we establish the perfect "law" for conduct: "You shall love your neighbor as yourself."[4]

A Universal Principle

The *Law of Reciprocity,* a kingdom principle revealed in these teachings of the Lord, is relatively easy for us to identify since it is so visibly pervasive in the physical world. As we noted in the previous chapter, a basic law of physics says that for every action there is an equal and opposite reaction. The jet age in which we live is founded on it.

Scientists some years ago must have said, "If we can push a jet of hot air out the back end of an engine, there has to be an equal and opposite reaction going forward. Now, if we can attach this to an airplane, the thrust will be unprecedented."

Of course the logical, parallel step produced rocket engines able to generate enough backward thrust to provide forward speeds necessary to break the hold of gravity and send machines and men into outer space.

In the interpersonal realm, we find the same principle prevailing. If you smile at someone, he most likely will smile back. If you strike someone, the chances are he will hit you back. If you express kindness, you are almost certain to have someone express kindness in return. If you are critical of everything and everyone, you can expect to receive critical judgment from others.

A number of years ago, not long after our family moved to the Tidewater area of Virginia to begin the Christian Broadcasting Network, I remarked to my uncle, a man of admirable maturity, "The people in Tidewater are so very nice, far more so than I had even expected."

My uncle's eyes twinkled and he spoke a powerful, homespun version of the Law of Reciprocity that I hope I never forget: "I tell you what, young man, you will find nice people anywhere you go if you're nice to them."

It is a principle built into the universe. Even international relations respond to it. We Americans saw it at work from the earliest days of the conflict that escalated into the Vietnam War. The escalation was gradual at first. The North Vietnamese and Viet Cong would push at our allies and us. And we would push back, a little harder. They would retaliate, harder, and then back we would come. In such fashion, the United States participated in a dragged-out war that sapped its resources and resolve, simply because of an unwillingness on either side to break the cycle.

This should have been done in one of two ways.

First, we could have loved the enemy and all Southeast Asians, giving them food, clothing, and housing, and doing everything possible to establish them in freedom and the love of God. Love is able to absorb evil actions without fighting back, thus disrupting the cycle of tit for tat. Great faith and courage would have been required while awaiting reciprocal love.

Second, we could have hit the enemy so fast and so devastatingly as to nullify reciprocal action. Because of the ultimate infallibility of the Law of Reciprocity, however, it seems almost certain that the latter course would have at a point in history, perhaps distant, produced reciprocity from some source. Recall, for instance, the low estate to which Babylon fell from its days of great, but frequently cruel, empire. Consider how even today, as by the recurrence of an ancient debt, the modern nation of Iraq continues to incur the wrath and scorn of both God and man. The Persian Gulf War was just one more stage in a longstanding chain of repercussions arising from the laws of God.

The point, however, is that the Law of Reciprocity functions in international relations—for good or for evil. It is immutable.

The Individual Level

I want to look first at the personal level, for that is where our walk with God must begin. The Christian faith is personal, although it quickly spreads to the interpersonal, the national, and the international. It is rarely private for long.

115

Nonetheless, individuals today are in crisis, and the Law of Reciprocity is important to them.

Jesus, as we have seen, said, "Give, and it shall be given unto you; good measure, pressed down, and shaken together, and running over, shall men give into your bosom."[5] What words for those today who are suffering economically, threatened with unemployment or foreclosure! They, quite bluntly, need money. The stories are much the same: "What do I do? I'm using everything I have, and still my bills aren't paid. It seems I've been in debt forever."

As simple as it might look, the Law of Reciprocity is the solution. The world sees such thinking as foolishness, but the Lord says it is wisdom—because it is founded on truth.

As we hear Christ's words, "Give, and it will be given to you,"[6] they take us immediately to His commandment to "seek first the kingdom of God and His righteousness, and all these things shall be added to you."[7] We saw that "all these things" means whatever is needed to provide what we need to live fruitful and productive lives.

Giving is foundational. You have to give of yourself. You have to give of your money. You have to give of your time. And this foundational truth works in both the invisible and the visible worlds.

It is not complicated. If you want a higher salary in your job, you have to give more. Those with good salaries are not people who sit back and scheme and spend all their time thinking of ways to promote themselves. The people who are recognized in an organization are those who work harder, think more creatively, and act more forcefully in behalf of the enterprise. They give. They are rewarded.

So many people in our age go for a job with one thought in mind: "What will I get out of it?" Their only concerns are salary, fringe benefits, and title. They are takers, not givers. And takers do not go to the head of the list. The top people are those who say, "I want to do this to help you. Your company has a product that I can help make successful. I have a plan that I'm certain will work." They are givers.

We tend to justify our shortcomings in comparison with

these people by hinting at "lucky breaks" or "knowing the right people." But we're wrong. Invariably, those who give concepts, extra time, personal concern, and the like are the receivers. They are giving to an organization—and, indirectly, to individuals in that organization—and they are bound to benefit.

The hard work and overtime must also be accompanied by a proper attitude, of course. Those who give meanness or anger or trouble will get it back. "Do not judge lest you be judged,"[8] the Lord said, which drives directly at attitudes. Anyone who is critical, constantly faulting others and cutting associates, will not rise to the top. He will get back what he gives. The one who makes his department look good, including his boss, is the one who will get the salary increase he needs. "The way you give to others is the way God will give to you."[9] That's a law.

The Issue of Giving

We cannot talk about a need for money without running headlong into the matter of giving to the Lord. Since everything is His—the cattle on a thousand hills, silver, gold, governments— He obviously is the one we should be turning to in our need. "Give, and it shall be given to you," Jesus said. And that includes our dealing with God Almighty.

The prophet Malachi was precise in speaking the thoughts of the Lord regarding such dealings.

> "From the days of your fathers you have turned aside from My statutes, and have not kept them. Return to Me, and I will return to you," says the Lord of hosts. "But you say, 'How shall we return?' Will a man rob God? Yet you are robbing Me! But you say, 'How have we robbed Thee?' *In tithes and contributions.* You are cursed with a curse, for you are robbing Me, the whole nation of you! *Bring the whole tithe* into the storehouse, so that there may be food in My house, and *test Me now in this*," says the LORD of hosts, "*if I will not open for you the windows of heaven, and pour out for you a blessing until there is no more need.*"[10]

The passage shows how seriously the Lord God takes the matter of giving. Obviously, He owns everything. He doesn't really need our tithes and offerings, but He has gone to great lengths to teach us how things work. If we want to release the superabundance of the kingdom of heaven, we must first give. Our Father is more than ready to fulfill His side of the Law of Reciprocity. One can almost imagine His heavenly host standing on tiptoe, brimming with anticipation, gleeful, awaiting the opportunity to release the treasures so badly needed in our visible world.

Note the promise of abundance in Malachi's words. Some translators render the promised blessing as "so great you won't have enough room to take it in!"[11] In the world, we measure return in percentages of 6 or 8 or 10, and sometimes 15 and 20. In the kingdom, as we noted earlier, the measures are 3,000 percent, 6,000 percent, and 10,000 percent—thirty, sixty, and a hundredfold.

That is a beautiful promise for those facing economic distress today. "Test Me," says the Lord. "Prove Me."

I am as certain of this as of anything in my life: If you are in financial trouble, the smartest thing you can do is to start giving money away. Give tithes and offerings to the Lord. Give time. Give work. Give love. That sounds crazy. But we have seen how the plan of God is filled with paradox. If you need money, then begin to give away some of whatever you have. Your return, poured into your lap, will be great, pressed down, and running over.

A Case in Chile

A missionary to Chile shared some insights into this law of the kingdom some time ago. As pastor of a group of extremely poor peasants, he did everything he could to minister to their needs. He revealed what he considered to be the full counsel of the Lord, teaching the Bible as the Word of God and leading them into many significant and deep understandings. But one day the Lord spoke as clearly as if He had been standing face to face with him. "You have not declared My whole truth to these people," He said.

"But Lord," the missionary replied, "I don't understand. I've taught them about justification by faith and forgiveness of sins and baptism in the Holy Spirit, about miracles and walking in Your power. I've taught them about the church, about history, about doctrine. I've taught them about godliness and holy living, about the Second Coming.

"What, my Lord, have I failed to teach them?"

He waited a moment. The voice was very clear. "You have not declared My tithe to them."

The missionary was stunned. "But Lord, these are very poor people! They hardly have enough to live. I can't ask them to tithe. They have nothing."

Again, a silent moment. "You must declare to them My tithe."

He was a faithful, obedient man. And the debate ended.

The next Sunday morning, with heavy heart, he stepped into the pulpit of the little rustic church in that poor, backward community, took a deep breath, and began.

"My beloved brethren," he said, looking into the open, uplifted faces of his flock, "God has shown me that I haven't been faithful in declaring to you His whole counsel. There is something you have not been doing that I must tell you about. You have not been tithing to the Lord."

And he began a trek through the Scriptures with them that lasted nearly an hour. He explained everything, including the Malachi portions urging that the Lord be proven on the matter.

The next Sunday, it was their turn. In they came, obedient to the Word. They didn't have money, so they brought eggs, chickens, leather goods, woven articles, and all manner of things from their poor peasant homes. The altar area was heaped high.

The missionary felt badly about taking the gifts, but he too was faithful, so he sold some and used the money for the work of the church. He distributed some of the gifts to the destitute in the neighborhood and kept some for his own sustenance, in lieu of income.

The same thing happened Sunday after Sunday. The people tithed.

119

It wasn't long before the effects of drought were seen throughout the countryside. Poverty gripped the people of the land worse than ever. Crops failed; buildings deteriorated; gloom covered everything.

But, miraculously, this was not so with the members of that little church. Their crops flourished as though supernaturally watered. But more than that, the yields were extraordinary, bounteous, healthy, flavorful. Their fields were green, while those around were withering. Their livestock were sleek and strong. Relative abundance replaced abject poverty.

They even had an overflow of crops and goods that could be sold, and before long their tithes included money. They were able to build a much-needed new meeting house.

Despite his misgivings, the missionary and his people had learned that no matter how desperate the situation, no matter how deep the impoverishment, the principles of the kingdom can turn deprivation into abundance.

They touch the visible world.

What Is a Tithe?

Lest we become rigid and legalistic, we need to understand the tithe quantitatively. The word, of course, means a "tenth." People quibble over such questions as whether it is before or after taxes, whether it should go to a single ministry, whether it should be put ahead of absolute necessities, and the like. Such niggling misses the point.

The Lord cherishes a ready giver whose heart puts Him and His service ahead of everything. The apostle Paul had a lot to declare on this point:

> Now this I say, he who sows sparingly shall also reap sparingly; and he who sows bountifully shall also reap bountifully. Let each one do just as he has purposed in his heart; not grudgingly or under compulsion; for God loves a cheerful giver. And God is able to make all grace abound to you,

that always having all sufficiency in everything, you may have an abundance for every good deed. . . . You will be enriched in everything for all liberality.[12]

According to the dictionary, the original definition of tithe was one-tenth of the annual produce of one's land or of one's annual income. According to the Bible, that is merely the *starting place* of giving to the Lord. The Malachi passage refers to "tithes and offerings." One might say, then, that there is no offering until the tithe has been paid; it is the expected, minimum amount.

So a lot of people who practice this critical spiritual law give far more than 10 percent of their income to the Lord's work. It's all His anyhow, they recognize. King David voiced this when he said:

Both riches and honor come from Thee, and Thou dost rule over all. . . . But who am I and who are my people that we should be able to offer as generously as this? For all things come from Thee, and from Thy hand we have given Thee.[13]

He also wrote in one of his great psalms:

The earth is the LORD's, and the fulness thereof; the world, and they that dwell therein.[14]

Therefore, many people ignore any 10 percent cutoff and give out of the abundance of their provision. I know one New Jersey florist who had been thoroughly blessed by the Lord as he exercised the principles we are exploring in this book, and he frequently gave 90 percent of his annual income to the service of God. And the prosperity simply mounted. He was not able to outgive the Lord. That law is built into the kingdom. It never changes.

One of the saddest things that can happen to people comes about so naturally. When hard times come, when they are thrown out of work or inflation runs wild, the first place they cut is often their tithe. Usually their intentions are good. "I'll make it up next week," they rationalize. And God lets them go. He does not pressure. But that is the worst thing they can do. That, I believe, is the time to step up your giving. That is the time you need something from God. "Prove Me," the Lord says. "Give, and you will receive."[15]

The Fruits of Neglect

One of the many men who served the Lord in the rescue missions and other street ministries during the Depression of the thirties has reported very moving accounts about those who would pass through the soup kitchen—broken, smashed men, virtually destroyed—where he would often ask them about their spiritual lives.

"Tell me, friend, were you faithful to the Lord with your tithes?" he would inquire.

And the man would shake his head no, clutching his cup and plate in front of him, staring vacantly ahead.

And he'd ask the next one, "When you were prosperous and all was well with you, did you give to the Lord? Were you faithful with your tithe?"

The man would shake his head no.

Never once, this worker reported, did he find a man living in poverty who had been faithful to the Lord and His principle of giving. And that fits exactly with what David said thousands of years ago: "I have been young, and now I am old; / Yet I have not seen the righteous forsaken, / Or his descendants begging bread."[16]

We must not misunderstand any of this to say that should there be a general economic collapse, we will see Christians riding in Rolls-Royces, wearing big jewels and rich furs, and living in mansions while everyone else lives in poverty. That would be contrary to the nature of God. It merely means that, if we have been faithful to the Lord, given to Him, given to the poor, given to our neighbor, then we will receive according to the prosperity of the Lord, not the prosperity of the ungodly.

We will experience the fulfillment of seeking first the kingdom of God and having the things necessary for life given to us additionally, even matter-of-factly, if you will.

Those who ignore God's principles, on the other hand, can be expected in a moment, a flash, to find themselves totally stripped of what they thought was theirs.

> Yet a little while and the wicked man will be no
>   more;
> And you will look carefully for his place, and he
>   will not be there.
> But the humble will inherit the land,
> And will delight themselves in abundant
>   prosperity.[17]

Negative Reciprocity

As we have noted, the Law of Reciprocity works in all the affairs of men. It can work for our good, or it can work for our harm. Americans saw it fulfilled in racial relationships, with roots going back to the days of slavery.

In one of the horrors of history, our representatives went to Africa, seized human beings, stored them in ships, and brought them here to treat like property. We sold them and put them out as forced labor, mistreating them, breaking up families, and ignoring their rights and dignity as people created in the image of God.

"Give, and it will be given to you . . ."

It took a hundred years, but our land has been reaping what it sowed. In many cases, blacks were forced into a matriarchal society as men were totally destroyed emotionally, psychologically, and spiritually. Women struggled to put bread on the table for their children, who soon perceived the cause of their suffering and were ripe for hatred.

Guilt and resentment often overtook the whites. The sides of conflict were locked in. And it came. A good nation was battered, its regions divided, its people torn.

Even though education has been improved, rights defended, and poverty relieved, the suffering continues. The government itself teeters under the threat of bankruptcy as it is unable to meet the demands of sickness, unemployment, welfare, inner-city redevelopment, and other social distress, much of it traceable to the deprivation of the black man centuries ago.

Signs of a possible turnaround through proper use of the Law of Reciprocity, which again identifies slavery as the cause of much that went wrong in America, can be seen in the economic recovery of the South. For many years, the Southern economy foundered, hostage to the Northern banking and commercial interests, because the region did not have properly trained and educated people capable and desirous of working in factories and offices. Without these wage earners, there were also few customers for Southern manufacturers, and prosperity eluded all.

But once the South began to give freedom to the black people, providing education and taking other steps to lift their standard of living, the economy edged upward and soon reached boom level in many places. The South prospered as it never had.

Quite simply, the society had cursed itself. But the Law of Reciprocity, still lacking in many dimensions of life, had made it possible to reverse the curse.

Getting Back in Kind

I saw the very opposite of the national racial experience unfold on the streets of Portsmouth, Virginia, one day in 1960, only to be snuffed out, all through the working of the reciprocity principle.

A friend, Dick Simmons, was visiting shortly after my family and I had moved to Tidewater, and he asked if we could go preach on the streets in some of the poor sections of the city. We ended up going to a shopping center in the middle of an area of recent racial violence.

We began by engaging a number of black youths in conversation, and before long several dozen had gathered. Dick preached to them about Jesus. The Holy Spirit moved upon all of us, and after a few minutes. Dick said, "Now if you want to meet Jesus, the One I'm talking about, you can do that right here, right now. You bow your head and kneel right here on the sidewalk and pray and ask Jesus to come into your life."

What a unique gathering that was! In the middle of one of the city's tensest areas, where violence had already erupted, love and peace and beauty descended. Here were two white men giving love and knowledge and experience—giving the truth of the gospel—to a group of deprived, volatile black youngsters, and what did we get in return? We received love and kindness and warmth back from them.

In an instant, even as the youngsters were praying the sinner's prayer and lives were being changed, everything exploded into a surrealistic movie scene. Two cars of police with trained dogs wheeled to a stop. Men and dogs piled out and charged the kneeling black youngsters. The policemen had jumped to a hasty conclusion, prompted by a phone call from a bystander, that a racial protest was mounting, and they intended to break it up. They chased the youngsters across the street as growls and yells filled the air.

In a twinkling, the Law of Reciprocity set in. The youngsters began to throw rocks at the policemen. Yells turned to curses. And the violence escalated, with all the potential of the devastation that shattered American cities in the sixties.

Dick and I had given love; we had received love. The police had given harshness; they had received harshness. Unhappily the latter pattern prevailed through most of the land.

Potential for the World

Convinced that the Law of Reciprocity could bring relief, if not total solution, to the major problems of the world, I began shortly after dawn one morning early in the decade to make notes on these problems. In less than an hour I had covered the spectrum: The Law of Reciprocity without question affects the way

125

people and nations live with each other. It has the potential to bring peace to the world.

Following are merely a few of the issues I jotted down, but they are widespread enough to make the case. Remember, under the Law of Reciprocity, men everywhere would operate under the principle of giving what they expect to receive, treating others the way they want to be treated, and loving their neighbors as themselves.

War. The need for standing armies would be removed as nations give as they receive and love their neighbors as themselves. The threat of invasion would be gone. Defense appropriations would be unnecessary. Huge governmental spending and the cruelty of high inflation and high taxes would be relieved.

Trade. There would be no need for tariff barriers because nations and companies would not be dumping products and damaging domestic industries. Trade would occur as needed and desired, fostered by healthy, imaginative competition, uninterrupted by runaway greed. Terms like "Third World" would become meaningless.

Injustice. Incredible extremes of wealth and poverty would be evened out simply by human kindness and generosity. The unjust privileges of wealth and other types of status would diminish, melting away envy, jealousy, greedy ambition, and perverted competitiveness.

Crime. Burglary, theft, and vandalism would vanish, along with personal assaults, murder, rape, and kidnaping. Narcotics usage and traffic would cease. Business and securities fraud would pass, cheating at every level would fade, along with price fixing, monopoly and cartel abuse, and influence peddling. International terrorism would end. Prisons would become obsolete.

Pollution. Air, water, and land could be cleaned up. There would be no more factories belching acid smoke into the air and draining chemical waste into rivers. Beer cans, bottles, and garbage would vanish from the roadsides and campsites. Parks would retain their beauty. Wildlife would flourish.

Productivity. As the Japanese have learned from their change of heart after World War II, moving from a people known for cheap merchandise to one prospering from excellence, nations would see their economies improve radically through increased productivity in every sector. Employers and employees alike would see sharp changes in their motivation, satisfaction, and collective prosperity. There would be no more shoddy products, no more dangerous construction in which buildings collapse and hundreds are injured or killed, no more unsafe toys to maim children.

Government. Huge governmental bureaucracy would disappear as overdrawn, rigid regulation and enforcement becomes unnecessary, along with most of the social services. As men begin to treat one another as God intended, the governments could concentrate on those relatively few things that must be done collectively.

The Foundation of Society

The Law of Reciprocity is the fundamental principle of social development. It is the foundation for development between people and communities. Great things happen when people follow this principle, but devastation comes when it is ignored. Consider, for example, the crisis of the family and all the aftermath that follows the breakup of the home in our culture.

We see the repercussions of disobedience of this law in international affairs as well. When Saddam Hussein went up against a defenseless neighbor and did to those people what was unjust and unfair, the nations of the world came against him. As a result, there was great suffering; there always is when somebody violates the fundamental law which says, "Do unto others as you would have them do unto you."

In the troubled economy of the 1990s we can see better than ever that this principle is the real reason for Japan's emergence as a world leader in industry and technology. When I wrote the first edition of *The Secret Kingdom*, the Japanese were not the power they are today. True, they were coming, but they had not yet reached the levels they would eventually attain. They had not yet become America's rival, dominating several key high-tech industries worldwide.

But what the Japanese discovered through the guidance of the brilliant American teacher, W. Edwards Deming, was the principle of the Golden Rule. The strategic factor behind Japan's success involves the whole idea of service; it is a combination of the Law of Greatness and the Law of Reciprocity. They found that in order to win, they had to give service. If they served their customers, the customers served them in return. If they served their employees and gave employees a voice in decision making, the employees worked even harder and helped the company to grow.

Jesus said, "Give, and it will be given unto you." And He said to the disciples, "Let he who would be greatest among you be the servant of all." Companies, individuals, and nations who follow His guidance will attain prosperity.

In his celebrated books, *In Search of Excellence* and *Thriving on Chaos,* author Tom Peters explored the factors that contribute to the success of America's greatest, most prosperous companies. What he found was that the industry leaders in virtually every case made, in effect, a fetish out of customer service. In *Thriving on Chaos,* Peters makes a strong point that the top companies have virtually a fanatical desire to serve their customers at any cost. Successful companies, here or anywhere else, do everything they can to serve the customer.

Genuine Concern

Stores he pointed out, like Nordstrom's, which is famous for its service, ranked at the top of their industry. And the example can be extended in many areas, not just businesses. We work very hard to do the same type of thing at CBN. For instance, we have a telephone ministry where we call people and simply ask how we can serve them. Counselors ask, "How can we pray for you? How can we help you?" People are sometimes surprised by this type of service. They ask, "Where's the pitch?" But there is no pitch. We tell them, "We just called to see if we can be of help to you in some way." What has pleased us is the bonding this kind of personal service produces. When people feel that you genuinely care, they respond. And in this cold, impersonal world, people are so desperate to have someone care for them.

It is such a tragedy that in this densely populated, highly social nation, we have the loneliest people who have ever lived. In an age that has produced miracles in communications technology, there is little communication on the human level, or personal contact, or touching, or genuine love. History shows that caring attention and service is the way to bridge the emotional gap between people. It says that when you give personal service, you always win. But somehow that message has to be understood and adopted on a much greater scale.

When you contrast the incredible debt and lingering recession of the United States with the incredible prosperity and financial achievements of Japan, you eventually have to realize that the Japanese are simply practicing what we used to preach. As a result, they have built an economic colossus on this one principle.

In the past few years Japan has made some mistakes, grown too fast, leveraged too much. But even if the recent problems in their economy were to lead to some kind of collapse, the fact remains that they built their success on service. The Law of Reciprocity was the underpinning of their achievement, and when it is followed faithfully, it will always bring positive results.

I have pushed and tested these principles for many years now, and they work in every situation. It's just a matter of having our minds open to see the correlation between current events and God's Word and how they fit.

Renegades Excluded

Many people rightly ask, "Can this law be made to work in the world today? Can we simply begin to live this way?"

I believe the answer is yes, with an exception.

The Law of Reciprocity when practiced by law-abiding people and nations will not work with a totally lawless renegade. To begin to practice this principle with one such as that is extraordinarily dangerous, and a distinction must be made.

However, if you analyze it, you will see that even this exception is a fulfillment of the reciprocity principle. As the renegade gives (living outside law and decency) so will he receive from the entire society, in force. He will be ostracized. That, in a sense, was God's answer to the problem when He called forth His people, Israel. They were not to temporize—to try to disregard God's principles because of convenience or expediency. The renegade was removed from society and rendered incapable of such conduct through very harsh punishment.[18]

For us, the example is found in the New Testament. Jesus did not turn the other cheek to the devil or anyone governed by the devil through His ministry. Instead, He exercised His authority. As James said: "Stand against the devil, and the devil will run from you."[19] Oppose him and those belonging to him. They are renegades.

It should be noted that the need to act quickly against the renegade in our society explains why the Law of Reciprocity does not encompass pacifism. For domestic tranquility, there must be a police force and a system of justice capable of bringing sure and swift punishment upon those who rebel against society. Injustice in the administration of the law will bring on revolution. But lack of diligence in the punishment of crime will promote anarchy.

So also in the international realm, the family of peace-loving nations must be able to protect itself against renegades. The Law of Reciprocity would forbid two equals from beginning a fight to settle a dispute. However, a miscreant is not the equal of law-abiding persons. A rogue nation is not the equal of the family of nations. A rebellious child is not the equal of his parents. In each of these cases, the lawful and just application of discipline or restraint does not violate the Law of Reciprocity. Such discipline is in fact a God-given, albeit temporary, method of dealing with evil in a still imperfect world.

But in all other cases, I believe we should exercise the Law of Reciprocity to the fullest, even among those not yet committed personally to God Almighty. For it is a principle that will work in the visible world—now.

8

The Law of Use

*T*he next seven years are going to be absolutely critical for Western civilization and the United States. If our culture continues the present, accelerating moral decline, the demise of our society seems virtually inevitable.

In Western Europe and the United States large numbers of people have forsaken the principles of the kingdom of God while their elites have exerted every effort to undermine the organizing premise of this society. The media, the intellectual community, government officials—those responsible for policy at every level—from the local school boards to the United States Supreme Court—seem determined to subvert and undermine the Christian principles and traditional family values that have upheld this society from its beginning.

On the global scale a concerted effort has been launched to establish a new world order based on a vague amalgam of socialism, humanism, and religious syncretism of values, while the traditional Western Christian heritage is abandoned. During the past fifty years these utopian dreamers have all but destroyed public education in America while they have fastened upon our nation a wasteful and profligate governmental system.

But instead of acknowledging their failures, these liberal manipulators and demagogues are stepping up their demand for more of the same. They want more failed policies instead of fewer; they seem not to have understood the lessons we have just learned from the fall of Communism.

I believe all this gives a great sense of urgency to the issues being discussed in this book. But when you look at the approaching financial collapse that may well be upon us—either a deflationary collapse or a hyperinflationary blowout—you have to see that we are in very real danger of destabilizing governments worldwide.

Anarchy, a revolution, emerging dictatorship, or worse, a worldwide dictatorship could well emerge from such an extraordinarily serious debacle. Most of the problems we have in the world today could be solved if we would simply adopt and implement God's principles of success. But short of a powerful spiritual revival and the concerted effort of America's Christians to bring about dramatic moral and political change, the future is not promising.

There is hope for a bright future, but we must act now! If we are to survive this momentous time in our nation's history, we must return to the laws of the kingdom or it will be too late for all of us. The secular world as presently constituted will not do it. The task is the responsibility of Christian people. Christians must boldly proclaim the truth of the kingdom, then as citizens of this world insist that the common-sense principles of God's kingdom be reflected in public policy for the good of all.

The term "from Christ to chaos" expresses our current dilemma. Surely, unless we adopt the wise principles of the Bible to bring order to our government and our lives, we are going to see the unavoidable collapse of what has been called Western Civilization. It will follow moral collapse as surely as night follows day.

Christ's Sense of Urgency

But we must not lose hope; great things can be done out of a sense of urgency. An exceptional urgency seemed to have gripped the Lord's ministry by the time He reached the teaching I wish to examine in this chapter. He had so much to impart and seemingly so little time to do it. Everything was speeding up.

In the midst of rapid-fire teachings about the kingdom of heaven, He began this story:

> For it is just like a man about to go on a journey, who called his own slaves, and entrusted his possessions to them. And to one he gave five talents, to another, two, and to another, one, each according to his own ability; and he went on his journey.[1]

Then unfolds the development of what I have come to call the *Law of Use*. To me this is the most important principle for human growth and development to be found in our world. It touches every facet of personal and communal life. We follow it to our benefit; we ignore it to our peril. Here is the setting.

Servant number one received five talents. The parable says he went out and "traded with them." We can imagine what happened. Perhaps he bought some commodities, sold them at a profit, and reinvested the entire amount. Or perhaps he took a journey and returned with valuable goods, and he added to the value of those goods through work he or someone else did to them. Regardless, he worked with his master's money and eventually doubled it.

The man with the two talents acted similarly. He may have bought wool, handed it over to a weaver, and then sold the woven cloth at a profit, only to quickly reinvest it and keep all the money working. Eventually he had doubled the amount left with him.

The third slave acted differently, however. The parable says he took the single talent, dug a hole, and buried it. He was afraid, Jesus said—afraid that if he went out and bought wool or oil or some such item, a depression would come and he would lose the money. Or maybe robbers would steal it. Or maybe someone would outsmart him or cheat him, say, at the weights and balances. Perhaps he would make a wrong decision. So, impotent with fear, he preserved his lord's investment by hiding it in a safe place.

After a long time, the lord returned and called the slaves to him. "Tell me," he said after a brief exchange, "how did you do with my money?"

The first servant quickly replied, "Master, I took the five talents and I traded with them. I bought and sold, and leveraged your money, but I made five more talents. Here is the original and five additional."

He had covered his overhead and still doubled the amount.

The master was pleased: "Well done, good and faithful slave; you were faithful with a few things. I will put you in charge of many things; enter into the joy of your master."

The next servant stepped forward and reported: "Lord, I took your two talents, and I went out and bought and sold. I entered into some business transactions, and I took some risks, but I made money. I've got two more talents. Here are the two you gave me and two additional."

The lord replied in the same way he had to the man with five talents.

Then it was the third man's turn. "Tell me what you've done with my money while I've been gone," the master said.

"Lord, I knew you were a hard man," he began. "You reap where you don't sow. You gather where you don't even plant. So I was afraid. I figured the best thing to do was play it safe, so I wrapped the talent up nicely and hid it. Here it is; I didn't lose anything."

Most of us today can sympathize with this fellow. After all, if you're a trustee over somebody else's property, you have to be careful. You can't take risks. It's even worse in an economically volatile world like ours.

What did the master do in this illustration to prepare us for the kingdom?

You wicked, lazy slave, you knew that I reap where I did not sow, and gather where I scattered no seed. Then you ought to have put my money in the bank, and on my arrival I would have received my money back with interest. . . . Cast out the worthless slave into the outer darkness; in that place there shall be weeping and gnashing of teeth.[2]

The man was considered wicked and sinful, given to evil, and because he refused to take what his lord had given him and put it to work, improving upon it.

Note that quantity wasn't the key. Their use of what they had been given was what mattered. Proper use gave them entry into the place of joy. Improper use barred the third man.

However, the startling point of the parable is the following conclusion: "to everyone who has shall more be given, and he shall have an abundance; but from the one who does not have, even what he does have shall be taken away."[3] During my extended time of seeking wisdom from God, the magnitude of that sentence crystallized for me. I perceived that it presented a principle, a law, that was as important for day-to-day life as any there is.

"To everyone who has shall more be given." It seems shocking, particularly to those tending toward a welfare state or socialism, as so many in the world do today. We have a poor man with only one talent and another who has improved his lot, and we take the one away from the former and give it to the one who already has ten. It goes against the grain, simply because we have failed to see how important God views our use of what He has given us.

Use It or Lose It

Despite our preconceived attitudes toward social justice, God's Law of Use controls the ultimate distribution of wealth. We must be willing to take the world as He made it and live in it to the fullest. For He says, in fact, that if we are willing to do that—if we are willing to use what He has given us—we will have more. But if we are not willing to use what He has given us, we will lose it.

As we will see, this is not mean or unfair. It is the way *God* wants the world to be. And as we begin to understand the Law of Use, we will soon realize that this is the only way it can be.

Our bodies give us a perfect illustration of the working of the Law of Use. For instance, let's say you would like to learn to do push-ups. Perhaps you've never been able to do them well.

I will assume the Lord has given you the strength to do one, perhaps only the kind from the knees, but you can do that. And so you take what you have, and you put it to work. Do one a day for a week or two and before long you'll find it's not hard. Then go to two, and do two for a week or two. They'll get easier, and then you can move to three, and so on. Before long you'll be doing ten, and you'll start to wonder, "Why did I think these were so hard?"

Do you see the same principle? To everyone who has, and who uses what he has, more shall be given.

Now, you could do the very opposite. You could take what you have, refuse to use it, and ultimately lose it. For instance, you could tape you hand to your side in such a way that you would be unable to move it. If you left it there, totally unused, for six months, the muscles would wither and an arm that had had unlimited potential would be useless. Even what you had would have been taken away.

The same would hold true for the development of your mind and resultant skills. If you were a doctor and wanted to master a particular type of treatment, you would begin simply with the knowledge you had. You could study everything available, and you could practice your knowledge, simply at first, perhaps under close supervision. You could stay at it for a year or two and before long, you would master the subject. You would have expertise and a specialty that others would covet, all acquired through using what you already had.

Of course, if you thoroughly neglected study and abstained totally from practice, you would gradually reach a point of deterioration and incompetence where no one would want to trust himself in your hands. You would lose what you started with.

So also in our spiritual lives. If we pray, read the Bible, and exercise the understanding we already have, we will grow. If we don't, we will weaken and diminish in effectiveness.

Carver and the Peanut

One of the geniuses of our country was the son of a slave, a black educator and botanist named George Washington Carver. He perfectly illustrated the Law of Use in a different fashion.

Carver was an agricultural chemist and researcher, and he suspected that there were many wonderful treasures still hidden in God's kingdom. So, the story goes, one day Carver went before the Lord in prayer and said, "Mr. Creator, show me the secrets of Your universe."

It was a big request, but he believed in asking boldly.

He received a bold answer, although it might not have seemed so at first.

"Little man," God said, "you're not big enough to know the secrets of My universe."

One can almost feel the sense of repudiation. However, God was not finished with His reply. "But I'll show you the secret of the peanut."

From the universe to the peanut! "Take it apart," God said.

Undaunted and obedient, Carver did just that. He took the peanut apart and discovered several hundred elements in that little seed and its shell.

Still God wasn't finished. "Start putting it back together again, in different form," the Lord instructed.

He did. And from that work came food of many kinds, plastics, paint, oil, and seemingly endless products. He revolutionized Southern agriculture and industry just by using what God had given him—boldly, creatively, patiently.

The Exponential Curve

Working hand in hand with the Law of Use is a mathematical phenomenon known as the exponential curve. Actually Jesus set forth the first step in such a curve when He told the parable of the talents. It fits perfectly into our principle. The Lord told how two of the servants doubled what had been given to them. Had they done that at regular intervals, such as annually, then their increases, placed on a graph, would have established an exponential curve that would have proved astounding.

For example, if they began with $100 and continued to double the amount each year, the graph would proceed along at a rather ho-hum level for a few years and then it would skyrocket. At the end of twenty years, the $100 would have grown to $50 million. In just five more years, it would have soared to $1.6 billion. By the thirty-five-year mark, it would be $1.6 trillion, and at the end of fifty years, it would be $12.8 quadrillion, which is more money than exists in the world.

This shows dramatically what can happen through a joining of the Law of Use with the exponential curve, simply accomplishing at a set rate what Jesus was teaching in the parable.

Of course, such 100 percent increases are not necessary for the exponential curve to be effective with this law. Take the $100 and compound it at 6 percent for fifty years and it is transformed into nearly $2,800. Increase the percentage to 15 or 20 percent and you end up with several hundred thousand dollars.

So phenomenal is this principle that Baron Rothschild, the financier, once described compound interest as "the eighth wonder of the world." Bankers throughout history have enriched themselves enormously by way of this "wonder." The key is consistency and longevity, to the point where the exponential curve makes its sharp upward turn, and the escalation defies the imagination.

I was in Zaire in June 1991, addressing a group of government leaders. I wanted to explain these principles as clearly and as memorably as possible, so I took hundred dollar bills and gave one to each member of the cabinet. I told them, "You now have in your hand the wealth of the world." Then I explained to them how it works. I said that at the end of fifty years, if the money in their hands doubled every year, they would have $12.8 quadrillion.

"You'll have more money than there is in the world today," I told them. "On the other hand, I said, if you start out with all the money in the world and continue to live under 230 percent inflation, you'll be back to a hundred dollars in just thirty-two years. You can take all the money in the world and reduce it to a hundred dollars if you allow the economy to stagnate. If you tolerate the kind of inflation you have in this country today, the only possible result is absolute and total collapse."

I am sorry to say that they didn't listen to me. I said, "If you don't stop printing money, you're going to have riots, looting, and violence in the streets." Within three months inflation had gotten so bad that the army revolted and did more than a billion dollars' worth of damage. There was killing, bloodshed, and devastation, and it all came, just as I had said, within three months.

Dealing with Reality

But we need to understand that the secret of growth applies in every area. It applies in areas such as church growth just as much as it does to individual, family, corporate, or any other kind of growth. These laws apply wherever people work for specific goals.

It says, "unto him who has, more will be given." The principle exploded for good with our Project Light initiative. I had visited Nicaragua, El Salvador, and Guatemala. I saw the beginning of a powerful spiritual revival. Then I realized the mass communications expertise our organization had accumulated during thirty years of intensive use. We were experts in television, radio, film, art, billboards, printing, and mass marketing.

So I challenged our staff to assemble all of these skills for one massive media blitz in Central America. We called it *Projecto Luz* ("Project Light"). And blitz we did. As a result we had the largest television audience in the history of those nations, and 3 million people made decisions to accept Jesus Christ as their Savior. It was amazing, and it was thrilling, but it was the result of the application of the Law of Use. We had worked with what we had, allowing God to multiply our efforts.

As I have said before, I only had seventy dollars in my pocket when we started CBN. But I used what I had, and God blessed it beyond measure. Now we operate in seventy nations, and just one division, Operation Blessing, has had the joy of giving $340 million to the poor and needy over the past fourteen years. This is no boast; it is merely evidence that we have discovered, firsthand, that God's law of growth and development really works!

Certainly, the Lord Jesus did not intend to lay down for us a principle whose purpose was to allow the rich to get richer and the poor to get poorer. No, He was showing how the world works and how, through the diligent, patient exercise of the gifts He is constantly bestowing, we can enter into the prosperity and abundance of the invisible world.

We need to see that the truths He disclosed are available to everyone—now. The sad fact is that not everyone—not even those committed to Him—will enter in. We are too much like the servant who took his talent and buried it.

The Politics of Envy

The problem often is that we will look at someone who's successful in a field where we would like to be, and we say, "I wish I were like him." We want to have the success without having applied the Law of Use and the exponential curve. We want to go from obscurity and poverty to fame and riches in one quick jump, without realizing that we have to first take what God has given us and then multiply it, steadily and patiently. If we do in accordance with His will, success will come.

To want full accomplishment immediately is lust. It is a sin and calls for a violation of the pattern of God. It is wanting something for nothing. Socialism and Communism feed on such lust, calling for taking from the rich and giving to the poor, for leveling society in such a way as to deprive individuals of the learning and maturity necessary to handle abundance. It is characterized by demagoguery and the politics of envy.

So many well-meaning people have in fact done harm to individuals and indeed to nations by short-cutting God's plan and short-circuiting the blessings intended. They want to give everything to everyone immediately, not only stirring up lust, but also fulfilling it, and ultimately harming those they want to help.

From Small Seeds

God's way is the way of gradual, sure growth and maturity, moving toward perfection. It can be compared to an airplane during take-off. If the trajectory is too low, then time will overtake it; the plane will run out of runway and crash, or it will get a few feet off the ground and not rise fast enough to avoid the trees or buildings.

People are the same. If their goals are too low, too stretched out and easy, they will never rise to any significant potential before time overtakes them.

On the other hand, if the pilot sets his angle of climb at take-off too high and the plane rises steeply too soon, it is likely to stall and crash.

The same is true with people. Set your economic growth too high, and you will stall; try to make your child learn too much too fast, and he will become discouraged and give up; try to do fifty push-ups without practice, and you will encounter agony.

Thus, although there is nothing but abundance in the kingdom of heaven and nothing is impossible with God, the Lord's plan is for us to set realistic goals with what He has given us. He wants us to have goals that are demanding enough to keep us occupied, but are not overtaxing, and to stick with them long enough for them to come to fruition. The key is to set a percentage to add to your performance each day, week, month, or year and then let God's Law of Use take you to undreamed of heights of achievement and blessing.

We find clues to this in other parables of the Lord.

Then Jesus told another story: "The kingdom of heaven is like a mustard seed that a man planted in his field. That seed is the smallest of all seeds, but when it grows, it is one of the largest garden plants. It becomes big enough for the wild birds to come and build nests in its branches."

The black mustard of the East starts with the tiniest seed imaginable, but from that tiny beginning comes a strong plant often running to heights as tall as a man on horseback. The grown plant is tens of thousands of times as big as the seed from which it began. Remember the Christian church, which started with just one tiny baby in an obscure stable, now numbers nearly 2 billion members.

Similarly Jesus told of what might be called unconscious growth from small beginnings:

> Then Jesus said, "The kingdom of God is like someone who plants seed in the ground. Night and day, whether the person is asleep or awake, the seed still grows, but the person does not know how it grows. By itself the earth produces grain. First the plant grows, then the head, and then all the grain in the head. When the grain is ready, the farmer cuts it, because this is the harvest time."

We must never despise or be impatient with small beginnings. The increase will come, almost unconsciously, imperceptibly, in the early stages, but suddenly there will be a burst of growth as the exponential rate takes hold and reaches maturity. Before long, it's harvest time.

Remember, everyone has some talent. With some, it's music. With some, it's athletics. With some, it's technical skill. Even a quadriplegic confined to bed cannot feel left out of this marvelous principle. Perhaps more important than anything else, he can consistently exercise the great gift of prayer, maturing to remarkable spiritual depths and affecting the entire world.

Touching the Family

Families in the world are in crisis, but an understanding of the Law of Use can help dramatically.

One of the most serious problems confronting families is the lack of even growth and shared interests between spouses.

Many couples begin life fresh out of school and with few material possessions. Then one spouse, typically the husband, begins to grow intellectually, professionally, and financially. His interests and scope grow little by little until after ten or fifteen years he is a different person. His wife, on the other hand, does not read, does not learn, and does not grow intellectually or socially. She is still the sweet girl he married, but he is no longer the young man she married. He wants to share his life with her, but she is now incapable of doing so. Often she will become jealous and resentful of her husband's new interests and circle of friends. As she becomes withdrawn and hostile, he begins to seek companionship with someone more compatible—with a physical relationship that is often the consequence of such shifts in interest. We say that they have grown apart. Indeed they have. Separation and divorce are often not far behind.

In today's world, women often become the professional achievers and grow ahead of their husbands. The same problems develop, but the roles are reversed.

Both spouses must exert an effort to grow spiritually, intellectually, and socially during their marriages. Each must ensure that he or she, in addition to his or her own personal role, keeps up with the interests and growth of the mate.

This is not an invitation to competition and rivalry, but an admonition to complement one another. Marriage is a shared life between two people. To build a life together, they must grow as individuals so that they can grow together as a couple.

Financial pressures are second only to the lack of communication in undermining marriages. Couples must establish early on in their marriage the Law of Reciprocity and the Law of Use. If they are faithful in giving to God's work, not only will He "open the windows of heaven and pour them out a blessing," but He will also "rebuke the destroyer" for their sake. In other words income will come, and the tragic outlays caused by accidents and sickness will not come.

Second, they must establish a budget that not only causes them to live within their income but also contributes to a modest and regular program of savings and investment. Then their marriage will not be torn apart because they are having to work and slave to pay usurious interest rates to credit card companies and merchants. Instead, they will have the shared joy of knowing that their little nest egg is growing at an exponential rate which will either permit a comfortable retirement or the acquisition of things that will enrich their lives and the lives of their children. Instead of working for money, they will have money working for them.

Not only will such stable families help stabilize our nation by reducing health costs, welfare costs, and delinquency, this pool of savings brought about by a nation of savers rather than a nation of consumers will enable businesses to find capital at lower rates to create jobs, which in turn will create more revenues so that we can have government services without crippling deficits.

It is all so simple, but it is true because it comes from God, and it works.

Wrong Side of the Curve

Human tragedy occurs when people get on the wrong side of the exponential curve, which can work against us as well as for us. Both individuals and nations can be its victims.

The United States and many of its citizens are prime examples. Singly and collectively we have allowed the exponential curve to plunge us into enormous debt. In most cases, the beginnings were innocent, but the exponential rate is merciless if it's working against you. It can destroy people who borrow money at high interest rates. Obviously, vast numbers of Americans are caught in such debt traps right now, and our government is the worst offender.

Consider the facts. From our early beginnings as a nation until 1981, a period of 205 years, the United States accumulated a debt burden of $1 trillion. Then as exponential compounding kicked in with a vengeance, the total jumped to $2 trillion in just 5 years, then $3 trillion in 4 years, then $4 trillion in a bit more than 2 years. Think of it: in 11 years we have accumulated three times the debt accumulation of the preceding 205 years of our history. At these rates our total stated national debt will be $10 trillion by the year 2000 and interest alone at that time may well approach $1 trillion every year! It doesn't take a genius to determine that our currency will lose its value, prices will skyrocket, and somewhere there will either be a dramatic crash or a massive repudiation of debt. All because as a nation we violated God's Law of Use.

Private and public debt usually comes from an inability to defer gratification. It comes from lust and covetousness, the insistence on having everything now. "I want my furniture now," the housewife cries. Meanwhile her husband demands his new, bigger car—now. Neither wants to await the accumulation of the resources necessary to avoid sending compound interest careening into action. On a wider scale, our national attitude views many luxuries as necessities. We override the Law of Use when we attempt to put the biggest, most modern television sets and gadgetry in every home and apartment through consumer debt or even through welfare laws. The national debt soars, credit card bills reach astronomical heights, and the exponential curve zooms upward to hopelessness and collapse.

Jesus Himself, coming in the flesh as man and suffering temptation just as we do, ran into a test on this score early in His public ministry. It came during His temptation in the wilderness: "Again, the devil took Him to a very high mountain, and showed Him all the kingdoms of the world, and their glory; and he said to Him, 'All these things will I give You, if You fall down and worship me.'"[6]

Satan, described in the New Testament as "the ruler of the world" (although destined to be cast out),[7] promised Him everything, right then, if He would just do it his way. But the Lord said He would do it God's way—gradually, the way of sacrifice and suffering, the way of work, the way of the cross.

The law of Satan's kingdom is: Have it now, with a splash. Quick money, quick things, quick success.

The Key to Security

In God's kingdom, the Law of Use governs, providing genuine and lasting security, genuine and lasting prosperity.

Because of the power of the Law of Use and the exponential curve—along with man's seemingly incurable weaknesses—God many centuries ago established two rules for the people of Israel of which we should be aware.

First, He decreed that the Israelites were not to take usury of one another: "You shall not charge interest to your countrymen: interest on money, food, or anything that may be loaned at interest."[8]

They were permitted to charge interest to foreigners, which would agree with the parable of the talents in the New Testament, apparently because the Lord intended to give the Jews dominance over other nations: "For the LORD your God shall bless you as He has promised you, and *you will lend to many nations,* but you will not borrow; and *you will rule over many nations,* but they will not rule over you."[9]

Modern experience has shown that usury ultimately leads to subservience, and God did not want that for His people, but rather intended for them to rule.

Second, God set up a year of jubilee for His people to counteract the fact that through the compounding of debt a few eventually gain control of all wealth and land. In short, He directed that every fifty years all debt be canceled, all accumulated property be redistributed, and the cycle of use begin again.

It was part of His marvelous plan under which the land would have a sabbath year to the Lord. For six years, the land would be worked, "but during the seventh year the land shall have a sabbath rest, a sabbath to the LORD."[10] Then He laid out the jubilee plan:

> You are also to count off seven sabbaths of years for yourself,
> seven times seven years, so that you have the time of the seven
> sabbaths of years, namely, forty-nine years. You shall then
> sound a ram's horn abroad on the tenth day of the seventh

month; on the day of atonement you shall sound a horn all through your land. You shall thus consecrate the fiftieth year and *proclaim a release through the land* to all its inhabitants. It shall be a jubilee for you, and each of you shall return . . . to his family.[11]

The "release" or "liberty" was multifaceted and touched much of the life of the Israelites, specifically through the cancellation of indebtedness. It was as though God said to a man who perhaps was twenty at the beginning of the cycle and who is now seventy: "You've had your day in the sun, your time of opportunity, so now you should step aside, cancel the debts, and let people start over again."

I believe it is quite possible that the year of jubilee will be the only way out, short of collapse for our world in its current economic slide. The United States government, and indeed all governments, have gotten on the wrong side of the exponential curve and the Law of Use and have reached the point of insupportable debt. Trying to meet the demands of the people who are screaming "We want it now!" the governments, along with individuals, are running major deficits, borrowing huge sums of money, always at compound interest. By 1991, the estimated worldwide total of public and private debt was in excess of $25.6 trillion. In fact, I observed in the *Weiss Money & Markets* a 1992 estimate of an astounding $50 trillion debt worldwide. Interest payments have reached the point where some nations can no longer meet them.

Notwithstanding the sneers of many in the banking community, it may be that God's way will be the only one open to us—a year of jubilee to straighten out the mess.

We should also be fully aware of the fact that finance is not the only area in which the exponential curve can work against us. We need only look at the snowballing evils of pornography, adultery, divorce, alcoholism, and drug addiction to grasp this. Such evil began small and steadily increased, almost unconsciously it seems, until the unprecedented surge of recent years and today's raging flood tide.

The Most Powerful Principle

In the previous chapter, I said the Law of Reciprocity was probably the most encompassing of the kingdom principles, virtually undergirding every aspect of life and revealing a course of conduct that could change the world.

The Law of Use, meanwhile, coupled with the exponential curve, is probably the most powerful of the principles in terms of day-to-day life. It is the fundamental law for the growth and development—or the decline—of all organizations and societies in both the invisible and the visible worlds. Beginning with the cradle, it touches everything—child development, intellectual development, professional development, physical development, social development, and on and on.

Together the Law of Reciprocity and the Law of Use are the core of the way the world works, the invisible world and the visible one.

We have already explored major areas touched by the Law of Use and the exponential curve, but we need to see the never-ending, ever-increasing potential. There is, in fact, a principle of increasing opportunity. For example, the man with $100 has certain vistas of opportunity before him. By applying the Law of Use, he can increase that sum to $1,000, and immediately his opportunities for expanded use of the law are increased. Quite simply, the man with $1,000 has more clout than the man with $100.

If he presses on with the Law of Use, he will rise to the $10,000 level and his vistas widen; then $100,000 and he finds bank doors and credit open to him that he hadn't dreamed of. A million dollars opens an entirely new class of opportunity, and so it goes—never-ending opportunity for the person involved in the Law of Use.

I found that the broadcasting world follows the same principle. To him who is faithful in a little will more be given. When we owned five stations we had a far easier time acquiring a sixth than the person just starting out has in acquiring his first. A five-station owner is experienced and knowledgeable. He knows when and how to move. He has access to money markets that the inexperienced, struggling beginner lacks.

So it is with people in science. The one who has mastered fundamental and intermediate theorems is far more capable of going on to an advanced theorem than is the youngster who hasn't had his first high school science course.

In politics, the person who has successfully run for a city council seat is more likely to succeed in a race for mayor than someone who is unknown and untested. The mayor is then in a stronger position to move to the state legislature than the beginner, and on up the line to governor, senator, and perhaps president.

The same holds true for spiritual life. The opportunities steadily increase as we move from one level of understanding and maturity to the next. Mastery of one small principle of faith opens up new horizons for even wider growth. Prayer and intercession for our families build us up for prayer and intercession for our church, and then our town, our state, and our nation. Similarly, public ministry to fifty people will open opportunities for ministry to one hundred. We are then far better prepared to minister to one thousand, then ten thousand, then twenty thousand.

No, we are not to despise small beginnings, but rather to exercise the eternally established Law of Use.

I am convinced that this law—put to work with the commitment, the virtues, and the accompanying subprinciples—can produce giant steps toward easing and ultimately removing the crises that grip the world. It will touch world hunger, the economic quagmire, energy depletion, Third World needs, educational and social injustice, church evangelism, moral decadence, disease, and inadequate health care.

The only thing lacking is for us to hear with understanding the words spoken by God to Moses regarding the sanctuary Israel was to construct for the Lord: "According to all that I am going to show you, as the *pattern* of the tabernacle and the *pattern* of all its furniture, just so *you shall construct it.*"[12]

"Do it MY way," says the Lord. He has given a pattern for the secret kingdom. We merely need to follow it.

9

The Law of Perseverance

*A*s we move on from the Law of Use, I want to be sure that we understand that success in this life comes through industry. By industry I mean those traits of character such as dedication, commitment, patience, self-discipline, and hard work that bring positive results—in short, perseverance. So to prepare the way for what follows, we need to examine this next principle, the *Law of Perseverance*, and how it relates to each of the other kingdom principles.

We caught glimpses of this law in previous chapters, but we need to see clearly that the ways of the universe yield to perseverance. God does not give the good things of this world to those who will not work. There are times when, in His grace, He may just hand us something, for whatever reason. Sometimes in His favor, God brings unexpected, perhaps even undeserved, blessings into our life. But no one who is successful can afford to stand around and do nothing while waiting for such a gift. God never rewards sloth and indolence.

When Jesus told his followers to "keep on asking," as we will see in the following pages, He meant that they were to be persistent in their endeavors. If we are persistent, if we keep on asking, and if we keep on knocking, the doors will eventually be opened. But we must keep on until they do.

Anyone working in sales can tell you that sometimes it takes five or six calls in order to close a sale. If you are doubtful, unprepared, and easily defeated, you will not make that sale. But if you are prepared and persistent, sooner or later you will succeed. So, in addition to all the other positive values needed for doing anything successfully, there has to be effort and perseverance.

We see this principle in the homey story of the chicken and the egg. The baby chick, still living in his shell, finds himself in a nice, safe environment, dark and quiet. For a period of time his home, the egg, keeps him warm and cozy; everything is more or less perfect.

Soon, however, the chick becomes aware that the shell keeping him so comfortable and safe is also circumscribing his life. He begins to feel restricted. He is growing by the hour, and the egg is not as pleasant as it once was.

You see, there is something in life that says, "I have to grow." Every living thing on this planet is designed to grow; that's the way we are made. Humans and animals have within them an inborn need to grow and develop their full potential.

So the little chick begins pecking at the shell. He doesn't understand it, but things have been set up so that he has to peck and peck and peck. He works very hard, gaining strength hour by hour from that God-ordained struggle. Before long, he has attained the strength and the endurance to cope with a new environment, and he breaks through the shell. He pecks some more, and soon he is free, ready for a new level of life.

People have tried to help little chicks speed the process of cracking the shell and opening it for them. But if they try to short-circuit God's process, they will kill the chicks. They are stillborn, unable to handle for even a few moments the rigors of their new environment.

Positive Signals

Supporting each of these various keys of the kingdom is the understanding that everything in this world is controlled by spirit.

For God Himself is spirit, and through the spirit He controls everything that is. He created the earth, the universe, and everything that is in them. Paul tells us that Jesus Christ, the Son of God, was at work in the creation, and that He was the agent of creation. He says:

> For by Him all things were created that are in heaven and that are on earth, visible and invisible, whether thrones or dominions or principalities or powers. All things were created through Him and for Him.[1]

Spirit is the ultimate power of the universe. The spirit can transmit the messages of God, or your own messages, to the mind; and it is mind that controls the events of nature and the world around you. And as I said briefly in chapter 4, in such matters a positive mental attitude is absolutely essential.

The way you transmit the thoughts in your mind is twofold. First, we have, in effect, an AM/FM transmitter in our brains that can send out impulses around us. Second, we can also speak the word out of our mouths and transmit the voice of spirit into the material world. Does this sound incredible?

Admittedly, certain New Age teachers have attempted to appropriate some of these Bible truths and apply them to their own false doctrines. Over the years, a number of authors have written popular secular books on these ideas. But that does not limit their application and value for the believer in Jesus Christ. These truths are eternal laws of the kingdom, and even if New Age mystics and gurus attempt to pirate what rightfully belongs to God's people, we should not allow them to damage or discredit what is rightfully ours.

Still, if this sounds too metaphysical or strange for you, please recall the apostle's words when he wrote:

> . . . we do not look at the things which are seen, but at the things which are not seen. For the things which are seen are temporary, but the things which are not seen are eternal.[2]

In the creation, God had a creative thought transmitted and empowered by the Spirit. By the spoken Word God said, "Let there be light," and it was so. That's the way He brought the world into existence. He has given us a portion of this same power in our daily lives. Here's how it works. If you think failure, impossibility, and negative thoughts, then you will indeed forecast your own failure. You will have what you say and what you think. You transmit failure to yourself, to other people, and to the world around you. Furthermore, your negative message will be transmitted to angels and demons, which are very real (though unseen) beings in our midst. But if you transmit faith, hope, and love, you will be sending a very different message.

The Source of Power

Paul said, "I can do all things through Him who strengthens me."[3] He spoke positive words. He said: "we are more than conquerors through Him who loved us."[4] Paul's own spirit was indomitable; his mind was full of the thoughts of God; his voice spoke forth faith and conviction. "Be anxious for nothing," he said, "but in everything by prayer and supplication, with thanksgiving, let your requests be made known to God; and the peace of God, which surpasses all understanding, will guard your hearts and minds through Christ Jesus."[5]

Compare that to someone who says, "I just can't do it. I've tried everything and nothing works. I can't do mathematics; I can't make sales; I can't hold a job; I can't make a go of my family. The whole world is against me. It's not what you know, it's who you know that counts. I'm a born loser." How can anyone hope to succeed with such destructive attitudes? That kind of thinking is a self-fulfilling prophecy for failure.

On the other hand, enthusiasm is contagious, and if you believe in the future, if you have faith, and if you are enthusiastic about what is to come, other people will catch that spirit. They will want to participate. In reality, they sense the spirit of God within you, and suddenly the Red Sea begins to part, Pharaoh lifts you out of prison and puts you in charge of things, and miracles begin to happen because you are sensing God's favor; you have humbled yourself before the Lord, and you have followed the principles of the kingdom. Suddenly your mind is filled with unlimited possibilities.

This is the attitude you must have for financial success; this is how you begin to approach the world. If you know Jesus Christ as your Savior, you have the ultimate hope. Your spirit lives forever; you are, at this moment, a child of the kingdom, and you will not see death.

In Christ you have new life. Jesus said, "I have come that they may have life, and that they may have it more abundantly."[6] Jesus did not bring us a spirit of defeat or despair, but of victory and hope. Are you certain that you are living in this kingdom? Are you a child of God?

If you are not certain of your eternal hope in Christ Jesus, I would invite you now to claim Him by simple faith as your Savior. Trust Him now and be certain that you are a member of this dynamic kingdom. Its privileges and promises—and, yes, its demands—are yours as you enter into a new relationship with God and discover the new freedom He offers.

The Risks of Freedom

These are elements of what I call the Law of Perseverance. It is critical to success in life generally and to life in the kingdom especially.

But certain risks go with new life and growth—the risks of freedom, we might say—but God prepares us for those risks, through perseverance and struggle, building our muscles, as it were, for each new phase. To refuse to struggle is to stand still, to stagnate.

Jesus taught the Law of Perseverance in a passage well known to most Christians:

> Ask, and it shall be given to you; seek, and you shall find; knock, and it shall be opened to you. For every one who asks

receives, and he who seeks finds, and to him who knocks it shall be opened. Or what man is there among you, when his son shall ask him for a loaf, will give him a stone? Or if he shall ask for a fish, he will not give him a snake, will he? If you then, being evil, know how to give good gifts to your children, how much more shall your Father who is in heaven give what is good to those who ask Him![7]

We grasp His meaning more fully when we understand that the verbs "asks," "seeks," and "knocks" were written in the Greek present imperative and are to be understood in this manner: "*Keep asking,* and it shall be given to you; *keep seeking,* and you shall find; *keep knocking,* and it shall be opened to you." The Father gives "what is good to those who *keep asking Him.*"

He also said, as we have noted, that "the kingdom of heaven suffers violence, and violent men take it by force."[8] It does not come easily. The little chick we spoke of was violent; he had to be. Most of the secrets of God come forth with effort; the blessings of God are the same.

Some Christians have been taught that all one has to do to get things from God is to speak the word of faith, believe, and receive. That comes close to the truth, but it neglects the universal Law of Perseverance. God slowly yields the good things of the kingdom and the world to those who struggle. Jacob, for instance, wrestled all night with an angel before he became Israel, a prince with God. Abraham waited a hundred years before he received Isaac, the child of promise. The people of Judah waited and struggled seventy years in captivity before God brought them home.

The Necessity of Faith

This does not negate the necessity for asking in faith, the believing, and the receiving. But many times those steps are only the beginning of the process. The fulfillment may take years.

Jesus gave this illustration of perseverance:

Now He was telling them a parable to show that at all times they ought to pray and not to lose heart, saying, "There was in a certain city a judge who did not fear God, and did not respect man. And there was a widow in that city, and she kept coming to him, saying, 'Give me legal protection from my opponent.' And for a while he was unwilling; but afterward he said to himself, 'Even though I do not fear God nor respect man, yet because this widow bothers me, I will give her legal protection, lest by continually coming she wear me out.'" And the Lord said, "Hear what the unrighteous judge said; now shall not God bring about justice for His elect, who cry to Him day and night, and will He delay long over them? I tell you that He will bring about justice for them speedily. However, when the Son of Man comes, will He find faith on the earth?"[9]

Jesus knew men inside out. He knew our tendency to give up quickly, to become inconsistent and lackadaisical. Yet He pleaded with us to persist, in prayer and in all aspects of life.

And He said to them, "Suppose one of you shall have a friend, and shall go to him at midnight, and say to him, 'Friend, lend me three loaves; for a friend of mine has come to me from a journey, and I have nothing to set before him'; and from inside he shall answer and say, 'Do not bother me; the door has already been shut and my children and I are in bed; I cannot get up and give you anything.' I tell you, even though he will not get up and give him anything because he is his friend, yet because of his persistence he will get up and give him as much as he needs."[10]

Keep on asking, He said, keep on seeking, and keep on knocking. Don't be afraid even to make a ruckus. God prefers persistence much more than slothfulness and indolence. He wants people who will travail and perhaps stumble a bit, but keep on going forward, just like a toddler who's trying to learn to walk. The child builds muscles and learns. One day he will run.

Strength Through Testing

In the early, trying days of the church, according to the Book of Acts, Paul and Barnabas traveled through Lystra, Iconium, and Antioch "strengthening the souls of the disciples, encouraging them to continue in the faith, and saying, 'Through many tribulations we must enter the kingdom of God.'"[11]

There was to be conflict, they said, using a word that most translators have rendered "tribulation" but which carries the idea of "pressure," especially pressure on the spirit. This pressure, or tribulation, was understood in New Testament times to build stamina and staying power, leading to fullness of character.

We are to remember that there is an adversary. He is called Satan. One of his favorite techniques is the unrelenting effort to trip the people of God to foster discouragement and depression. That is why the Bible says repeatedly that Christians are to be patient, to hold on, to persist.

Satan is continuously pouring into our ears such negatives as these: "You're not accomplishing anything. . . . You're on the wrong course. . . . You don't have the necessary skill and ability. . . . Everyone else has failed so why do you think you'll succeed? . . . Those promises you thought were from God are nothing. . . . You're unworthy. . . ."

So we often grow discouraged and quit. Then the principles of the kingdom cease to function in our lives. And we fail.

The ultimate personal failure, of course, is suicide. It is the number two killer of our nation's youth, next to automobile accidents. So many people have given up in hopelessness, finding their problems overwhelming, the world a mess beyond repair, the possibilities of life too dark. And they slip into the horror of taking their lives, which truly are not theirs to take.

Even the great prophet Elijah reached such despair. Having experienced one of his great triumphs, the defeat of the priests of Baal through a powerful miracle of God, he obviously was exhausted mentally, emotionally, and physically. Jezebel was trying to kill him. He fell into gloom.

"It is enough . . . ," he cried out. "O LORD, take my life, for I am not better than my fathers."[12]

But God would not let him give up. Neither does He want us to quit.

Instead, we are to be constantly alert against discouragement and depression. We are to be aware of what our enemy is trying to do. We are to reject him and he will flee. God will not let trial and temptation overcome us if we will stand, but rather will make a way of victory for us.[13] He wants us to persevere and will make it possible.

Remember that the Law of Use and the exponential curve will bring wealth, physical strength, spiritual growth, expanded knowledge, organizational growth, and national prosperity. But none of these things will happen unless we persevere long enough for the blessing to be realized. How many overweight people begin a sensible weight-loss plan that is guaranteed to give them a slimmer body only to quit after three or four weeks? How many people begin a modest savings plan that compounded could yield them a million dollars in thirty years only to withdraw their savings to buy a stereo or an automobile? How many gifted children with the potential to be leaders drop out of school or lack the perseverance necessary to work through college and graduate school? How many gifted musicians never progress because they refuse the daily discipline of practice? How many treadmills and exercise machines that would bring physical vitality and strength gather dust in spare rooms and garages because of lack of perseverance?

God's tangible blessings are there for all. But only those willing to persevere in their exercise will receive them.

Lessons of History

Had God given us no more insight than the Law of Perseverance together with the Laws of Reciprocity and Use, we would have enough to change the world. We need only think of examples from our own national history.

Consider Abraham Lincoln. He became one of the greatest governmental and moral leaders in American history. But the achievements didn't come until he had passed through many personal failures, including bankruptcies and endless humiliating labors to make ends meet. The struggles, the battles, the wounds—they equipped him for the environment in which he would make his greatest contribution.

Consider Thomas Edison. This greatest of inventors went through hundreds of experiments that were failures before he achieved success with the electric light. He attributed his incredible accomplishments to "2 percent inspiration and 98 percent perspiration"—a formula for struggle and perseverance.

Consider the Wright Brothers. On the lonely sands of North Carolina's outer banks, they battled the elements, the ridicule of men, the lack of resources. They built; they failed; they rebuilt and failed again. Finally, they flew, and the world was forever changed.

In my own life's work, through the grace of God, I learned the centrality of perseverance. In 1959 my family and I arrived in Tidewater with seventy dollars and a God-planted desire to establish a broadcasting ministry that would glorify the Lord. We went through two years of personal and corporate struggle before getting on the air with our first station. Then came ten more years of striving, anguish, and hardship before we obtained our second station. Steadily the growth increased as we persevered and learned the lessons of the kingdom.

In that pressure cooker, which in so many ways resembled the trials of the chick with the egg, we matured to the point of readiness for a worldwide ministry. With hindsight, it is amusing to note how the Lord forced us to use everything He had given us to its very limit before He provided something new. Before establishing us in our new Virginia Beach international center, He had us using every nook and cranny of space available to us. We had trailers lined up all over the land, jammed with people and activity. We had rented property all over Tidewater, taxing our ingenuity and patience daily. Through it all, we were getting ready for the next phase of our work; we were being strengthened for a new environment and new challenges. We were getting maturity the only way a Christian can get it.

In 1979, I examined CBN's history and found that in those twenty years, the Lord had taken our initial seventy dollars and caused it to double exponentially every year during that time. By sheer mercy and grace, He had led us in the Laws of Reciprocity, Use, and Perseverance.

Had He led us otherwise, dumping on us too quickly the responsibility for a worldwide ministry and budgets of tens of millions of dollars, we would have crumbled. But He is wise enough to lead His people according to His laws even before we are able to know and articulate them.

As the great Bible teacher Donald Gray Barnhouse put it, "God uses oak trees, not mushrooms." Are not perseverance and strength the great virtues of oak trees?

10

The Law of Responsibility

A person, a business, a charity, or a nation that diligently and conscientiously applies the Laws of Reciprocity, Use, and Perseverance must succeed. There will be prosperity, strength, and blessing. The consequence of following the laws of the kingdom are inexorable. The results over time are nothing short of incredible.

But did God put His laws in the universe so that men might heap up boundless riches for their own pleasure, or have muscles like Arnold Schwarzenegger for men and women to admire, or have wisdom like Edison to gain popular acclaim, or be a famous and powerful world leader for the purpose of controlling others? Of course not.

Jesus made it clear that with the blessings also come responsibilities. He summed it up succinctly: "unto whomsoever much is given, of him shall be much required: and to whom men have committed much, of him they will ask the more."[1]

Using a parable on watchfulness and preparation, He made clear that rejection of this law leads to suffering. Those who are given understanding, ability, goods, money, authority, or fame have a responsibility that the less favored do not bear; failure to fulfill it produces fearful punishment.[2]

Jesus was precise in showing that the parable was for the favored in every category, spiritual and physical, those living in the invisible world and those living in the visible.

Whatever level of opportunity is given to us, both God and man expect us to give a certain standard of performance. Favor carries with it responsibility. As the favor increases, the responsibility increases.

If, for example, I am the steward of $1,000 for someone, that person may expect a profit of some $100 on his money. But if I am the chairman of multi-billion-dollar General Motors and report a profit of only $100 to the stockholders, I would be forced to resign in disgrace.

If I am a weekend tennis player who manages to win a few games with friends, my friends and I will be satisfied. But if after years of training I have the skill to be ranked first in the world, I must beat the world's best lest the fans, my peers, and the press diminish my stature rapidly and I feel disgraced.

Artur Rubinstein, the great pianist, capsulized this principle when he remarked that should he fail to practice one day, he would know it; should he skip practice for two days, the critics would know it; but should that extend to three days "the whole world knows it." A part-time church pianist might get away with a bit of a letdown, but not an internationally acclaimed musician. More is required of the professional.

Harry Truman said it well when remarking on the burden of the presidency: "If you can't stand the heat, get out of the kitchen." The presidency of the United States carries heavy responsibilities, he related, and if one doesn't want to face the responsibilities, he should not seek the favor of the people in the first place. For, as he said at another time, "There is no end to the chain of responsibility that binds [the president], and he is never allowed to forget that he is president." The sign on his Oval Office desk said, "The buck stops here."

The Burden of Favor

At CBN, we have found the burden of favor to be a responsibility never to be forgotten and never to be neglected. In 1991 CBN telephone counselors received more than 1.5 million calls, most with prayer requests. Of those, 430,130 asked for prayer for healing; 205,343 needed help with finances; 388,913 were having family problems of one kind or another; and more than 3,000 were contemplating suicide. Most exciting was the fact that in the same year 27,000 people called to say they had prayed to receive Christ with the hosts of our "700 Club" broadcast, and another 33,000 prayed for salvation with our phone counselors.

In 1991, CBN International was overwhelmed by the incredible response from people seeking God in countries around the world. In the former Soviet Union, for example, where CBN programming in Russian went out to more than 103 million viewers, more than 20 million viewers prayed with the show's hosts to accept Christ as Savior. Throughout the Commonwealth of Independent States, more than 150 million men, women, and children watched these broadcasts, and more than 30 million accepted Jesus Christ.

Such news is thrilling to anyone who understands what God is accomplishing in the world. But it is also a burden to know that God uses our skills and talents in this way to build His kingdom. I recall my emotions a few years ago when we calculated that we had led seventy-five thousand people to faith in Jesus Christ through CBN. From that point on, there is no way we could be satisfied with leading one thousand people to the Lord. Indeed, one thousand decisions for Christ in one year is a wonderful achievement. But the Lord has given us equipment, personnel, and opportunity, and of those to whom much is given, Scripture tells us, much is required. So we are determined to be faithful to the high calling to which we have been called in Christ.

The Church Must Listen

Leaders of the church should be especially careful to rise to the responsibility given to them, for the Scripture is so clear on this point as to be somewhat frightening. I am always stopped momentarily when I read the words of James regarding teachers: "Let not many of you become teachers, my brethren, knowing that as such we shall incur a stricter judgment."[3]

Those who have been shown enough to teach can be expected to practice what they teach, at the very least. The office carries a great responsibility.

Paul's letters to Timothy and Titus show the great expectations of God and man from those desiring to be overseers ("bishops" in the older translations).

> What I say is true: Anyone wanting to become an elder desires a good work. An elder must not give people a reason to criticize him, and he must have only one wife. He must be self-controlled, wise, respected by others, ready to welcome guests, and able to teach. He must not drink too much wine or like to fight, but rather be gentle and peaceable, not loving money. He must be a good family leader, having children who cooperate with full respect. (If someone does not know how to lead the family, how can that person take care of God's church?) But an elder must not be a new believer, or he might be too proud of himself and be judged guilty just as the devil was. An elder must also have the respect of people who are not in the church so he will not be criticized by others and caught in the devil's trap.

He goes on to point out that those seeking the lesser office of deacon, while not required to measure up to the full responsibility of overseer or bishop, must nevertheless bear a burden greater than that of most, first being "tested" and found "beyond reproach."[5]

Christ's first disciples, especially the Twelve, carried extraordinary burdens and responsibilities, as the New Testament shows in detail. They had been "given the mystery of the kingdom of God"[6] by the Lord Himself while others heard only in parables. This great gift, in a sense, carried with it the load of the world, and those apostles paid a great price—ridicule, ostracism, persecution, martyrdom—for the opportunity of spreading the gospel. Their sense of responsibility was always before them. In his letter to the Romans, Paul summed up that responsibility with these words: "I am under obligation both to Greeks and to barbarians, both to the wise and to the foolish."[7]

Even the ordinary, little-known people who have received the inexpressibly rich gift of eternal life—by grace through faith—are called to a life far more responsible and demanding than they led before. Knowing the Lord, who is "the way, and the truth, and the life,"[8] sets a standard for us in the sight of God and people that we should always keep in mind. Paul referred to it as knowing how to conduct yourself "in the household of God, which is the church of the living God, the pillar and support of the truth."[9] It is a significant responsibility each Christian must meet. We need only look at the Great Commission given by Jesus to His people just before His ascension.

> All authority has been given to Me in heaven and on earth. Go therefore and make disciples of all the nations, baptizing them in the name of the Father and the Son and the Holy Spirit, teaching them to observe all that I commanded you.[10]

Even though He had said He Himself would build His church,[11] the responsibility for carrying that plan forward for the entire world was put into the hands of His people. *That* is responsibility.

Rank and Responsibility

Early in the nineteenth century, a French duke, Gaston Pierre Marc, wrote in a collection of *Maxims and Reflections* a two-word statement that has become part of our language: "*Noblesse oblige.*" Despite historical abuses, it expresses the essence of the Law of Responsibility. "Nobility obliges" or, better, "nobility obligates" states the obligation of people of high rank, position, or favor to behave nobly, kindly, and responsibly toward others.

The idea, of course, did not originate with the Frenchman. The ancient Greeks reflected such attitudes in their writings, as shown by Euripides—"The nobly born must nobly meet his fate"[12]—and by Sophocles—"Nobly to live, or else nobly to die, befits proud birth."[13]

Men have known almost instinctively that as accomplishment and position rise, so do responsibility and burden. With each achievement, society raises its expectation a notch.

With the British of the nineteenth century, the concept of *noblesse oblige* reached its zenith, sometimes for good, sometimes for not-so-good. Regardless of mistakes, the British nobility perceived that if they were to have their country houses and servants, their privileges and honors, they in turn had to be responsible for the working people.

In the case of Great Britain as a whole, she felt a responsibility for the entire world, a duty to Pax Britannia—the British peace—on every continent. She called it the burden of empire, sending young men and women to India and the four corners of the earth, challenging any she felt would disrupt the peace of the world.

In a pattern that would be repeated, Russia threatened to enter Afghanistan in the late nineteenth century as a move toward a warm-water port in the Middle East. The British, accepting the responsibility accompanying their position as the world's greatest power, challenged the Russians and prevailed. To them, it was *noblesse oblige,* protecting the people from invaders, pirates, and brigands. To others, it often was unadulterated colonialism, in which people were exploited, confined to subservience and poverty. Both views contained truth. Humility and purity, among other virtues, were lacking. Nonetheless, Victorian Britain instinctively realized that the Law of Responsibility was a foundational corollary to her preeminent position in the nineteenth-century world.

Having witnessed the Soviet invasion and occupation of Afghanistan—during virtually the entire decade of the 1980s—it is fascinating to see what consequences have ultimately befallen these nations. Many have said that, as Vietnam was a fatal stumbling block to American supremacy in the world, so Afghanistan was the ultimate undoing of the Soviet Union. In nine years, the Soviets lost fifteen thousand lives, untold millions of dollars' worth of armaments, equipment, and supplies, and ultimately their prestige and self-confidence.

The lesson of Afghanistan was a bitter and tragic pill for the Communists. They did not come responsibly to build up and bring freedom, but to tear down. They gained nothing. The Afghan republic is still splintered and torn by civil war, and within months of the Red Army's retreat from Kabul, their own government collapsed. God had given the Afghans a somber role in world history for they were, at least in current events, the straw that broke the Soviet camel's back.

The United States Faltered

Contrasted with the British leaning toward *noblesse oblige* were the frequent failures of responsibility by the government of the United States during the second half of this century. To begin with, Americans during most of their history worked hard under the Law of Use. They were frugal, disciplined, and moral. Furthermore, they persevered, and following World War II became the strongest power on earth. With that stature came responsibility, especially, in my judgment, the responsibility to accomplish two goals: To order the world economy and to keep world peace.

On the first, we began to fail rapidly in the sixties, refusing to measure up to the responsibility. We were profligate in our spending, igniting the time bomb of inflation, which we exported overseas since every other currency was tied into the American dollar. We printed money faster and faster, sending more abroad than we got back through sales of our own goods, eventually reaching a point where more than $600 billion of our money was held in foreign banks. This showed little sense of duty, strength, courage, or determination.

In 1971, shirking our responsibility even more, we went off the gold standard, having little choice in light of overseas claims against our currency. Thus inflation exploded across the world.

Second, as the leader of the free world, we faltered in our duty to lead in keeping the peace. It became especially critical after the Vietnam debacle, in which our course cost us severely in morale, determination, economic strength, and lives of more than fifty-eight thousand valiant youths. From that point on, our neglect went on the downhill slalom. We neglected to keep the peace in Africa, allowing the Communist-led world to take several countries in an unprecedented display of international burglary. We allowed similar conduct in Latin America and put up only token resistance as the Communists came in to take over and destroy Nicaragua. They tried the same subversion in El Salvador, Honduras, and other countries throughout Central and South America.

All of this merely solidified a trend that had been building momentum since the end of World War II. Although as a nation we have been extraordinarily generous, for many reasons, we Americans seem to have no stomach for the full burden of leadership and responsibility demanded of someone to whom much has been given. We apparently want the position of power but not all the sacrifices of duty that accompany it. Because of historical and cultural factors, we have not developed a national fiber of *noblesse oblige*.

Yet God and man insist on it. The parable told by Jesus about the slave who was made steward over his master's possessions said this about failure to fulfill responsibility: "And that slave who knew his master's will and did not get ready or act in accord with his will, shall receive many lashes."[14]

Despite a certain euphoria over our success in the Persian Gulf, the apparent collapse of Soviet Communism, and economic gains in foreign markets, we are experiencing the pains of our neglect and are beleaguered at every turn. We are plagued by insoluble tensions, a persistent recession, constant acrimony and bloody battles between liberal and conservative factions, and an electorate that has lost faith not only in the candidates for public office but in the elective process itself. In the 1990s, the ship of state in America is veering off course, listing under intolerable financial burdens, straining at the mercy of insensitive leaders, and drifting in angry seas because we first lost our moral compass and the *foundation* of our freedom.

The Issue of Capitalism

Although I believe Communism and capitalism in their most extreme, secular manifestations are equally doomed to failure, likely to result in tragic dictatorship, at the same time I believe free enterprise is the economic system most nearly meeting humanity's God-given need for freedom in existence. The freedom of self-determination in an open economy is, in my view, an ideal system, but when greed and materialism displace all spiritual and moral values, capitalism breaks down into ugliness. In his instructive and provocative book, *Wealth and Poverty*,[15] widely circulated in the early days of the Reagan administration, George Gilder makes a convincing argument that capitalism at least *sets out* to fulfill generally what I am calling the Law of Responsibility.

"Giving is the vital impulse and moral center of capitalism," Gilder argues, adding:

> Capitalists are motivated not chiefly by the desire to consume wealth or indulge their appetites, but by the freedom and power to consummate their entrepreneurial ideas. Whether piling up coconuts or designing new computers, they are movers and shakers, doers and givers, obsessed with positive visions of change and opportunity. They are men with an urge to understand and act, to master something and transform it, to work out a puzzle and profit from it, to figure out a part of nature and society and turn it to the common good. They are inventors and explorers, boosters and problem solvers; they take infinite pains and they strike fast.

Then the author drives to the heart of the criticism leveled at the capitalists—their preoccupation with money. But his answers are logical and need to be heard.

> Are they greedier than doctors or writers or professors of sociology or assistant secretaries of energy or commissars of wheat? Yes, their goals seem more mercenary. But this is only because money is their very means of production. Just as the

sociologist requires books and free time and the bureaucrat needs arbitrary power, the capitalist needs capital. . . . Capitalists need capital to fulfill their role in launching and financing enterprise. Are they self-interested? Presumably. But the crucial fact about them is their deep interest and engagement in the world beyond themselves, impelled by their imagination, optimism and faith.

Gilder's assessment is on target, I believe. Capitalism satisfies the freedom-loving side of humanity. It has an inherent quality of giving, of breaking through into new levels of experience. It uses that which it has and fully exploits the exponential curve, and perseverance is one of its tested virtues.

Responsibility Grows, Too

But what about responsibility? As success grows, the responsibility grows. Has the level of fulfillment of that responsibility kept pace? That is the problem.

Gilder's argument, while touching on "religious" factors, becomes muddy on the point of God and faith. He is imprecise, as in the case of the last word in the above-quoted passage when it comes to what precisely this "faith" is in. The fact is that everything else rests on that foundation. Ultimately, imprecision in this area will produce shakiness. Jesus said, "Have faith in God."[16] That principle was the umbrella for all activities.

If the faith is in God, then this quite naturally flavors the question of responsibility. Faith in God presumably will produce an acknowledgment of responsibility toward God—and an ongoing and rising responsibility toward men. This is where the capitalists most frequently stumble.

And they are not alone. Other conservatives have fallen short, too. This is exemplified by the evangelical Christians who so often find themselves in league with economic and political conservatives. They have been given great understanding, and often they have given much in return. However, they have concentrated almost exclusively on personal salvation, neglecting responsibility for intelligent public policy, international affairs, the poor, the oppressed. To whom much enlightenment has been given, much will be required.

We in the developed world—capitalists, evangelicals, everyone—will be held accountable for all that has been given. The people in Africa and South America will not be held to the same level of accountability simply because they have not received as much.

Just think of the Western world! Think of the revelations in law, justice, science, medicine, technology, religion. Think of the rewards that have come through capitalism and evangelical Christianity as merely two examples. Those revelations, those rewards, govern what is demanded of us—by God and by men.

The responsibility is great. And this may not be comprehended to the fullest by Gilder and his fellow conservatives and capitalists. We all need to hear Isaiah, who in his great prophecy spelled out this responsibility, mincing no words in reporting God's instructions. We will look at only one section of them,[17] for they alone are enough to set us in motion with the Law of Responsibility.

> Shout with the voice of a trumpet blast, tell my people of their sins! Yet they act so pious! They come to the Temple every day and are so delighted to hear the reading of my laws—just as though they would obey them—just as though they don't despise the commandments of their God! How anxious they are to worship correctly; oh, how they love the Temple services![18]

Being Doers of the Word

The words echo throughout the New Testament. How God deplores those who hear His word and do not *do* it![19] They wonder why they don't see power in their lives. Isaiah looks at the kinds of questions they throw at God.

"We have fasted before you," they say. "Why aren't you impressed? Why don't you see our sacrifices? Why don't you hear our prayers? We have done much penance, and you don't even notice it!" I'll tell you why! Because you are living in evil pleasure even while you are fasting, and *you keep right on oppressing your workers.* Look, what good is fasting when *you keep on fighting and quarreling?* This kind of fasting will never get you anywhere with me.[20]

No, the Lord says, your revelation carries a responsibility to Him and to people. He hits the point on workers hard.

No, the kind of fast I want is that you stop *oppressing* those who work for you and treat them fairly and give them what they earn.[21]

Then He broadens it.

I want you to share your food with the hungry and bring right into your own homes those who are helpless, poor and destitute. Clothe those who are cold and don't hide from relatives who need your help.[22]

Fulfill your responsibility at the level to which He has raised you, God says, and He will raise you even higher.

If you do these things, God will shed his own glorious light upon you. He will heal you; your godliness will lead you forward, and goodness will be a shield before you, and the glory of the Lord will protect you from behind. Then, when you call, the Lord will answer. "Yes, I am here," he will quickly reply. All you need to do is to stop oppressing the weak, and to stop making false accusations and spreading vicious rumors![23]

From the beginning of the Scriptures to the end, a theme flows relentlessly: *God is the enemy of oppression.* So must His people be. In His behalf, Isaiah pounds at the issues even more boldly.

> *Feed the hungry! Help those in trouble!* . . . And the Lord will . . . satisfy you with all good things . . . and you will be like a well-watered garden, like an ever-flowing spring.[24]

Give and it will be given to you. Fulfill your responsibility at your current level if you would rise to a higher one. Blessing carries responsibility.

Unending commitment to the truth would advance the cause of capitalism and free enterprise immensely, carrying it perhaps past the dangers of anarchy and dictatorship. It would also advance the cause of evangelical Christianity, perhaps to the point of winning the world, a feat that has thus far eluded us.

11

The Law of Greatness

*A*ll people desire to be great.

Because of human frailty, however, this can turn out badly, especially if we think in terms of comparison with others, for that usually spells pride.

But we need to think more deeply than that. Pride is still a hazard, but one can set goals of accomplishing tasks rather than of performing better than someone else. It's a fine line, but it exists.

Jesus, pointing to that line, spoke of the possibilities of greatness—a purity of greatness, we might say. Indeed, He set forth a two-part principle that I have labeled the *Law of Greatness*. The world needs it desperately at this hour.

It is easy to forget that the people surrounding Jesus during His earthly ministry were just that—people. Plain, simple, ordinary people. They exhibited the frailties of all of us. For example, at one point, acting a bit like twentieth-century kids quarreling over who's the greatest shortstop in the American League, the disciples came to the Lord and asked, "Who then is the greatest in the kingdom of heaven?"

The answer was remarkable, flying in the face of everything we expect in our day.

> Jesus called a little child to him and stood the child before his
> followers. Then he said, "I tell you the truth, you must change

and become like little children. Otherwise, you will never enter the kingdom of heaven. *The greatest person in the kingdom of heaven is the one who makes himself humble like this child.*"[1]

At another time, they fell into a dispute over which of *them* was regarded as the greatest. They, like us, were very concerned about their status from time to time. But the Lord showed great patience with them.

And He said to them, "The kings of the Gentiles lord it over them; and those who have authority over them are called 'Benefactors.' But not so with you, but *let him who is the greatest among you become as the youngest, and the leader as the servant.* For who is greater, the one who reclines at table, or the one who serves? Is it not the one who reclines at table? But I am among you as *the one who serves.*"[2]

Every time the question arose, the answer was the same two-pronged directive: If you want to be great, become like a *child* and become a *servant*. And that answer reverberates down through human experience to our day, yet so few of us grasp it.

"Oh, that was OK for what He was doing then," we say, "but He didn't understand what it was going to be like in the modern world." Or we mumble something like, "That may be all right for church, but you'll get killed in the real world."

Facing Reality

If you're honest, you have to admit those remarks seem true as the twentieth century winds down. Knowledge has exploded all over the planet and, through the space program, even onto other planets. Man is doing things never dreamed possible in earlier generations. Furthermore, we are in a life-and-death struggle for the hearts and minds of the next generation. It is what my friend, Dr. James Dobson, described in his book, *Children at Risk,* as a civil war of values. Greatness in this world will be measured by success on these fronts. Trying to live as a little child in this modern world, we tell ourselves, would be suicide.

We all rationalize that way. We argue with the things we learn from Scripture as if the Bible were no longer relevant to our world, and we are in a terrible mess as a result. We should look at what Jesus was showing us.

What is there about a little child that He wants us to copy? If they're very little, they cry a lot and seem to be pretty much governed by what their stomachs tell them. If they have pain, they cry; if they're wet, they cry. As they grow, they're apt to be spoiled by their families. They may become extraordinarily self-centered; they may whine a lot. In time, they may become unruly and undisciplined. All parents know the pattern.

Is this what Jesus wanted us to be?

No, He had something else in mind. He spoke of three qualities that under normal circumstances predominate in little children: They are trusting. They are teachable. They are humble.

To begin with, little children trust their mothers and fathers. They have to. A baby relies upon his mother to feed him, trusting that she is not going to put poison in his mouth. As he grows, he believes in his parents, usually certain that his daddy is absolutely the greatest man in the world. We all know that many things can work to warp that trust, but basically all children, if treated the way God would have parents treat their offspring, will have incredible faith in their mothers and fathers. They won't worry about being fed, clothed, or housed. They will simply trust that their parents will meet their needs.

Such total trust in the provision and protection of God is the first giant step toward greatness.

As for being teachable, children, most significantly, will listen. They have voracious appetites for learning, and, since they're starting from zero, they know the best way to feed those appetites is to listen. They may ask a lot of questions, but they listen to the answers. "Daddy, why is the grass green?" "Daddy, why are the birds flying?" "Daddy, why is the car running?"

It never stops. Their minds are set in the inquiry mode.

Too often parents become annoyed, but they need to understand that this is a mark of intelligence. It is desirable and pleasing to the Creator. A child between the ages of four and five will learn more in that one year than a student will in four years of college.

This teachableness has an interesting side effect that I'm sure Jesus had in mind. Children, hungry to learn, will experiment. They are quick to master new ideas, new languages, new techniques. Their minds are open. If we think of this in the context of God's instruction to Adam and Eve to master and subdue the earth,[3] we see the importance of such inquiry and openness.

They are steps toward greatness.

Innocent As a Child

Then, little children are humble—at least until someone spoils them. You seldom see a young child vaunting himself as if he is something special. This virtue is eventually corrupted by a society that has become increasingly warped through the centuries, but in his very early years a child doesn't care if his dad is a prince or a pauper, highly educated or lacking in training. All he cares about is that this man is Daddy, and he loves him. Usually this carries over to attitudes toward others; he loves people as people, regardless of social status.

Quite simply, children love life, until we train this quality out of them. When you watch them play, they are free; they throw themselves into situations with abandon, even getting a little reckless. And they'll throw themselves into your arms with absolute delight. Their innocence is beautiful. While fully content in the fact that their parents are sovereign—it's so good and natural that they never even think to challenge it—they are free to be free.

They wear no masks. They're innocent, transparent, and genuine. Jesus says, become like them and you're on the road to greatness.

The New Testament is jammed with urgings toward humility, and we have noted the importance of this virtue in simply moving toward the kingdom of God. But we should observe that Jesus, in a parallel passage on greatness, reemphasized that insistence on humility. It is a virtue with more than passing importance. After having said that "the greatest among you shall be your servant,"[4] He continued: "And whoever exalts himself shall be humbled; and *whoever humbles himself shall be exalted.*"[5]

With that principle, Christ was pointing to a truth that Solomon had unfolded in a different way: "The reward of humility and the fear of the LORD / Are riches, honor and life."[6] Greatness, summed up as "riches, honor and life," is the reward of those who are humble, which is the necessary ingredient for fearing the Lord. And that, psychology confirms, is what men long for—financial reward, recognition, and a good, satisfying life. It all awaits the little child, epitome of the humble.

So, in short, Jesus said greatness begins with being trusting, being teachable, and being humble. The three traits go together—not merely in children, but in adults as well. The trusting person puts away criticism and skepticism, and becomes open. He doesn't have to be right all the time. Then he is able to learn—from God, from people, from circumstances. He'll listen; he'll try new things. And *that* is the humble person.

Do you see the circle? Trust. Teachableness. Humility. They run from one to another, backward and forward.

The businessman who becomes like a child in this regard will rise to greatness. So will the scientist. So will the minister.

Learning

In God's order it is the poor in spirit, the "spiritual beggars," who are given the kingdom of God. In God's order it is "little children" who make up the kingdom of God. In God's kingdom the servant becomes the greatest. Yet in the material world as well it is these very heavenly characteristics which, despite our preconceptions, make for success.

In politics the winner is usually the man or woman who goes door to door shaking hands, asking for votes, offering to serve the people. Those office-seekers who are too arrogant to "beg" for votes sooner or later lose.

In business, the most successful entrepreneurs are those who have a childlike curiosity and a childlike, contagious enthusiasm. They always want to learn more. How can they improve production and sales techniques? How can they streamline costs? What are the latest consumer trends and marketing techniques? What are their competitors doing? What ways can they find to copy, improve, extend? What better and more profitable uses can be made of existing product lines?

These successful men and women are always listening and learning. They listen to their customers, to their employees, to experts, to the man on the street. They and their companies will always defeat the man or company that says, "I know it all. My product is the best. My techniques have worked for years and they are the best. No one can teach me." The successful are innovative and adaptive. Whatever the business climate they will succeed. They become great. The other is rigid and autocratic. Their position and power will carry them for a time, but like dinosaurs in the Ice Age, when dramatic change comes, their pride and unwillingness to learn guarantees their defeat.

A Difficult Concept

In the second episode we examined at the beginning of this chapter, Jesus added another criterion for greatness. Quite paradoxically, He said the secret of greatness is service. If you reflect on it, you see that it fits well with being childlike, but it begins to rub. It goes against the grain of society.

That is why we should be serious and careful on this subject. We are dealing with a law that turns everything upside down. Little children soon yearn to grow up so they can "be somebody." But Jesus says, "Be a child if you really want to *be* somebody." Servants, meanwhile, usually hate their position, yearning to earn enough to have their *own* servants. But Jesus says, "No, become a servant if you wish to be truly great."

184

This pushes us into a corner where we have to ask, "Do I really want this?" We should weigh it carefully, for the Lord said to count the cost of the things we set out to do.[7]

If you're an average working man, you may have been striving all your life to escape any image of servanthood, trying to rise to the point, perhaps, where you work for yourself and not for someone else.

If you're a black man or woman, you have known the effects of the struggle against slavery all your life, and chances are one of the most disturbing facts you have lived with is the tendency to think of blacks as service workers. But what happens when a black man or woman works hard to get a good education and moves into one of the higher professions? Will the idea of being a "servant," as Christ commanded, have any appeal to him or her? Can we honestly expect anyone escaping from "servant" status to volunteer for servanthood in another form?

If you have ever been exposed to management-labor relations, you know that no manager has any true desire to be a servant of the labor ranks, and no union member will accept the slightest hint that he or she is a "servant" of management—or anyone else. That kind of thinking would be anathema to both sides.

If you're a politician, you smile indulgently when someone refers to you as a "public servant"; you really prefer the role of celebrity.

If you're a minister of the gospel, "successful" and well known on the speaking circuit or perhaps on television, the chances are very good that you are far more comfortable signing autographs and sitting at head tables than being a servant to the flock.

You see, there will be a cost if we seek true greatness. For our attitudes—wrong ones—are well solidified, despite the fact that we have had examples of true greatness over the years.

Judging Greatness

My generation considered Albert Schweitzer to be a great man, and most—even those who disagreed with his theology—

would acknowledge that his was true greatness. Why? Because he became like a little child and like a servant. He gave his life for the sick and the oppressed. He was trusting, teachable, and humble. He was a servant.

A scientist, musician, philosopher, and theologian, Schweitzer left what the world would have considered to be the road to greatness in Germany and went to Africa to labor among primitive, underprivileged people in a remote, little village. Establishing a hospital, he lived his life out in full service to others, continually learning, continually enthusiastic, continually innocent.

Even the modern world came to understand that his greatness was somehow different from the greatness most men sought. Year after year, he was numbered at the top of the list of outstanding people.

Similarly, polls measuring the ten most admired women in the world place a remarkable Roman Catholic nun, Mother Teresa of Calcutta, at the top. This is a woman who has given up everything, in a materialistic world's terms, to go among the poor, downtrodden masses of India to feed them, clothe them, house them, and love them.

Hers is a role of a servant through and through, a refusal to lord it over anyone, and yet we somehow know she has achieved greatness.

Stepping back through history, we encounter Father Damien, the Belgian priest who gave himself entirely to service to the leper colony on the Hawaiian island of Molokai in the mid-nineteenth century. His was true greatness.

And there is Hudson Taylor, the missionary who turned away from a life of comfort in Britain to throw himself into service of the suffering and lost Chinese. His greatness still rings in the annals of missionary service.

And there was Florence Nightingale, the English nurse who served heroically in the Crimean War and became known as the founder of modern nursing.

These unusual humanitarians were among those who found the key to success through the Law of Greatness.

The business world, too, has produced greatness. And we need to understand that the principles set forth by Jesus are pragmatic and effective in the hard-nosed give-and-take of free enterprise.

Henry Ford was a good illustration. He wanted to make inexpensive, efficient transportation available to as many people as possible. So he came up with the Model T. Before long he was serving thousands with cheap transportation. The more he served, the more money he made, and the greater his business became. He became the greatest figure in the auto industry.

Management Insensitivity

The Law of Greatness did not gain a permanent foothold in the American car industry, however. Confrontations gradually replaced service. Management and labor lost all semblance of unity, and the thought of serving one another became a joke. The industry also confronted the public, steadily losing awareness about changes in society, consumer economics, and fuel outlook. It designed cars the way *it* wanted them.

The early tolling of the death knell went largely unnoticed. While there has been a concerted effort in Detroit in the past decade to reverse this trend and to put the customer and the worker back in the driver's seat, it remains to be seen if the American auto industry can ever regain its position as the world leader in this field.

For a long time, the deterioration in the concept of service reached the point where car manufacturers decided that fully effective quality control at the factories was too expensive. Their surveys convinced them that they would be better off to repair mistakes at the dealership level.

So cars came off the assembly lines with little things untended. Buyers drove them a short while and things started going bad. When they took them back, the dealers made the repairs and sent the bill to the manufacturer. Almost inevitably something else would happen to the same car, and the process would be repeated. It was terribly inconvenient for car buyers, but it was less expensive for the manufacturer.

The tolling of the bell grew louder as the principle of service fell by the roadside.

Consider the kinds of arrogant and destructive self-interest that brought men like Ivan Boesky, Charles Keating, Michael Milken, and Donald Trump into the headlines between 1989 and 1992. Along with the virtual collapse of the savings-and-loan industry, the international BCCI banking scandal, and a litany of insider-trading scams and stock fraud cases, American industry has been shaken to its foundations. No longer were businesses looking after their customers' interests; they were catering to the personal fortunes of a few unscrupulous top executives.

This, as we noted in an earlier chapter, was not the case in the booming Pacific-rim countries like Japan. There, thoughts of service penetrated deeper into the industrial consciousness. Until the mid-1960s Japan was known only as a country of cut-rate merchandise and cheap knock-offs, but one day that situation came to an end. A desire emerged among Japanese managers and workers to end shoddiness and to give their customers the best products available. Industry would serve the people; and particularly in the automobile market, their achievement speaks for itself.

In Japan, following the teachings of W. Edwards Deming, management and labor began to work on the idea of becoming servants of one another. Companies took pains to instill in their managers the thought that they were servants of the workers. "We're here to make their jobs better, to improve their environment, to solve their problems," they repeated. Furthermore, they became like little children and listened to their workers.

"We want to learn from you," management said. Japanese automobile workers were each submitting eighteen and nineteen suggestions a year for improving their automobiles, and management was adopting at least 80 percent. While Japanese automobile companies led by servant managers were seeing stunning success, American managers remained autocratic and rigid. Here workers offered only two suggestions a year and only one of them was adopted by management.

Japanese employees, meanwhile, were constantly reinforced in their understanding, through attitudes and material rewards, that they were servants of the customers and the society. United States employees were locked in hostile confrontation with management.

Principles That Really Work

Serving is a concept that works at every level, even in an enterprise as massive as the automobile industry of a major, very prosperous nation. For, as the world knows, the Japanese auto industry overwhelmed everyone, even gaining a foothold in America that resulted in a major share of sales.

The principle works in other industries, too. J. C. Penney, for example, embraced the concept of giving a square deal to everyone—honest merchandise, honest measure, honest price. With that in mind, he developed a giant chain of stores across America, becoming a great man in merchandising. More recently Sam Walton, founder of Wal-Mart and Sam's wholesale stores, built one of the world's most prosperous retail chains by bringing mass merchandising and low prices to small towns and rural communities all across America that had never seen a discount store. His venture paid off in many ways, and at his death in 1992 Walton and his family were reportedly the richest in the world. So a life principle emerges. Those who serve others—whether in religion, philanthropy, education, science, art, government, or business—are the great ones. Indeed, the deeper the sacrifice or the broader the scope of service, the greater the individual becomes.

And rarely will our society award the status of greatness to those who lust for personal power and seek to exalt themselves. How often we hear applied to such persons the phrases "petty tyrant," "little Caesar," "self-seeking," "ruthless," "vain." And though occasionally these people rise to prominence, they never touch greatness. Invariably the Law of Reciprocity brings them down.

Looking around us in this last decade of the twentieth century, we would certainly find a consensus that if ever greatness was needed in the world, it is now. We have few statesmen of international stature; few political leaders we would trust in a personal relationship; few heroes in any field. Instead of greatness of spirit, more often we find meanness. Our vision is dim.

Frankly, we need leadership at every level, especially in the international realm. As Armageddon looms closer with each passing day, there is every reason to fear that the kinds of mismanagement and insensitivity we have witnessed during most of the past generation will lead us to the brink of catastrophe. We need men and women to lead our nation in taking on the responsibilities and the risks of serving other nations, helping them to achieve their potential, helping them with education, agriculture, and industry. We need to cast off the paternalism and exploitation that has passed for foreign relations.

We need to dare to live the Beatitudes at this level, to be trusting, teachable, and humble, to discover perhaps for the first time in history how a true servant can lead.

In addition to being spiritually and biblically sound, this course has a very practical result. The nation that does the most for others will be the one growing in greatness. That nation will be the one other nations, as customers, will turn to, the one whose products will sweep the world. That nation will be exalted, elevated, enlarged as the Laws of Reciprocity and Use take hold.

As with nations, so with all of us.

12

The Law of Unity

*F*rom the beginning of His revelation to mankind, God has held forth a difficult principle that flows naturally into and out of the concept of serving. Men have continually stumbled over it.

I call it the *Law of Unity*. It is simple to understand, and for some, difficult to obey. But it is essential to success. God has been trying to explain that to mankind for thousands of years, for unity is central to the working of the universe.

Perhaps the most powerful illustration of the creative power of perfect unity is found in God Himself. At the very moment of creation there was unity. "Then God said, 'Let *Us* make man in *Our* image, according to *Our* likeness.'"[1]

This is the only part of the Creation where such language is used and, admittedly, we do not know with great precision what the Lord was inspiring the writer to communicate. He probably was referring to the Godhead, the Trinity, when He spoke of "Us." But He could have been speaking to the angelic court of God or perhaps even the multifaceted majesty of God. Regardless, there was some form of conversation involving more than one Person, and *there was unity*.

Although the passage presents many significant facts, this is the one we should see here: Within the Godhead (or the court of heaven) there was agreement and harmony. God moves in unity.

Thus, the principle is first stated: Great creativity occurs where there is unity. God's unfathomable power is released where there is harmony.

The early Genesis accounts add another piece of insight in this regard. After man had refused to obey God and live under His sovereignty, the half-truth of Satan, the liar and deceiver, came to pass: Adam and Eve became "like God."[2] We are not able to comprehend the seriousness of that moment. It was history's terrible tragedy. Man, the delight of God's heart, had fallen. And we read these words:

> Then the LORD God said, "Behold, the man has become like one of *Us,* knowing good and evil; and now, lest he stretch out his hand, and take also from the tree of life, and eat, and live forever"—therefore the LORD God sent him out from the garden of Eden.[3]

Judgment flowed from unity. Just as the magnificent power of creation had sprung from the perfect harmony of heaven, so had the dreadful power of judgment and justice come from the awesome unity of the Almighty.

The examples are clear. God moves in unity. Harmony is central to the unleashing of God's incredible power.

Furthermore, unity in the invisible world governs the visible world. If it works in heaven, it works on earth. "Thy kingdom come. / Thy will be done. / *On earth as it is in heaven.*"[4]

This operation of the Law of Unity on earth was the point of one of the Lord's most-quoted statements:

> Again I say to you, that if *two of you agree on earth about anything* that they may ask, *it shall be done* for them by My Father who is in heaven. For where two or three have gathered together in My name, there I am in their midst.[5]

He was calling for agreement, but not merely for agreement's sake. He was calling for unity. Since He would be in their midst when they gathered to consider some issue, they would be expected to agree with Him. Their unity would be an external manifestation of their internal agreement. Since He was there, He would bring them to harmony if they genuinely laid aside their own preconceptions and centered on Him.

Then, and only then, would power flow, just as at the creation. For unity is the fountainhead of God's creative power.

There is a multiplication factor in that unity too. We see it in a song of Moses spoken to all of Israel as he approached the end of his life. One standing on the Rock, he said, would chase a thousand of the enemy, while two would put ten thousand to flight.[6] Unity does not cause a mere doubling or tripling of power; the progression explodes.

The Early Church

The biblical accounts of unity within the early church show the power of the Law of Unity. For example, the fledgling assembly (the *ekklesia*, or church) continued to stick together after Christ's crucifixion, resurrection, and ascension—still weak, still uncertain, still afraid. But an enlightening verse says, "These all *with one mind* were continually devoting themselves to prayer."[7] They were in accord in unity.

Then, the Bible says, power flowed through and from that unity. The Holy Spirit, the giver of life and power, was sent forth upon the people of God as never before. The church was on its way.

At another critical stage, as the people reached unity and harmony, we see the launching of the missionary outreach that was to change the world. This occurred in Antioch, where the Lord's followers were first called Christians.[8]

In the church at Antioch there were these prophets and teachers: Barnabas, Simeon (also called Niger), Lucius (from the city of Cyrene), Manaen (who had grown up with Herod, the ruler), and Saul. They were all worshiping the Lord and giving up eating for a certain time. During this time the Holy Spirit said to them, "Set apart for me Barnabas and Saul to do a special work for which I have chosen them." So after they gave up eating and prayed, they laid their hands on Barnabas and Saul and sent them out.

The Lord acted in that setting of harmony, in which those great and diverse leaders centered in on Christ—"ministering" to Him, worshiping Him, turning their full devotion upon Him, feasting upon Him rather than upon ordinary food. He called out Saul, whose name was changed to Paul,[10] and Barnabas, the "Son of Encouragement" whose name had already been changed from Joseph, and sent them forth in power.[11]

We see in all of these reports evidence that people will not hear the voice of God clearly unless the unity of the Spirit is maintained. Disunity will cause the Spirit to flee.

If we need further support for the point, we have only to look at the recent history of the church. Division and disunity have been its most distinguishing characteristics, with the result that it has been impotent to move the world. It has lacked the power that flows from unity. It is small wonder that Jesus, on the night of His betrayal, prayed so movingly and powerfully for the harmony of His people, asking that they might be "perfected in unity."[12] He knew how critical it was.

For Good or for Evil

A fascinating aspect of unity is that it apparently generates a power that can work for good or for evil, at least for a time. We find this illustrated early in the Bible in the story of the Tower of Babel.

After the Flood, we read, "the whole earth used the same language and the same words."[13] The people were becoming gradually unified and beginning to work in harmony. They discovered the use of bricks and mortar, for example, and set out to build themselves a city with a great tower "whose top will reach into heaven." They wanted to make "a name" for themselves and to grow as a unified force.[14]

If we read carefully, we see that their motive reflected pride. Their plan actually constituted man's first effort to glorify himself.

They wanted to build a memorial to themselves, a symbolic assault on heaven in defiance of God.

God viewed this as sin, and Scripture records His reaction as follows:

> "Behold, they are *one people*, and they all have the same language. And this is what they began to do, and now *nothing which they purpose to do will be impossible* for them. Come, let Us go down and there confuse their language, that they may not understand one another's speech." So the LORD scattered them abroad from there over the face of the whole earth.[15]

God Almighty saw that the people were of one mind and one language; they were unified. Nothing would be impossible for them, whether for good or for evil.

God's assessment is blunt: Mankind in unity becomes absolutely overwhelming. Here we must emphasize in the strongest terms possible what God is saying. To a group, a business, a church, a family, a nation that is of "one mind and speaks one language" *nothing will be impossible. Absolutely nothing.* Conversely, if a house or a kingdom is divided against itself, *it cannot stand. The lack of unity is destroying our families and the increasing lack of unity in America is guaranteed to destroy our nation!* Divided against itself, it cannot stand! Not "might not stand"—it "cannot stand."

There are those who might think God's action against Babel was harsh and unreasonable, so we must make sure we comprehend the truth of the episode. The Lord instantly understood that the people's intention was to unify in glorifying man, which meant the same thing as unifying in rebellion against God. The Bible, as we have seen, tells us that God resists the proud but gives favor to the humble. Indeed, He resists pride in any form. Any expression of rebellious pride, especially the pride of a unified group, wherever found, will ultimately draw opposition from Him.

It is noteworthy that pride, which leads to the glorification of man, continues in the world today in a subtler, yet similar manner. It goes under the label of secular humanism, which, in truth, is a religion of man. Its intention is to build great towers, as it were, to the glory of man. Moving slowly but persistently across the earth and capitalizing on the natural pride of man, it has been gaining adherents. Its final aim is the rejection of the centrality of God and the removal of religious freedom from society. The unity of its believers has given it unprecedented force in our time. It's ultimate goal is the establishment of a new world order in defiance of God that one day will, according to the Bible, be ruled by Satan's emissary on earth.

Bible believers draw confidence, however, from the fact that the Scripture announces that such forces as those gathered under the banner of humanism or those who rallied at Babel, as long as they remain in opposition to God, will be defeated. The Bible places them under the name of "Babylon," which is doomed to annihilation.[16] It is noteworthy that the presumed site of the Tower of Babel was at or near historical Babylon in modern-day Iraq.

The lesson we are to learn from all of this is that the Lord God takes the matter of unity very seriously. We, His people, should do no less.

Unity of Quest

Unity must begin with the individual. If you are going to experience the power that can change the world, you must be unified within yourself. You must have internal harmony. In the Bible, James addresses this point specifically. A "double-minded man," he says, will not receive anything from the Lord.[17]

One mind believing or desiring one thing and in the same person another mind believing or desiring something else will not work. And there can be no doubting, James added, "Anyone who doubts is like a wave in the sea, blown up and down by the wind."[18]

Instead, the Bible says, you must be as Abraham was when, at a hundred years of age and sonless, he was told he would be the father of many nations. He did not "waver" regarding the promise, but remained fully assured that God would perform what He had said.[19]

Abraham had unified his quest in life. He did not fall victim to spiritual schizophrenia, which wracks so many in their walk with the Lord. People can be torn between the pursuit of worldly goals and the pursuit of the Christian life. They can't make up their minds which to put first, needing desperately to hear the words of David: "My heart is fixed, O God, my heart is fixed."[20]

The well-known story of Mary and Martha illustrates the problem.

> Now as they were traveling along, He entered a certain village; and a woman named Martha welcomed Him into her home. And she had a sister called Mary, who moreover was listening to the Lord's word, seated at His feet. But Martha was distracted with all her preparations; and she came up to Him, and said, "Lord, do You not care that my sister has left me to do all the serving alone? Then tell her to help me." But the Lord answered and said to her, "Martha, Martha, you are worried and bothered about so many things; but only a few things are necessary, really only one, for Mary has chosen the good part, which shall not be taken away from her."[21]

We must not interpret that passage as approval of laziness or irresponsibility. Jesus loved Martha and her willingness to serve, but He was concerned about her attitude, her internal unity. Mary had "chosen the good part"; her quest had been unified. If need be, she would sacrifice all else for it. But Martha wanted to be recognized as a follower of Jesus *and* as a good organizer *and* as a good cook. She wasn't single-minded, and she had no peace. She was "worried and bothered about so many things."

We cannot serve two masters.[22] We cannot put our spouse and Jesus first in our lives at the same time. We cannot put our job ahead of everything and serve Jesus as Lord at the same time. Our problem is that we make a gap between the two, seeing them as two masters, and try to put each one first. That leads to schizophrenia and breakdowns.

The solution, of course, is to be single-minded. Put Jesus first, and then He will say, "Love your wife as I loved the church."[23] A spouse can get no greater love than that. Similarly, put Jesus first and He will say, "When you undertake a task, do it with all your might."[24] A job can get no more attention than that.

Single-mindedness is the solution to the internal desperation so many people regularly experience. It removes the terrible burden and dark heaviness that weigh upon the chest as they teeter on the fringes of nervous collapse.

A Collective Principle

The Bible is precise in showing that what is true for the individual is true for the family, the group, the organization, and the nation. When the Pharisees accused Him of being in league with Satan, Jesus countered with the following universal principle: "Any kingdom divided against itself is laid waste; and any city or house divided against itself shall not stand."[25]

His point was simple. Without internal unity in a group—whether a family, a business, or a political entity—that group will ultimately collapse. Vacillation and dissension will lead to tearing and destruction.

Jesus, in this verse, was talking about the kingdom of Satan, showing that such universal principles as the Law of Unity apply everywhere. They are broader than religion. Even works of evil will collapse unless the evil forces are unified.

Unity produces strength; disunity produces weakness. Obviously, this was not a New Testament revelation. The Lord's words quickly remind us of the teachings of the man credited with unimaginable wisdom, Solomon: "He who troubles his own house will inherit wind."[26] This proverb was thoroughly supported throughout biblical history. Houses of leadership would often fall to scheming and fighting among themselves, and then the leadership would crumble.

In my generation, the name of Kennedy immediately comes to mind when we consider the strength derived from unity within a house or clan. Working together and for the good of the family or for one of its members, the Kennedys of Massachusetts achieved remarkable political success. The power of the individual was geometrically multiplied by the harmony of the group. We have fewer and fewer examples of such family unity.

When any family is supportive in unity it can succeed even in a hostile environment. The husband and wife support each other. The children are together and honor their parents. All members work for the good of the family. It is this family unity that above all else accounts for the remarkable rise of immigrant Vietnamese, Korean, and Chinese in our society.

But consider the tragedy that comes when husbands and wives battle each other and seek to undermine one another. When children are neglected and grow up estranged, even hating their parents. The economic and social cost of the lack of unity in families is appalling. When families lack unity and cohesion, all society begins to suffer. The hatred engendered by disunity in marriages leads to racial, ethnic, and class warfare, which rips society apart and destroys cities, states, and nations. "A kingdom divided against itself cannot stand!"

Corporate Disunity

The same is true of the business world. We need only think of those businesses that have fallen on hard times because they abandoned a clear-cut unity of mission in favor of diversification. A great electronics company floundered because it tried to make large computers. A chemical company ran into trouble when it tried to be a land developer.

Successful organizations, as well as successful individuals, are those unified around a relatively simple statement of goals and mission. A double-minded man is "unstable in all his ways."[27] So is a double-minded business.

At the national level, the problem is just as great. Turning back into history we see the roots of modern-day Italy, whose turmoil may be greater than any developed country in the world despite its conspicuous marks of great civilization. Before the time of Guiseppe Garibaldi's efforts to unify Italy in the nineteenth century, that land witnessed the struggle of little city-states to prevail over one another and maintain their autonomy. Garibaldi brought them together in a fragile alliance, but following the wars in our century and the conditions in modern Europe, Italy is probably best described as "the sick man" of the continent, owing almost exclusively to the absence of harmony.

The factions in that nation simply will not come together. The house is divided. Consequently, the economy is sick; the society with its unbelievable terrorism and crime is unstable; governmental services falter. Life is a shambles.

In the United States, the history is different and the symptoms vary, but the disease is the same. From its founding until about 1960, Americans were united by at least a common ethic. Essentially, the country had been founded as a Christian nation, adopting biblical principles and governing itself pretty much under biblical countenance. There was a work ethic and moral restraint based on an underlying philosophical system of honor and decency that prevailed even in the face of frequent and flagrant violations.

Today, the United States struggles under a social philosophy of "diversity" and "pluralism." There is no unified reality. Many disparate, frequently cacophonous voices echo from one shore to another. Unity is no longer the goal of secular society, but disparity, difference, and diversity. Consequently, confusion is triumphant.

A "700 Club" guest once asked a question typically heard in the current atmosphere: "Whatever happened to the concept that 'I am my brother's keeper?'"

The answer was easy. It vanished with the Christian ethic. Such concepts spring from a God-centered society, but we no longer have that unifying force. We are now fragmented, and each fragment spawns its own jealousy and self-concern. If this continues and the rival factions increase and strengthen, the country will fall quite simply from violation of the Law of Unity.

Unity with Distinctiveness

It is important we understand that unity springing from the truth of the kingdom of God does not insist on, or even desire, uniformity. Lessons from the Bible about the unity of the Godhead make this abundantly clear. There is distinctiveness even with the oneness of the Trinity.

We see this point in the lives of Christ's disciples, too. They were unified in their quest, but they were a diverse lot, thoroughly nonconformist in several instances.

Paul the apostle taught on this in a spiritual lesson that has physical applications:

> Now there are *varieties* of gifts, but the same Spirit. And there are *varieties* of ministries, and the same Lord. And there are *varieties* of effects, but the same God who works all things in all persons. But to each one is given the manifestation of the Spirit for the common good.[28]

Variety is God's way, he said, even invoking the Trinity to make the point—Spirit, Lord, God. Variety and distinctiveness serve God's purpose, working differently but pointedly to arrive at the common good.

No, in families, businesses, churches, and nations, the Lord is not seeking a collection of robots. He is seeking people with varying personalities, talents, and styles who are unified in purpose and will work toward the common good.

Using His principles harmoniously, they can overcome the crises of our century.

Keenly aware of this the night before He was crucified, Jesus prayed to His Father in this manner:

> I do not ask in behalf of these alone, but for those also who believe in Me through their word; *that they may all be one;* even as Thou, Father, art in Me, and I in Thee, that they also may be in Us; that the world may believe that Thou didst send Me. And the glory which Thou hast given Me I have given to

them; *that they may be one, just as We are one;* I in them, and Thou in Me, that they may be perfected in unity, that the world may know that Thou didst send Me, and didst love them, even as Thou didst love Me.[29]

He knew that the fulfillment of the purposes of God would require unity. Without it, there would be no flow of power to save the world and to perfect the people of God.

13

The Law of Fidelity

A woman once approached Billy Sunday, the great evangelist of the World War I era, with this question: "Reverend Sunday, tell me how I can stop exaggerating?" Sunday shot back, "Call it lying."

To many in our culture there are euphemisms to describe conduct that is prohibited by God's clear command. The woman in the story was lying repeatedly, but her conduct was somehow made acceptable by calling it "exaggerations" or "little white lies."

Unmarried men and women are not fornicating, they are "living together," "having an affair," or "making love." Homosexuals aren't sodomites. They are "gay." The killing of unborn babies is not murder, it is a woman's "freedom of choice." Looting and pillaging by ghetto youths is no longer theft, it is an act of "cultural deprivation." Workers do not steal tools and parts from their employers; they temporarily "borrow" or, in wartime jargon, they "liberate" them. We don't slander and gossip, we show "concern."

In each case we can then say we are truly "good" people, but, of course, we, like everyone else, are guilty of all of the "little" sins that don't really matter because everybody is doing them.

But in God's eyes there are no "peccadilloes" and "mortal" sins. Either we are living for God, or we are not. Either we are sinning, or we are not.

Jesus laid out the universal principle in what I call the *Law of Fidelity.* He said, "Whoever can be trusted with very little can also be trusted with much, and whoever is dishonest with very little will also be dishonest with much. So if you have not been trustworthy in handling worldly wealth, who will trust you with true riches? And if you have not been trustworthy with someone else's property, who will give you property of your own?"[1]

The story is told of a private dinner which found the witty and irreverent playwright, George Bernard Shaw, seated next to an attractive young actress from London. "Tell me," Shaw began, "would you consider sleeping with a strange man if he paid you a million pounds sterling?" The young lady thought for a moment and then coyly said, "Yes, I would." Then Shaw asked, "Would you sleep with a strange man if he paid you five pounds?" "Of course not," was the angry reply. "What do you take me for?" "I have already discovered that," said Shaw. "Now I am trying to determine the price."

A person who would resist a five-dollar bribe but yield to a million-dollar bribe is not honest. And conversely, if a man would steal one dollar from the company stamp drawer, he will also steal ten thousand dollars from a trust account if the opportunity presents itself.

If a worker will not work hard and conscientiously for ten dollars per hour, he will not suddenly become conscientious if paid a hundred dollars per hour. An employee who will lie on his résumé to get a job will lie about his performance in order to keep his job. A husband who cheats on his wife under extreme temptation will also cheat under more normal circumstances.

A Matter of Degree

Recently a New Hampshire-based manufacturer of hand guns dismissed a longtime employee because, when he found himself without change for the coffee machine, he took thirty-five cents from the desk of a fellow worker. Most people who heard of that action, including me, felt that the company had acted with excessive severity. Apparently there were other instances of petty theft concerning this worker which justified his dismissal. Nevertheless, knowingly or unknowingly, the company realized that a man who takes thirty-five cents will also take thirty-five dollars or thirty-five hundred dollars because that is the truth of the Law of Fidelity.

In our permissive society there is so much petty theft, shoplifting, insurance fraud, and tax cheating, that losses are considered an ordinary part of doing business. The New Hampshire incident is an aberration, not the rule in our society.

Nevertheless, the Law of Fidelity has much wider application for it speaks not just of isolated acts, but tendencies. And it really deals more with ultimate rewards in the kingdom of heaven than reward for conduct on earth. Jesus was contrasting material wealth with "true riches" and "someone else's property" versus "your own" property.

Here is the concept. Each of us is only a life tenant of the property we possess on earth. Whether we live ten years or a hundred years, whether we drink from a beggar's cup and live in a shanty or drink from fine crystal and live in a mansion we cannot take anything material with us to our permanent home in heaven. When we die, all of it is taken from us—stocks, bonds, bank accounts, insurance policies, pensions, farms, ranches, office buildings, houses, cars, boats, furniture, jewelry—everything is left behind. Then, we learn from the Bible, one day all of the material things will "melt with fervent heat." Nothing on earth will remain for eternity. All will be destroyed by fire. Every single thing!

Jesus is telling us that earthly possessions, including our life, our health, and our abilities, are on loan to us to determine what we will do with them. Will we lie and cheat to acquire them? Will we trample upon the rights of others to gain our success? Will we neglect and dissipate the stewardship of our earthly talents and resources? Will we hoard them selfishly for our own pleasure and glory? Will they become a source of arrogance whereby we exalt ourselves above those who have less than we?

Or will we consider ourselves as holding stewardship under Almighty God of whatever He places for a time in our hands? Remember the parable of the talents. The servant who used to the fullest that which had been temporarily entrusted to him in order to enhance his lord's estate was called "good and faithful." The servant who out of fear or indolence refused to use what had been temporarily entrusted to him was called "wicked and slothful." The faithful servant who created ten talents for his lord was given a permanent possession of ten cities. The servant who failed to use his one talent at all not only had that talent stripped away from him, he himself was "cast into outer darkness."

Starting Small

Obviously the Law of Fidelity applies to the material world. The faithful employee in little things is entrusted with bigger things. Some years ago at the tender age of thirteen I was given the role of Sir Joseph in the Gilbert and Sullivan operetta "*HMS Pinafore.*" The story that I had to sing was that the great Sir Joseph—the "monarch of the sea"—started in life as an office boy in an attorney's firm whose task it was to polish the handle on the big front door. Then the line, "I polished up the handle so carefully that now I am the ruler of the Queen's Navy."

"*Pinafore*" is a delightful spoof, but it reflects the clear-cut expectation in our material world that those who are diligent and faithful with small responsibilities will over time be entrusted with larger responsibilities.

But the material expectations are just a prelude to the true meaning of the Law of Fidelity which our Lord was careful to repeat in various contexts for emphasis.

The basic rule is this: Every person will be held accountable for whatever talent, ability, or opportunity that is afforded to him. All of these things are, like the talents, not our personal property but the property of the Lord. There will be an accounting at the end of each of our lives. For those who have been faithful in the "little things," such as the material world, they will be given "true riches" as a permanent, eternal possession. The measure of the scope of our responsibilities in the eternal and never-ending kingdom of God will be determined by our fidelity in managing our Lord's affairs here on earth.

To say that this is an awesome concept is a vast understatement. Henceforth, we cannot think that a tithe of money belongs to God and 90 percent belongs to us to do with as we please. None of it is ours; it is all, 100 percent, God's. We are merely its stewards who can use and enjoy it for His glory. So also our time. We cannot think that one or two or three hours a week spent in church belongs to God and the rest belongs to us to use or waste as we please. All of our time is His. We are stewards of God's time to use and enjoy it for His glory.

No Surprises

When the final judgment comes, those surprised by the outcome will comprise a multitude beyond reckoning. Many who have regularly been excused by society for "little sins" will find heaven's doors slammed in their faces. Revelation makes it clear, "Outside are the dogs [cult sodomites], those who practice magic arts, the sexually immoral, the murderers, the idolaters [those who worship the material] and everyone who loves and practices falsehood."[2]

Why is God being so harsh? Remember His law. Everyone who is unfaithful in the little things will be unfaithful in the big. Imagine what would progressively happen to the teller of "little white lies" during the first million years of existence in heaven. The monstrosity of the eventual falsehoods possible to him could rival those of Satan himself.

And think of those who will enter the kingdom of God by the grace of God because they have received Jesus Christ as their Savior and have been born again, yet they have done nothing with their lives or their talents or their material resources to extend their Lord's kingdom. If they have not been faithful with what belongs to another, who will give them "true riches"?[3] For them, the Lord says, "The servant who knows what his master wants but is not ready, or who does not do what the master wants, will be *beaten with many blows!*"[4] The apostle Paul put it another way when he wrote, "We all shall appear before the judgment seat of Christ to account for the deeds that we have done in our body."[5]

Of course, many will be surprised when they find that their stewardship of their meager possessions to feed the hungry, to clothe the naked, to visit the sick and those in prison, to intercede in prayer will open for them entrance into the true riches, "the joy of the LORD"![6]

The Law of Fidelity is at once a solemn warning and a promise of eternal blessing. Even as I write these words I am solemnly praying, "Lord, when it's over, will you say to me, 'Well done good and faithful servant. . . . Enter into the joy of your Master'?"[7]

14

The Law of Change

The French have a saying: *Plus ça change, plus c'est la même chose* ("The more things change, the more they remain the same"). The writer of Ecclesiastes expressed it this way, "What has been will be again / what has been done will be done again; / there is nothing new under the sun."[1]

God has said, "I am the LORD, I change not."[2] God is spirit, and spirit is changeless and ageless. My good friend, the late Father Dennis Bennett, put it this way, "We have sinned and grown old. Our father is younger than we."[3]

It is a sobering thought to realize that the One who is called the Ancient of Days is actually younger than I am. The earth is running down; our sun is gradually running out of energy; all stored energy in the universe is running down. In fact, all living things in the created universe experience a life cycle of birth, growth, and death.

Yet God, the Creator of all, is continually fresh, new, vibrant, and a source of life. According to the psalmist, He "will neither slumber nor sleep."[4]

We are told in the Bible that the "elements shall melt with fervent heat" and the "sky will be rolled up like a scroll."[5] Yet the invisible world of the secret kingdom and the laws that govern it will abide unchanged forever.

It is at this point that the parallels between the visible material kingdom and the invisible spiritual kingdom diverge. Although God never changes and His immutable laws never change—nor does His spiritual kingdom change—there have to be principles to govern existence in a world where there is an array of changing cycles—seedtime and harvest, birth and death, invention and obsolescence, flexibility and rigidity, enthusiasm and boredom, war and peace, wealth and poverty, revival and apostasy.

Here is the governing *Law of Change:* "No man puts new wine into old skins, lest the skins break and all be lost."[6]

What Jesus is telling us is that the spirit and message of the kingdom of God is always new, but that the receptacles prepared by human beings to receive it will age, become rigid and inflexible, and then must be replaced by receptacles that are new, pliable, and able to adapt. God is always the same; His plan is always the same. But the vehicles, the organizations, and the techniques of carrying out His program will always be changing.

A Mandate for Action

Many examples come to my own mind. In 1959, I was moved by a clear direction from God's Spirit to leave New York City with my family and to journey to the seacoast area of Hampton Roads, Virginia, to purchase a run-down UHF television station for God's glory. I had neither the money nor the knowledge to operate a television station. But I had a mandate for action from the Lord of the secret kingdom.

At the time, I could not have conceived in my wildest imagination that what was to be brought into being would result in more than 50 million people accepting Jesus as Savior in more than seventy nations; a cable network with 55 million subscribers; a daily television broadcast to millions; a relief agency that has distributed over $340 million to needy people; a fully accredited graduate university training future leaders; the preeminent

Christian public service law firm in America; a Christian coalition to mobilize America's Christians to resist the wasting secular trends in government; two large radio news networks; a motion picture company; and a personal run for the nomination of a major political party for the presidency of the United States.

I had within me new wine. God wanted to prepare a totally new wineskin to contain it. The old wineskins of the existing church structure were just not capable of what God had in mind. If I had tried to force it upon them, I would have brought about conflict, confusion, and failure. The new wine would have been lost and the old skins would have been destroyed.

I can still see the morning meeting of the Portsmouth, Virginia Ministerial Association when I tried to share the excitement of God's vision to use the powerful medium of television to reach the city for Christ. They nodded, asked a few questions, then adjourned for a coffee break. I went to a pay phone in the lobby to make a call. Imagine my surprise when I heard two of the pastors talking. Here were the exact words: "If we can't stop it, at least we can disassociate ourselves from it."

I was listening to tired old skins whose day of service in God's kingdom was coming to an end. Change was on the way in God's kingdom, but God Himself would have to show me how to put together the new wine flask for the new wine He was preparing. Had I insisted, despite objections, that the new wine be forced into the local denominational church structure of that one small city I would only have succeeded in destroying what they had and losing completely what God had given to me.

With Due Diligence

Moving to the present, in the spring of 1992 I read that the venerable news service, United Press International, was in bankruptcy and was to be sold to the highest bidder at the Federal Bankruptcy Court in Rutland, Vermont. Since our organization had a considerable news presence already, I felt that a worldwide news service would prove a logical extension of our activities.

So I flew up to Rutland, and in the company of a very able local bankruptcy attorney submitted what I considered to be a modest bid. Imagine my amazement when my bid proved to be the only one offered, and I walked out with a contract to buy the eighty-five-year-old news service after a thirty-day period of "due diligence."

My bid was welcomed by the management and most of the staff because it meant that the company had been saved from extinction. With a few exceptions, I found delightful, courteous, and helpful people. So, with a team of accountants, lawyers, journalists, broadcasters, and financial advisers we plunged into the books and records of UPI. After a few days the accountants said, "Don't do it." After a few more days the lawyers said, "Don't do it." After a few more days the journalists said, "Don't do it." Nevertheless, I was hoping to find something to salvage for what seemed a bargain price.

As I wrestled with the decision, I asked my wife, Dede, to join me at our breakfast table to ask God for wisdom. As I prayed, the quiet voice of the Lord spoke to me from the Gospel of Matthew. I opened my Bible and read these words:

> Neither do men pour new wine into old wineskins. If they do, the skins will burst, the wine will run out and the wineskins will be ruined. No, they pour new wine into new wineskins, and both are preserved.[7]

I called my news director, and asked his opinion. His reply, "UPI is about as tired an old wineskin as you can find. I think we should pass." And pass we did with great reluctance.

But in retrospect, there is no question that this was the course of wisdom. Our news has been on the cutting edge of technology—chip cameras, digital tapes, computer graphics, etc. The wave of the future is the satellite delivery of compressed digital information to computers, with television having a decided edge over print journalism. Everything about UPI was antiquated—old methods, old technology, old distribution, and in some cases old people. We needed to invest our time, resources, and talent into building the technology of the future, not in trying to keep alive the technology of the past.

The Law of Change was working.

Time for a Change

In 1992 there is an incessant clamor for change at every level of government. People not only have a disrespect for government, in many cases they actually loathe it. Tell a room full of businessmen, "I am from the government. I want to help you," and they will burst out laughing. The secretary of health, education, and welfare needed no further discussion to condemn a national health care plan than to say, "It would have the efficiency of the Post Office and the compassion of the Internal Revenue Service."

The federal government as we now know it started on its present course in 1932 under the administration of Franklin D. Roosevelt and what was known as the New Deal. Roosevelt took office in the midst of a desperate recession when 25 percent of the work force was unemployed, when long lines of helpless men queued up at soup kitchens for something to eat, and when the potential collapse of our society threatened. Roosevelt ran over a compliant Congress to jam through dozens of pieces of emergency legislation to transfer control of the economy from private industry to federal bureaucrats.

In a brilliant and prophetic article written for the September 15, 1934 issue of *Saturday Evening Post* former president Herbert Hoover made this comment:

> These proposals necessitate that a large part of leadership and managerial responsibility and authority in business and agriculture be taken from the hands of those who have risen in leadership . . . and placed in the hands of those who appear to merit political power. An enormous extension of bureaucracy is inevitable. . . . No one with a day's experience in government fails to realize that in all bureaucracies there are

213

three implacable spirits—self perpetuation, expansion, and incessant demand for more power.

Now after sixty years, the New Deal bureaucracy has grown even beyond the worst fears of Herbert Hoover. Each year it turns out more than sixty thousand pages of regulation to annoy and sap the vitality of the private sector. I recall reading one informal survey that placed the cost to the private sector of conforming to the bureaucratic regulation of the federal government at $450 billion per year.

Every four years, the American people vote for change, but nothing changes because the new wine is quickly lost in the old skins.

In the former Soviet Union, East Germany, Poland, Hungary, Czechoslovakia, and Romania, it became painfully obvious that no amount of *glasnost* or *perestroika* could cause Communism to adapt to free-market economics and capitalism. When a little new wine of change came in, the rigidly inflexible old system suddenly collapsed. Only then did it become possible to begin building new structures to house the new liberties demanded by the people.

The Change Movement

In the United States a movement is under way to limit the terms of congressmen. But even if this initiative succeeds in a few states, it will not be adequate to remove the deeply ingrained habits of wasteful spending, the multiple committees, and the utter venality that has taken control of that body.

But even if a reform effort changes both the chief executive and the Congress, they are still stymied by an intractable bureaucracy of nearly 3 million government workers. The old bureaucratic skin will frustrate and waste any reform effort from either party that is poured into it.

As frustrations mount in America, it will become crystal clear that a revolution—peaceful or violent—will come to pass to

214

break the gridlock of waste, ineptitude, and senseless regulation that has been strangling the productive energies of our nation. Vast changes are needed, including the wholesale elimination of federal programs, bureaus, agencies, and departments. Not only must the terms of congressmen and senators be limited, so also must the terms of bureaucrats be limited. Basically the structures of the New Deal, the Fair Deal, and the Great Society must be dismantled and replaced with a simple, efficient, service-oriented new wineskin into which we can pour a new birth of liberty in America.

The Bible says, "Where the Spirit of the Lord is, there is liberty."[8] Communism fell in Romania only after a protest when thousands of people jammed the streets of the city of Timisoara shouting, "God is alive!" Freedom came to East Germany directly as the result of prayer vigils in churches across the land. Christians around the world prayed for decades for the fall of Communism in the Soviet Union.

Where God's Spirit is, there is truth, justice, compassion, wisdom, liberty, free enterprise, moral self-restraint, evangelism, and usually humble simplicity. When the structures men build in the material visible world—whether in politics, law, business, science, health, social relations, education, and religion—begin to depart from the principles that characterize God's Spirit, the eternal, invisible kingdom begins to work quietly and secretly in the hearts of men to bring them new structures.

Without a doubt the authors of the American Revolution were moved upon by God's Spirit when they appealed to the Creator God as the author of their liberty and then framed a unique experiment in democracy dedicated to the proposition that all men are created equal.

Hope Against Hope

I recently returned from Zambia, where I visited at length with its new president, Frederick Chiluba. He is a fully committed, Spirit-filled Christian who was imprisoned by the tyrannical and corrupt regime of Kenneth Kuanda, the previous president. President Chiluba told me of a miracle that took place when God caused a man who was considered the most corrupt tyrannical judge in the service of Kuanda to dismiss all charges against him, even though this act later cost the man his judgeship.

Chiluba told me of God's intervention in his campaign for president, when the polls showed that he came from nowhere to defeat the powerful president of twenty-eight years. God put in his heart the ability to hope against hope and to believe for the electoral miracle that occurred.

Now a new structure exists in Zambia. President Chiluba declared it a Christian nation and then set about establishing freedom, cutting the bureaucracy, privatizing state-owned businesses, inviting foreign investors, and eliminating corruption. He plans to balance his nation's budget by the end of 1993, a feat that has steadfastly eluded our own government. The new government structure in Zambia can only lead to prosperity.

But to bring about this change, God was preparing a man, letting him suffer and grow, teaching him the Bible, giving him an understanding of the principles of the kingdom. Then with God's blessing, tyranny was overthrown; the old was swept away and the new began.

No one of us knows which people of the invisible kingdom are being prepared to change the visible kingdom. Someone reading this book may suddenly realize that he or she is God's agent for change. It may be a corrupt school board, an incompetent city government, a legislature controlled by selfish interests, or a church that has lost its vision of mission. Whatever the task, God is looking for people to say like Isaiah, "Here am I. Send me."[9]

Whatever changes may come about in institutions, God's principal mission is people. At the end of the eighteenth century, England was a cesspool of corruption, crime, drunkenness, and unattended poverty. Then God's Spirit moved upon several students at Oxford University who wanted their lives to stand for holiness, not debauchery. The leaders of this small band were two sons of an Anglican pastor and his godly wife,

Suzanna Wesley. These young men moved deeper into the truths of the invisible kingdom until their hearts were on fire for spiritual revival in England.

They attempted to pour their new wine into the Church of England, but this particular old wineskin was a major part of the spiritual problem in the nation. Instead of receiving the changes God was bringing by Wesley, the church forbade him to preach the truth in their churches. He turned from them, declared "the world is my parish," and set out with a zeal to change the hearts of his countrymen and, in the process, to create a new structure, the Methodist Church. Wesley, like John the Baptist in Jesus' day, called on men and women to repent—to have *a change of mind*— and be born again.[10]

Spiritual revival swept like wildfire throughout England and then jumped across the Atlantic. Tens of thousands of people turned out to giant open-air meetings to hear John Wesley or his contemporary, George Whitefield. England, which had been standing on the brink of moral collapse, moved to revival, public morality, and then a century of prosperity, while France was plunged into the horrors of the French Revolution and the excesses of Napoleon Bonaparte.

Targets for Change

We can be sure that even now the corrupt, outworn, ineffective, or ungodly structures of the material world have been targeted for change by those special agents chosen by God to represent the invisible world of God's kingdom. To them and to us the words of the apostle Paul ring out, "Do not change yourselves to be like the people of this world, but be changed within by a new way of thinking."[11]

This is the reason that we should never be discouraged or despair when we are confronted with entrenched evil or dogged mismanagement. The clearest reference to just such despair is found in the biblical account of the great prophet Elijah.

According to the record, the nation of Israel was ruled by

evil King Ahab and his malevolent wife, Jezebel, and had virtually abandoned the worship of Jehovah and turned to the worship of Baal.

As a consequence God sent a severe three-year drought which brought the nation to its knees. Then God directed Elijah to approach the king and demand a showdown with the priests of Baal at Mount Carmel, which overlooks the Mediterranean port city of present-day Haifa.

In that encounter, Elijah boldly proclaimed his faith in Jehovah God, was vindicated above the hapless priests of Baal, and then personally slaughtered 450 of the priests. The representative of the secret kingdom had won a smashing victory and the oppressive false system was crippled.

But Elijah did not stop there. He boldly reached into the invisible world through earnest, repeated prayer and brought forth a deluge of rain upon the parched land. But even though he had won, he fled for his life to avoid being killed by the vengeful Queen Jezebel.

His flight took him to the Sinai desert, to Mount Horeb, which we call Mount Sinai. There his exhaustion and the seeming impossibility of ever overthrowing Ahab and Jezebel led him to thoughts of death. So, he prayed to the Lord in despair, "Lord, take away my life."[12]

Then God quietly showed him that the plan of His invisible world was right on schedule. Hidden among the population was a faithful remnant of seven thousand people who had never worshiped Baal and from whom the Lord could build a new society.

Then God reached from the invisible world to the visible and ordered His servant to anoint the next generation of leaders who would bring about and manage the change that was coming: Elisha was to be the next great prophet to take Elijah's place, Hazael was to be king over Aram (Syria), and Jehu was to be king of Israel in place of Ahab and Jezebel. The Lord told him that these three were to replace the leadership of the old system of rebellion against God and bring in complete change.[13]

Elijah was one of the greatest and best of the prophets, but even the best and strongest and most godly can grow weary and discouraged by entrenched evil. The lesson of Elijah should encourage us all. In times of discouragement we need to remember that God rules in the affairs of men. When things get darkest, suddenly, unexpectedly, dramatically, His plan for change will burst forth.

A Personal Challenge

I would be remiss at the close of this chapter if I did not clearly point out the personal ramifications of the Law of Change. As we grow as individuals, each one of us develops habits, thought patterns, and conscious and unconscious attitudes that become more and more shaped by the secular world in which we live. We are shaped by a world system around us, the inner desires from within us, and the incessant urgings of a spiritual adversary we call the devil.

The force of God's Spirit becomes progressively dim as we progress in age and worldly experience. Our spirit grows callous and insensitive to communion with God. At this point, whether it occurs at age ten or age fifty, we are old skins.

If we sit in church in that condition and hear sermons and exhortations to righteousness, they will pass right over us. Our own attempts to pour New Year's resolutions or solemn resolves or moral rearmament into our lives is a waste of time. If we take these moral homilies too seriously, as many do, they have an absolutely deadening effect—taking away the pleasures and pursuits of a worldly, sinful life without having the ability to give the vibrant life of God's Holy Spirit in exchange.

I know of nothing sadder than the hapless drones who have given up a worldly life to try to please God by physical, legalistic means. In the process they become part of some extreme rigorous cult that demands abstinence, sacrifice, and poverty to serve their version of God, but these groups never offer the transforming gospel of Jesus Christ. Often it is just such unhappily legalistic people who become the pattern for "Christians" in motion pictures and popular fiction.

It is impossible to reform a tired, cracked, wineskin to receive new wine. And it is impossible to reform our cracked, broken, sinful lives by religious exercises. That is why it is absolutely imperative that worldly persons who want God must first have a change of mind, turn from the old life, and then allow Jesus Christ to remake them into vessels suitable for the new wine of God's Spirit.

Indeed God changes institutional structures and nations, but the greatest change is in the heart of the individual. To quote the apostle Paul: "If any man is in Christ, he is a new creation. Old things have passed away. Behold all has become new!"[14]

God's plan for you and me is not re-formation, but transformation into a new creation in Christ. No amount of rigorous asceticism, personal neglect, strict legalism, or even an extended devotional life will suffice. Only a new creation by the power of God's Spirit.

It should go without saying that in the final culmination of time, God will not try to place His new heavenly kingdom into a universe filled with decay and death. No, He is planning "new heavens and a new earth, wherein dwelleth righteousness" to receive his new reborn humanity. Then the invisible kingdom will become the visible kingdom and all else will "melt with fervent heat."

15

The Law of Miracles

Little by little over the past dozen chapters we have seen how the kingdom works. We have looked briefly at how our physical world appears to be approaching the outer limits of survival through its violation of the laws of the spiritual world on which everything we know ultimately stands.

We have considered how the invisible nature of that spiritual world does not diminish its reality, but merely governs who will understand it.

We have spoken of reaching into that spiritual world, touching the truth and power of God, and transferring them into the physical world. This is possible even as we hurtle toward that moment when the kingdom of God will burst into visibility and supplant all the kingdoms and powers on earth.

It is this point of reaching into the invisible and seeing its effects manifest in the visible that we should examine more closely. There is a *Law of Miracles.* It governs the question of God's willingness to disrupt His natural order to accomplish His purpose. When He does disrupt that natural order, the result is a miracle, a contravention of the natural laws through which He usually works moment by moment. He overrides the way in which things normally operate.

Since God is almighty, the only absolutely free person in the universe, not bound even by His own creation, He is perfectly able at any time to change the way things are done. He can heal a body instantly; He can still a storm; He can move a mountain. Those are miracles. Even then, however, He works within principles, and they frame the Law of Miracles.

Because of the desperate condition of our world, we still need miracles today. That means we need to understand the law and act on it, for Jesus introduced a new order of normality at the Day of Pentecost. With the power of the Holy Spirit, miracles were to be normal. He expected His followers to do even greater things than He did.[1] After all, during His incarnation He rebuked them for failing to do miracles like walking on water and casting out demons. And He praised an outsider, a Roman centurion, who perceived Christ's spiritual authority and discerned the relationship between the spiritual and the natural. "Just say the word and my servant will be healed," the centurion declared. Jesus marveled at the Roman's understanding. "I have not found such great faith with anyone in Israel," He said.[2] That is what we must recover.

The Umbrella of Faith

"Have faith in God."[3] In chapter 4, we saw that to understand how the kingdom works, we have to *begin* there. That was the umbrella given by Jesus in explaining the cursing of the fig tree. We have to *end* there, too.

Through the process of rebirth—by grace through faith—we are to see and enter into the kingdom of heaven, where the miraculous power resides. As the Lord explained to Nicodemus, this is the world of the Spirit, which is like the wind, invisible, yet frequently revealing its effects. We cannot see the wind itself, but we can see the things it moves. With the kingdom, we too observe its effects. Furthermore, we gain access to its power through our faith in Jesus Christ, through our rebirth.

We might think of ourselves as a people dying of thirst. But off in a distance there is a pool of water, a reservoir with a dam and beautiful pebble-lined banks. We can see the green trees and lush grass in its vicinity, but we can't see the reservoir itself. We desperately need to get to it.

By accepting Jesus, all that He is, all that He has done—by being born again—we gain access to this marvelous reservoir, this thirst-quenching pool of water, the kingdom of God. We are given access to an entirely new world, a heretofore invisible world—the secret kingdom.

"Have faith in God," Jesus said. Believe that God exists, trust Him, expect Him to enter into communion with you, to show you His will and purpose. Use the water in the reservoir. Remember that faith is the title deed to that pool of power.

It is all ours, if we know the *rules of miracles*.

First, *we are to take our eyes off the circumstances and the impossibilities and to look upon God and the possibilities.* We have good examples from the history of God's people for this. Remember Joshua and Caleb.[4] Representing the twelve tribes of Israel, they and ten others were sent as spies to determine if the people should enter the land promised to them by God. They stayed forty days and returned with reports of a marvelous land of milk and honey, but it was peopled with giants living in fortified cities.

"They are too strong for us," ten of the spies said.

But Caleb and Joshua, who were to figure prominently in Israel's future, were enthusiastic and eager to move ahead. "It doesn't matter how many giants there are. The Lord is with us." They looked at God and not at the circumstances, reflecting the attitude He expected of His people.

Yet the ten others prevailed, exploiting the fears of the Israelites existing since their flight from Egypt. They succumbed to their crisis, ignoring the principles of the miraculous, and failed to take what was theirs.

The biblical story of Jonathan, the son of King Saul, shows us how to focus on God rather than circumstances.[5] He and his young armorbearer, looking at a great field of enemy Philistine soldiers, put out a sign to see if God was with them. He was. So they moved to the attack, declaring that it was no harder for the

Lord to win with a few than with many. Their refusal to be de-terred by seemingly impossible circumstances led to an important victory by the entire army of Israel.

Have Faith, Never Doubting

Second, *we are not to doubt in our hearts.* We have seen that spirit controls matter, that lesser authority yields to greater author-ity, and that the mind and the voice are the instruments by which the will of the spirit is transmitted to the environment.

For miracles to happen through us, God's will must first be transmitted by the Holy Spirit to our spirits. Then, Jesus de-clared, we must not doubt in our hearts. The inmost center of our beings—which the Bible alternately terms the "heart" or the "spirit"—must be focused on the objective. Our hearts must be fully persuaded, without any doubt. We must be like Abraham, who against all hope believed God would grant him a son by his wife Sarah. "He staggered not at the promise of God through unbelief; but was strong in faith, giving glory to God; and being fully persuaded that, what he had promised, he was able also to perform."[6]

In fact, the persuasion in our spirit must be so strong that it seems to us the desired result has already taken place. As Jesus put it, "Believe that you have received" and you will have what you say.

I experienced this extraordinary *present* possession of a *future* miracle before I acquired CBN's first television station. Although my available capital was only seventy dollars, and I was without a job, and although I did not own a television set and was without any knowledge of broadcasting, motion pictures, or theater, the purchase of a station became for me a present reality. Even now it is hard to describe my inner experience at that time. The persua-sion in my spirit was so real that purchasing a station with seventy dollars seemed as possible as buying a bag of groceries at a super-market.

As an official of RCA later told me, "You sounded so positive that we thought you had the money in the bank."

To those around me who could see only the *visible* reality, I was on a fool's errand. The things I was attempting were clearly impossible. But God had given me a measure of faith, and my spirit counted God's resources as part of my reality. As Jesus said: "This is something people cannot do, but God can. God can do all things."[7]

The tentative, the hesitant, the fearful, the overly cautious, the half-hearted, and the half-persuaded will never know miracle power. They will never experience success or victory in the visible or the invisible worlds. The goals they seek will always elude them, and they will never understand why. Never, at least, until they understand that their divided minds and spirits are actually projecting the seeds of failure into every situation.

The Time to Speak

When Mark told in his Gospel of the cursing of the fig tree, he was careful to include the voice. Jesus *spoke* to the fig tree, and He told the disciples to *command* the mountain, which would do what they said if they didn't doubt in their hearts.

Scripture tells us further that Jesus stilled a storm by *speaking* to it,[8] raised three dead people by *speaking* to them,[9] cast out demons by *speaking* to them,[10] cleansed a leper by *speaking* to him,[11] and healed a Roman officer's servant by *speaking a word from a remote location*.[12]

Prayer for Jesus was communing with the Father, listening to the Father, watching the Father. What was the Father doing? What did He desire? Insight from the Father unified the heart and mind of the Son. Then, taking the authority that was His, the Son spoke the word of the Father. And the miracle happened.

So we see that miracles begin with certainty that God is present and that He has a purpose. Then we, His people, translate that purpose into the physical world by invoking His unlimited power. We do it with our mouths, speaking the word of the Lord to the mountain, to the disease, to the storm, to the demons, to the finances that God wants to send to us.

We do not pray further, unless the situation specifically calls for prayer. In one instance, Jesus said, "That kind of [unclean] spirit can only be forced out by prayer."[13] That means we pray in those cases. Jesus also prayed at the tomb of Lazarus, but He made it plain that He was doing so for the people to recognize that God was performing the miracle. Then He Himself approached the tomb and uttered the words, "Lazarus, come forth,"[14] executing God's will by speaking.

Prayer is extremely important, and we are never to neglect it. Jesus gave us example after example, going off by Himself to pray, often for hours. And the Scripture writers are relentless in their admonitions to pray. Paul went so far as to tell us to pray without ceasing.[15]

But once God's will is disclosed, then is the time to shift to speaking.

Because of the great power the Lord has given to speech, it is terribly important that we Christians not use our mouths to speak slander, profanity, lust, or foolishness. The last point is delicate. We are not to think that the Lord lacks humor or that we should not have fun. It means merely that we should avoid jokes and foolishness about sacred things, for that comes dangerously close to violation of the third commandment: "You shall not take the name of the LORD your God in vain."[16]

Why should the Lord be so deeply concerned about our use of His name that He would include the issue in the Ten Commandments? He was giving us insight into the power of speech. We have in our mouths the power to kill or to make alive. We must not take it lightly.

This significance explains why, on the Day of Pentecost when the power of the Holy Spirit came upon the disciples, an evidence of their anointing was their speaking in tongues.[17] Their voices were empowered by the Holy Spirit, a miracle that continues to be experienced by people of God today through what is known as the baptism of the Holy Spirit. From there, the disciples entered into ministry more miraculous than any they had known. They had been clothed with power from on high.[18] Their speech was a critical factor—again, not to be taken lightly.

The Major Hindrance

Having faith, seeing, refusing to doubt, speaking—all are critically important parts of the Law of Miracles. But Jesus made another point in the episode with the fig tree. Many people wish He hadn't.

> And whenever you stand praying, forgive, if you have anything against anyone; so that your Father also who is in heaven may forgive you your transgressions. But if you do not forgive, neither will your Father who is in heaven forgive your transgressions.[19]

With those few words, He set forth the major hindrance to the working of miracles in the visible world—the lack of forgiveness. Men and women, Christian and non-Christian, carry grudges. Any power of God within them is eaten up by resentment.

Is there any wonder that we see so little of the miraculous intervention of God in the affairs of the world?

We noted earlier that our initial view of God and our entrance into kingdom blessings depend on being born again and allowing the Lord to remove the cloud of sin between us and God. That unobstructed view must continue if we are to evidence the miraculous. Being born again merely sets the process in motion; we must then walk step by step in a state of forgiveness. John the apostle said it this way: "If we live in the light, as God is in the light, we can share fellowship with each other. Then the blood of Jesus, God's Son, [continuously] cleanses us from every sin."[20]

He went on to say that the one who hates his brother, who is not in a state of forgiveness with him, walks in the darkness and doesn't know where he's going. Thus walking in the light equates to living in proper relationships, which also means that we can be cleansed of our sins. The blood of Jesus does not cleanse in the dark or in a state of unforgiveness. Without forgiveness, our view of God and His kingdom is clouded. We will see no miracles.

In this matter, the Lord does not appear to be speaking of the loss of eternal salvation, for we have learned that this comes by grace through faith, not works. He is not saying a grudge will prevent you from ultimately going to heaven; He can be expected to deal with that at the proper time. Rather, He is declaring that if we want to experience now the miraculous power, say, of moving mountains, it is imperative that we live in a condition of forgiveness. Unforgiveness is not a characteristic acceptable in the kingdom of God. It contradicts the doctrine of forgiveness itself.

If all the law and all the prophets hang on loving God with one's entire being and loving our neighbors as ourselves,[21] then unforgiveness can shatter everything. It reveals, among other things, the horrible sin of pride. For only the humble can forgive—those who surrender anger, feelings, and reputation to the will of God.

No Small Matter

One well-known dialogue occurred with Peter right after a bit of instruction on unity: "Then Peter came and said to Him, 'Lord, how often shall my brother sin against me and I forgive him? Up to seven times?' Jesus said to him, 'I do not say to you, up to seven times, but up to seventy times seven.'"[22]

Increasing the impact of the lesson, the Lord went on to tell a parable about a nobleman's slave who was forgiven a debt of $10 million after coming close to being sold, along with his family, on the slave market to recover the money. The man turned around and seized another slave who owed him $100 and had him thrown into prison for nonpayment. Here is how Jesus concluded the parable:

> Then summoning him [the first man], his lord said to him, "You wicked slave, I forgave you all that debt because you entreated me. Should you not also have had mercy on your fellow slave, even as I had mercy on you?" And his lord, moved with anger, handed him over to the torturers until he should repay all that was owed him. So shall My heavenly Father also do to you, if each of you does not forgive his brother from your heart.[23]

It is no small matter, and I regret that the church through the years has not dealt more forcefully with it. As members of the kingdom, totally indebted to our loving heavenly Father, we must maintain an attitude and an atmosphere that promote harmony with our brothers. If we refuse to love our neighbors, we cannot receive blessings from our Father, and we block the flow of miraculous power.

Our principal weapon in the crises we face in the world is love, and love operates only in a state of forgiveness and reconciliation. Pettiness must go, and jealousy and pride and lack of concern for others, and neglect of the poor and needy.

Letting Go, Letting God

I have a close friend, Demos Shakarian, the founder of the Full Gospel Businessmen's Fellowship, one of the outstanding ministries in the world, who told me a story from his own life that reinforces the reality of the Law of Miracles as well as any I know.

At death, his father left a sizable fortune in property. In that period of grief and legal confusion, a family friend stepped in and legally, yet questionably, took advantage of the grieving children to gain control of a part of the estate.

Demos, when he realized what had happened, became angry and a seed of bitterness took root in him. A deep and churning resentment grew, worsening as he reflected on the nature of a man who would take advantage of those who trusted him.

One day God showed Demos that if he was to please Him, he would have to deal with this resentment. He would have to forgive the man.

That was a difficult instruction from the Lord. The family friend was guilty. He had done something wrong to make money. Yet God said, "You must forgive him."

So, despite the spiritual struggle, Demos telephoned the man and arranged a meeting. I'm sure the man expected a confrontation and perhaps a shouting match; that's the way those things usually work out. But Demos, Spirit-filled and familiar with the purposes of God, followed through and said: "I want to ask your forgiveness. I've harbored resentment against you over what happened. I've actually hated you. But I've been wrong and I've repented before God, and I totally forgive you for anything you may have done. And now I ask your forgiveness."

It was more than the man could stand. He began to weep, and the uniqueness of the moment broke him internally. Someone he had treated badly was actually asking him for forgiveness! It was upside down.

Demos recalled that he immediately felt the flow of God's power in his own life. He was thoroughly free.

The two embraced and were reconciled.

In a matter of days, Demos received a call from an official of a corporation that owned a store on another piece of his property. The corporation had closed the store, and the future of the building and lease were unsettled. However, the official said, "You've been so nice to us that we're going to give you the store."

Again, things were upside down. That sort of thing simply was not done.

Without lifting a finger, Demos had overnight received a building worth far more than the disputed inheritance. There was no quarreling or legal fighting. God had moved miraculously once the roadblock of unforgiveness had been removed.

Furthermore, his ministry, which centers on the miracle-working power of God, is flourishing to this day. Continuous forgiveness and continuous love are the crucial ingredients in the Law of Miracles.

Miracles Are Available

If we would live in the kingdom of God today, by grace through faith, we would see far more miracles. We need only look at Paul's relatively compact, but nonetheless illuminating, instructions to the early Corinthian church to discover the miracle experiences that were considered normal.[24] He spoke of the "manifestations" that the unblocked presence of the Holy

Spirit within God's people would bring forth, declaring that these were for the common good.[25] There was nothing elitist or abnormal about them.

> For to one is given the *word of wisdom* through the Spirit, and to another the *word of knowledge* according to the same Spirit; to another *faith* by the same Spirit, and to another *gifts of healing* by the one Spirit, and to another the *effecting of miracles*, and to another *prophecy*, and to another the *distinguishing of spirits*, to another *various kinds of tongues*, and to another the *interpretation of tongues*.[26]

These are the supernatural evidences of God's favor and grace. They are among the effects of the blowing of the Spirit in our lives that the Lord was talking about with Nicodemus. You can't see the Spirit, which He likened to the wind, but you do see His effects.[27] When the wind blows, tree leaves move. When the Spirit blows other things move as well.

In my unending quest for wisdom, it turned out that the "word of wisdom" was a miracle of God that developed special meaning for me. All the gifts of the Spirit are exceedingly important when springing from faith, hope, and love, but the supernatural bestowal of the word of wisdom is to be cherished.

The word of wisdom, as I indicated in chapter 6 when talking about wisdom in a broader sense, is a glimpse into the future regarding a specific event or truth. It is an unveiling.

Many people think prophecy is futuristic, and it often is. But not always. Prophecy specifically is "forth-telling"—speaking forth the Word of God. Quite often it deals with the present, or perhaps even the past.

I was praying one day early in 1969, and the Lord spoke plainly to my inner man: "Communism will collapse in the Soviet Union, but then they will be the most dangerous. Fidel Castro will fall in Cuba. There will be a great opportunity for the gospel. The stock market will crash. Only the securities of your government will be safe."

By 1992 I can surely say that Communism has fallen in the Soviet Union, and in the former Eastern Bloc there has been the greatest opportunity for the gospel in the history of mankind. Fidel Castro has not yet fallen, but rumors have it that he has been negotiating an exile in Spain. In 1969 there was a market crash as there was in 1974, but I believe the big one has not yet happened and may soon be upon us. Whatever happens, in this it is clear that God speaks today to those who will listen so that they may prepare His people for what is to come.

Passing on the Blessing

Part of my motivation for taking the time and effort to produce my newsletter, *Pat Robertson's Perspective,* for "700 Club" members is to transmit to the people of the kingdom the insights the Lord has given me concerning these matters. And the Lord has steadily increased this miraculous manifestation in my life and in ways more directly affecting the ministry than just the performance of the stock market.

One day some years later, at a prayer meeting regarding a then upcoming telethon in which we needed to raise the funds to meet the budget of our expanding outreach, the Lord spoke a word of wisdom as part of a prophecy. He responded to our concern about the burden we carried if we were to fulfill the mission He had given us.

I was speaking in prophecy about the presence of the Lord in what we were doing, and then the word of wisdom came regarding the telethon several days thence: "It will be so marvelous that you will not believe that it is happening. And yet this is going to happen before your eyes, and when it does happen, do not give credit to yourself, to your program people, to your computer operators, or to any of the things you have done. But give Me credit because I am telling you now that I am going to do it. And when it's over, you will see it and you will know who did it."

Of course, the word was fulfilled and we dramatically exceeded our goal. He met our need and the need of the people we were ministering to.

And we could give no one else the credit. Despite the difficulty of the circumstances, we were in God's will and He was with us. According to the pattern revealed by the prophet Isaiah, He had proclaimed the "new things" He was doing, even before they sprang forth.[28]

Probably the most frequent occurrence of the miraculous in my life has involved the word of knowledge, touching on physical or emotional healing or other interventions by the Lord in the lives of people. Such a word quite simply reveals information the natural mind would not know about a condition or a circumstance in which God is acting. And there have been memorable times when, quite unwittingly on my part, the "word of knowledge" has actually been an unveiling of something that was to occur in the future—a "word of wisdom."

For example, a woman in California was watching "The 700 Club" while sitting in a great deal of discomfort from a broken ankle encased in a cast. She heard me say on the air, "There's a woman in a cast. She has broken her ankle, and God is healing her."

The woman immediately knew, in a burst of faith in her spirit, that those words had been spoken for her. She rose from the chair, removed the cast, and, with increasing confidence, began to put weight on the broken foot and then to jump on it. The ankle bone had been healed.

The thing she did not know was that she had been watching a program taped a week earlier and shown in her area at that time. Further checking uncovered that I had actually spoken the words about her ankle before it had been broken. In a word of wisdom, I had spoken about something that was yet to occur. The Lord has caused this to happen many times over the years in my ministry.

He wants each of us to reach up into the invisible world and allow Him to perform miracles through us in the visible world. He will do it without limits of time or circumstances. He waits for us to practice the principles He has set forth in Scripture.

The University Miracle

One of the most miraculous moves in my life, covering numerous laws of the kingdom and spanning several years, involved the establishment of our CBN headquarters, a graduate university (Regent University), and a lovely hotel and conference center.

I had wanted to buy five acres in the city of Virginia Beach, which was burgeoning at that time, as a possible headquarters site. The owner of the land, however, refused to sell a portion of the 143-acre tract.

But the situation changed the day I was sitting in the coffee shop of the Grand Hotel in Anaheim, California. Invited to a conference at the Melodyland Christian Center, I had arrived late for the opening luncheon and was eating alone. When my meal arrived, I bowed my head to say grace—and the Lord began to speak to me about the site three thousand miles away. People around me in the busy shop must have thought I was terribly grateful for the simple cantaloupe and cottage cheese before me, for I remained in prayer for a long time.

"I want you to buy the land," the Lord said. "Buy it all," He said. "I want you to build a school there for My glory, as well as the headquarters building you need."

I had not thought of a school before. True, we desperately needed a headquarters building. But did we need 143 acres? When I returned to Virginia, I called the banker holding the major mortgage on the property and told him I wanted to buy the entire site and build a school on it. "Praise the Lord!" he exclaimed.

I hadn't been able to get anywhere with my small thinking about five acres, but suddenly I had acquired what God had directed—an interstate site worth $2.9 million, with a gift of $550,000 in equity, nothing down, no principal payments for two years, and the balance of the mortgage at 8 percent simple interest payable over twenty-three years.

The terms could hardly have been more favorable! Furthermore, the Lord wasn't finished. He later enabled us to acquire more than five hundred additional acres at prices that today seem nothing short of miraculous. The magnificent center standing on that property to-day is eloquent testimony to the power of God and the operation of the Law of Miracles. Although I didn't know it at the time, the story had begun long before my California dialogue with the Lord. I eventually learned the following facts.

First, seven years before our acquisition of the site for the center, an Assembly of God minister had seen and shared with a friend of mine a vision of an international center on that same land. It would be a center reaching out to the world with the gospel. It would have students and dormitories, among other things, and would serve missionaries from around the world.

Second, at a point just ten miles from the site I had purchased, the first permanent English settlers in America had planted a cross on the sandy shore and claimed the land for God's glory and for the spread of the gospel. After 370 years, the ultramodern television facility with worldwide capabilities began to fulfill their dreams.

But that was not the only tie to those English settlers. I learned that a college had been part of their vision. Indeed, they had planned Henrico College as a school to teach the gospel and train young men and women for Christian service, hoping to reach the world through education. The plans for the college did not succeed. But the settlers believed the vision would last, as revealed in an introduction to a sermon pertaining to the overall settlement activity: "This work is of God and will therefore stand. It may be hindered, but it cannot be overthrown." They expected their descendants to rise to the challenge.

Unknown to me at the time we bought the land, I am a collateral descendant of the man of God who led the first settlers in prayer in 1607, and a direct descendant of the surgeon who arrived in 1619 at Jamestown with those who were to build Henrico College.

Trust and Never Doubt

The miracle has enlarged beyond my dreams in 1975, when God said to buy and build. Regent University has a graduate population today of 1,450 students representing all 50 United States and 40 foreign nations. Our distinguished law school continues to grow at an incredible rate, and recently enrolled 121 first-year students. Registration is up more than 50 percent in the law school this year over the previous year, and interest is growing.

Associated with the law school now is our American Center for Law and Justice, headed by two of America's most outstanding lawyers, Keith Fournier and Jay Sekulow. Jay Sekulow has gained an international reputation for his success in defending cases involving Christian values and constitutional principles at the highest levels, including victories before the United States Supreme Court.

In addition to degree programs leading to the juris doctor degree, the master's degree, and the doctor of philosophy in communications, Regent University is now offering programs leading to the master of business administration, master of education, master of divinity, and a master of arts in biblical studies.

Clearly, this university is a miracle of God. God had a plan. If miracles were required to fulfill it, then He performed miracles—all according to the laws of His kingdom.

The Bible teaches that when Jesus Christ comes back to earth to rule His millennial kingdom, prophecy will cease, the gifts of knowledge and tongues will cease, and visions will cease because we will be in the presence of the living Lord.

We will not need those things at that time because Christ will reveal all things to us. He is Alpha and Omega, the beginning and the end. Things that are imperfect will be done away with, and we will see the essence of perfection revealed in Jesus Christ Himself.

Until that time, however, we need His life and His spiritual weapons. He has charged us to occupy until He comes again, and He has empowered us to do just that, because we need His miracle power today more than ever.

16

The Law of Dominion

I was praying and fasting some years ago, seeking to understand God's purpose more fully. I heard His voice, level and conversational, "What do I desire for man?"

A bit surprised, I replied, "I don't know, Lord. You know." Then the Lord directed me to open my Bible. "Look at Genesis, and you will see," He said.

Genesis is one of the longest books in the Bible, but I opened it at the beginning. As I read along, my eyes fell on this passage:

> And God said, Let us make man in our image, after our likeness: and *let them have dominion* over the fish of the sea, and over the fowl of the air, and over the cattle, and over all the earth, and over every creeping thing that creepeth upon the earth. So God created man.[1]

"Let them have dominion." My eyes went over it several times. Then I knew the Lord's purpose. He wanted man to have dominion—then and now.

It was very clear. This was a kingdom law. God wants man to have authority over the earth. He wants him to rule the way he was created to rule. You cannot help but juxtapose this desire of God with today's reality. The thousands of letters that pour into

CBN, the pages of the newspapers, the screens of our television sets reveal anything but a people maintaining authority over their environment.

Christians especially show the symptoms of a defeated people. Many are sick, depressed, needy. They live in fear and confusion. Where, observers fairly ask, is the conquering army sung about in the great church hymns? Where is the blessing promised in the Bible from beginning to end? Was Jesus wrong when He said, "I will build my church; and the gates of hell shall not prevail against it"?[2]

No, Jesus was not wrong. Hell will not prevail. But we are seeing an Old Testament warning lived out among the people of God, and indeed all mankind: "My people perish for want of knowledge."[3] Men haven't been taught the Law of Dominion and the other principles of the kingdom. That is why they are miserable.

But they can change immediately.

As in the Beginning

Almighty God wants us to recapture the dominion man held in the beginning. He has gone to great lengths to make that possible, sending His own Son as the second Adam to restore what was lost in Eden.

Remember, at the time of creation, man exercised authority, under God's sovereignty, over everything. He was God's surrogate, His steward or regent.

The Genesis account uses two colorful words to describe this. One, *radah,* we translate as "dominion." Man was to have dominion. The word means to "rule over" or "tread down," as with grapes. It comes from a Hebrew root meaning "spread out" or "prostrate." The picture we get from it is one of all the creation spread out before man, whose dominion would extend wherever his feet trod.

The other word, *kabash,* is translated as "subdue." Man was told to subdue the earth. The root means "to trample under foot," as one would do when washing dirty clothes. Therefore, in *kabash* we have in part the concept of separating good from evil by force.

With the first word, God gives man the authority to govern all that is willing to be governed. With the second, He grants man authority over the untamed and the rebellious. In both instances, God gave man a sweeping and total mandate of dominion over this planet and everything in it.

But stewardship requires responsibility. And implicit in the grant was a requirement that man order the planet according to God's will and for God's purposes. This was a grant of freedom, not of license. As subsequent history proved, God's intention was that His world be governed and subdued by those who themselves were governed by God. But man, as we know, did not want to remain under God's sovereignty. He wanted to be *like God* without having anyone to tell him what to do.

The progression toward the Fall is enlightening. First, note that God, after giving man dominion over the fish, the fowl, the cattle, and all the earth, specified that this authority extended to "every creeping thing that creepeth upon the earth."[4] Man specifically had dominion over serpents.

Then, we ask, what happened when Eve was faced with a challenge by the serpent? She faltered and allowed the serpent to convince her that God's grant of sovereignty was faulty. She refused to exercise her authority, and, worse than that, the serpent took authority over and manipulated her. Worse yet, with that first erosion, mankind allowed virtually all of his dominion to slip away.

It was the Law of Use in operation: Refuse to use what you have been given and you will lose it. Since that time, Satan has been exercising a type of dominion over human beings, deceiving them, destroying them.

God wants man to repossess that original dominion. He is ready to cause the Law of Use to work in our favor, if we will but begin to exercise what has been given.

A Shift of Allegiance

We need to understand that God did not actually take the dominion away from man. He simply took away man's access to

Him because of sin. Man still had dominion, but he lost the relationship and understanding necessary to exercise it properly. From there, the condition deteriorated as man voluntarily gave himself to the dominion of others.

As a result, man has for ages been neglecting and even misusing that which he was told to rule and subdue. He has, in effect, raped the creation rather than take care of it. He has lost the humility and discipline to exercise dominion as God intended. He has exercised it arrogantly, or not at all. He hasn't been a servant of the creation—the animals, the oceans and rivers and streams, the forests, the mountains, the resources. He has violated the Law of Responsibility.

It is clear that God is saying, "I gave man dominion over the earth, but he lost it. Now I desire mature sons and daughters who will in My name exercise dominion over the earth and will subdue Satan, the unruly, and the rebellious. Take back My world from those who would loot it and abuse it. Rule as I would rule."

Included in God's grant of dominion to man was sovereignty over flowers, vegetables, and fruit. The mandate was all-inclusive: "Behold, I have given you every plant yielding seed that is on the surface of all the earth, and every tree which has fruit yielding seed; it shall be food for you."[5]

In one of the tragic ironies of all history, the Fall meant not only that man became a slave of Satan and his own base passions, but also that a sizable portion of mankind would become slaves of flowers, vegetables, and fruit. We have learned that those three can be cruel taskmasters.

According to the statistics published by David Barrett and Todd M. Johnson in 1990, there are more than 650 million men and women worldwide, and a skyrocketing number of children, addicted to the tobacco plant. Of this number, there were 2.6 million tobacco-related deaths in 1990 alone. In addition, there are more than 170 million alcoholics worldwide—victims of corn, barley, rye, and grapes—with at least 20 million in the United States.

These products are involved in more than 70 percent of the fifty-five thousand accident-related deaths on American highways each year. What a fearful toll these addictive stimulants take on human strength, creativity, and happiness.

Yet even more insidious is the weed, *cannabis*—called grass, pot, or marijuana—which has sucked a staggering number of young people into deeper and more destructive addictions over the past three decades. Along with formulated drugs, such as amphetamines, and street drugs, such as crack, crystal, cocaine, heroin, and others—each in some way a corrupted derivative of a plant or natural product—addictive substances are destroying the brains and the futures of entire generations of Americans.

As I reported in more detail in my book, *The New Millennium,* U.S. Justice Department statistics show that 58.5 percent of Americans between the ages of twenty-six and thirty-four have used marijuana and nearly 25 percent have used cocaine. For many these easy-to-get drugs are considered "gateway" drugs to even harder and more dangerous substances. We shudder at the fortunes that change hands and the crimes that are committed by those under the dominion of the coca plant and the opium poppy. The number of people convicted of drug possession in this country doubled in the decade of the 1980s, and the number convicted for manufacturing drugs increased 180 percent.

The drug industry in North and South America is larger than the entire United States automobile industry and apparently more profitable. The alcohol industry rakes in more than $65 billion each year in the United States alone. Despite a growing public reaction against smoking, the tobacco industry gathers in billions more per year. So valuable is cigarette brand awareness that the trade name "Marlboro" and the companion cowboy were recently calculated to be worth $39 billion, more than any other trade name in the world. Of the 50 million deaths worldwide each year, fully fifty thousand are the result of "second-hand smoke"—that is, breathing the smoke exhaled by another person.

The evidence shows that well over half of America's staggering $738 billion medical bill can be attributed to illnesses induced by slavery to these items—vegetables, flowers, and fruit. Yet the statistics only reveal a part of man's slavery. The losses in terms of trials forced on the hearts and souls of these people, and on their mental, physical, and spiritual stability, are incalculable.

But almost every attempt to set people free from these forms of slavery is met with derision. It does not matter that they lead to death, disability, and degradation. Those living outside the kingdom clutch their "pleasures" to their bosoms as if they were holy and sacred rights.

A False Consensus

You see, when man broke free of God's authority, he lost control of himself. Without a clear relationship with God, he became unable to see where he was going, and he soon became captive of what the Bible calls "the world, the flesh, and the devil." His own fears, his animal drives, his lusts drove him. The devil, a malevolent power, played upon his base desires to seduce and entrap him. Then, as the human race grew, each man became a slave of mob psychology—the tyranny of the warped consensus of a sinful world.

Before the world can be freed from bondage, man must be made free from himself. This is why Jesus told the Jews of His day: "If you abide in My word, then you are truly disciples of Mine; and you shall know the truth, and the truth shall make you free."[6]

Again, the writer of the letter to the Hebrews, speaking of the effect of the death of Jesus for mankind, said: "that through death He might render powerless him who had the power of death, that is, the devil; and might deliver *those who through fear of death were subject to slavery all their lives.*"[7]

When man, through Jesus, reasserts God's dominion over himself, then he is capable of reasserting his God-given dominion over everything else. That is the way everything on earth will be freed from the cycle of despair, cruelty, bondage, and death.

I furthermore believe the Lord would have man subdue the natural forces in the universe. Jesus, who was our example as well as our Redeemer, did this, as we have discussed in earlier chapters.

Without in any way advocating fanaticism, I believe God would enable man, under His sovereignty, to deal successfully with the conditions that threaten the world with catastrophic earthquakes. Scripture makes plain that God uses natural disasters as judgment upon mankind, but I am convinced that were man to turn from his wicked ways and seek the Lord, he would be able to take dominion over the faults in the earth's structure and render them harmless. For the words of Jesus spoken to the tumultuous waters of Galilee still echo down through history with great power and authority: "Peace, be still."[8]

Similarly, man, taking his rightful place under God, would subdue the causes of drought and famine. World hunger would cease.

Dominion Theology

The Law of Dominion should not be confused with the teachings of what is sometimes called "dominion theology" or "reconstructionism." Reconstructionists believe that through the discipline and authority of the church and the empowerment of Christ, Christians will ultimately reclaim the earth as the kingdom of God and bring peace and unity to all mankind. It is the idea that man, through his own efforts, is going to reconstruct the fallen earth and bring in the millennial kingdom.

While there are elements of this belief which are biblical, in general this view is mistaken. It is a fairly extreme interpretation of the Scriptures, and that is not at all what I want to imply in this chapter.

We have more authority now than any of us dreamed possible, but I do not believe that man, through his efforts, is going to bring the world back to a time of Edenic innocence. The millennial kingdom will not come until Jesus Himself does it, but that does not mean that we should not strive in His name. The great commission says, "Go therefore and make disciples of all the nations, baptizing them in the name of the Father and of the Son and of the Holy Spirit, teaching them to observe all things that I have commanded you; and lo, I am with you always, even to the end of the age."[9]

When I was writing *The New World Order,* God revealed to me in the most palpable way that the biblical prophecies concerning the coming kingdom, given by the prophets Isaiah and Micah, are to be taken absolutely literally. The Law of the Lord is going to go forth from Jerusalem. All the people are going to say, "Let us go to Jerusalem, for there is the Law of the Lord, and we will walk in His ways." I have been privileged to live that out. When I travel abroad now, men and women at all levels of society, from heads of state to taxi drivers, are saying to me, "Teach us the Law of the Lord." The Bible proclaimed the people would cry out, "Teach us that we might walk in His ways."

A high official in Romania came up to CBN Vice-President for Development Michael Little and said: "Look, I am an atheist; I don't believe in God or Jesus Christ, and I don't believe in the Bible. But I know that if we are going to build a just society in Romania, we have to build it on the Bible."

He said, "We want your Bible on our national television in Romania." So, consequently, today CBN programming is teaching the Bible in animated Bible stories over Romanian television Monday through Friday at 7:30 P.M., throughout that entire nation. Not only that, the Romanians are inviting teachers of religion to come into their schools to instruct them in the Law of the Lord.

In Search of Wisdom

This same scenario is being repeated all across Eastern Europe, in Africa, and in many other Third World nations. The kings, presidents, and government officials are saying, "What is the ideal society?" "What is a Bible-based society?" "How do you organize and manage an orderly society?" They want to learn God's Law.

We broadcast a report from Russia on CBN News in the summer of 1991 in which a young woman who had grown up under Communism made a challenging comment. She said, "When we look at America, we see prosperity, comfort, success, and relative peace. When we look at Russia, we see poverty, despair, unhappiness, and strife. So we ask ourselves, what is the main difference between Russia and America? and the answer is, in America you have God; in Russia, we have no God. So now we are changing. We want to know about God. We want to know about the Bible. We want to know Jesus Christ."

If indeed all men would walk according to His Law, it would be a whole new world we would be living in, but obviously they are not. The idea that we are going to bring in the millennium by ourselves is, in my estimation, false theology.

God's Fellow Workers

The concept of man's dominion over the created order is too much for us to comprehend unless we get a secure grip on the fact that the Lord thinks of us as fellow workers with Him in the development and operation of His kingdom.

Mark, in his Gospel, tells how the disciples went out after Christ's ascension and "preached everywhere, while the Lord *worked with them.*"[10]

Paul, in his first letter to the Corinthians, reminded them that it was perfectly proper for both him and Apollos to be ministering to them. "We are God's *fellow-workers,*"[11] he said.

Later, in a passage describing Christians as "ambassadors for Christ" to whom God has committed the message of reconciliation, he spoke of "*working together* with Him."[12]

You see, the Bible's view is that God, in a mystery too great for us to fathom, has chosen to use men to carry the truth around the world. To accomplish this, He had to give them authority.

In addition, the Bible speaks of that time when God's kingdom and His Christ will visibly rule on earth. "If we endure," Paul wrote, pointing to the Law of Perseverance, "we shall also *reign with Him.*"[13] That will involve exceptional authority. God wants us to prepare for it.

We see this exemplified in the accounts of the Lord's sending His disciples out to minister: "Jesus called the twelve apostles together and gave them *power* and *authority* over all demons and the ability to heal sicknesses. He sent the apostles out to tell about God's kingdom and to heal the sick."[14]

Obviously, in the Lord's mind authority went hand in hand with the proclamation of the kingdom. Authority authenticated the kingdom. How would it be possible to say there was a kingdom of God that was to supplant the kingdom of Satan unless it carried power and authority?

Those two words, "power" and "authority," have a significance of their own, too. First, the passage says, the Lord gave them "power," which is translated from the Greek word *dunamis*. It means "resident power." Dynamite, for example, has that kind of power. Christians who have the Holy Spirit operating in their lives also have it. It is the power to perform miracles.

But the Lord also gave them "authority." This is translated from the Greek word *exousia*. It, too, carries with it the idea of force and power, specifically in the sense of authority like that of a magistrate or potentate.

Kingdom Authority

Quite simply, Jesus gave them power to perform miracles and authority to use that power over the devil and all creation. At another time, speaking to seventy people who had gone out to minister, Jesus said: "Listen, I have given you power to walk on snakes and scorpions, *power that is greater than the enemy has*."[15]

With that, He was referring directly back to the Fall, for serpents are a remembrance not only of the deception in the Garden of Eden, but also of the curse that followed. Serpents and men have been at enmity ever since God said the seed of Eve would one day bruise the head of the serpent,[16] pointing to the triumph of Christ over the devil and his works.

So, in giving His followers such authority, Jesus was indeed saying, "I reestablish your authority over the one who robbed you of it in the garden. You can reassert your dominion."

246

Our problem in the twentieth century, as we perish for lack of knowledge, is that it does us no good to have this authority if we don't exercise it correctly. And most of us don't.

Yet we have tried so hard in many cases to take seriously the words Jesus spoke to His people before ascending to heaven to sit at the right hand of His Father. We must examine those words closely and with understanding: "And Jesus came up and spoke to them, saying, '*All authority* has been given to Me in heaven and on earth. Go therefore . . .'"[17]

In the long and moving prayer Jesus spoke in the hearing of the disciples just a few hours before His arrest and trial, he prayed to the Father, saying "I [have] accomplished the work which Thou hast given Me to do."[18] He had destroyed "the works of the devil,"[19] which especially included the robbery performed in the Garden of Eden. He, the King of the kingdom, had "all authority."

"Therefore," He declared, "go!"

His people could move out to accomplish their worldwide task because He had restored man's dominion under God.

Satan's Strategy

Satan, although defeated, is alive today, of course, and is as dangerous as we allow him to be. His primary weapon is deceit, and he uses it to prevent Christians from exercising the authority that is truly theirs in this world.

First, of course, he tries to entice us into sin, which can cloud or obstruct our view of the Lord and His will and, untended, can separate us from God.

He also tries to lead us into another form of sin, through unbelief. He tries to make us feel unworthy of the grace in which we stand. If he gets the upper hand in this, then we neglect the authority and the power given to us. They fall into disuse and, ultimately, vanish like the mist. The dominion that has been so awfully and awesomely won for us serves no purpose if it is not exercised.

We must combat this with all our strength and all our alertness. We must not be deceived.

We should recognize that we, in fact, *are* unworthy but that through the Lord Jesus we become worthy in the sight of God. We are sinners but, like Paul, who described himself as chief and foremost among sinners,[20] we "can do all things through Him who strengthens" us.[21]

Too many times, people fall into the devil's trap of believing that we can somehow earn our dominion. If we fall for that, we will never feel worthy, and we will never use the dominion given us. And we will never overcome the crises in the world.

If Satan can keep us in a state of timidity, discouragement, or embarrassment, he will nullify our authority and delay the manifestation of the kingdom of God on earth. I have been amazed in recent years by the success of this very simple maneuver. He has rendered Christians ever so slightly embarrassed about being Christians. The world, for example, sees nothing wrong with a person carrying a copy of *Playboy* or *Penthouse* magazine around under his arm on the street, in the bus or subway. The same with a bottle of whiskey or a carton of cigarettes, with all of its life-threatening ingredients. Yet vast numbers of Christians have been intimidated about carrying a Bible on the street or bus or subway. They're afraid of being categorized as religious freaks, or perhaps old-fashioned and out-of-step with the world. They are nervous about being discovered in prayer or other attitudes perceived as different. As for authority—whether it be over Satan or over the natural order—their timidity is overwhelming.

And yet, as we have noted before, the Bible says, "God has not given us a spirit of timidity, but of power and love and discipline."[22]

Neither Satan nor the world has the authority nor the power to limit or impede the Lord's people. They are flying directly in the face of God's desire. He wants us to assume our rightful authority and to hasten the coming of the kingdom on earth. Jesus emphasized this when He said: "And this *gospel of the kingdom* shall be preached in the whole world for a witness to all the nations, and then the end shall come."[23]

You see, there are many signs of the times that we can watch for, but this one is most critical. The gospel of the kingdom in all its fullness and power, with all its authority, is to be carried to every nation. Timidity must vanish. There will be "signs and wonders"[24]—miracles and other evidences of the kingdom.

The Law of Dominion, properly exercised, will guarantee that.

It Must Be Voiced

In practical terms, the Law of Dominion works much like the Law of Miracles. It depends on the spoken word. We are to take authority by voicing it, whether it involves the devil or any part of the creation.

We should not argue with Satan. We merely tell him that he has to go, that he has no authority, that he must release this person or that situation. Quite bluntly, we say, "In the name of Jesus, I command you to get out of here, Satan!"

Also, reaching the mind of the Lord, we tell the storm to quiet, the crops to flourish, the flood water to recede, the attacking dog to stop. We simply speak the word aloud.

Again, the central point is to "have faith in God."[25] But we do not have to await a directive from Him in ordinary circumstances as to when to exercise the authority, assuming that we are walking in His will and yielded to His sovereignty. For He has already given us general guidelines: "Be fruitful and multiply, and fill the earth, and *subdue it;* and *rule* over the fish of the sea and over the birds of the sky, and over every living thing that moves on the earth."[26]

This especially covers "every creeping thing that creeps on the earth," symbolizing the one described in Christ's time as "the ruler of this world,"[27] who has now been utterly defeated. Even though we still must struggle against those forces that willingly choose to ally themselves with Satan, that struggle has already been decided.

The apostle Paul described it this way: "For our struggle is not against flesh and blood, but against the rulers, against the powers, against the world forces of this darkness, against the spiritual forces of wickedness in the heavenly places."[28]

But since the authority for winning that struggle has been granted, Paul was confident that Christians will "stand firm" in "the evil day." The instrument for wielding that authority, he said, is the Word of God, which he described as the "sword of the Spirit."[29]

We simply are to speak forth our God-restored authority, preparing for an even more amazing era.

17

The Coming King

*J*esus said an astounding thing to His disciples: "You have been chosen to know the secrets about the kingdom of God."[1] For three years, Jesus walked and talked with His disciples, and He taught them the principles of the kingdom in intimate detail. But when He commissioned that first group of twelve and sent them out into the world to spread the good news of salvation, He challenged them to "make *disciples*, . . . baptizing them in the name of the Father and the Son and the Holy Spirit." If you have received that good news and believed it, it follows that you, too, are a disciple, and you have been permitted to know the mysteries of the kingdom.

Why would the Savior of the world want to share His privileged secrets? The reason is simple, but very important. He wants all people to live in that realm right now, to master its principles so they will be ready to share in the culmination of the age—His divine new world order.

Uncovering the Mysteries

If you are not a disciple of Jesus, the mysteries of the kingdom are bound to remain clouded and confusing for flesh and blood cannot inherit the kingdom of God.[m] You must be born of the Spirit and receive access to that secret kingdom. That can occur this moment, merely by asking Jesus Christ to be your Lord and Savior and to take up a spiritual residence in your heart. For God desires that you not miss out on anything; that is why He has been so patient these thousands of years.[3]

From the beginning of man's history, the Lord has been intent on establishing—through love, not fear—a kingdom of people who will voluntarily live under His sovereignty and enjoy His creation. That is the thrust of His entire revelation made in what we call the Holy Bible. He is building a kingdom. And a new, major step in that building shows signs of being at hand. The invisible world may be ready to emerge into full visibility.

One can almost hear Jesus speaking to His church: "Beloved, be ready. I have shown you the laws of My kingdom, the way things truly work. Use them. Live them. They will work for good even now."

There is a new world coming. And we already know ten of its principles!

The Law of Reciprocity teaches the golden rule as the foundation of all personal, national, and international relations.

The Law of Use teaches the key principle of success in life.

The Law of Perseverance teaches that the best in life will only be given to those who struggle and persevere.

The Law of Responsibility teaches that God's increasing blessings bring increased obligations to others.

The Law of Greatness teaches that we achieve true greatness when we love others and serve them selflessly.

The Law of Unity teaches that those who share a common vision can change their world.

The Law of Fidelity teaches that true riches will only accrue to those faithful with what God has entrusted to them.

The Law of Change teaches that God's spiritual kingdom requires continuous change in the old structures of this world.

The Law of Miracles teaches that in the secret kingdom nothing is impossible.

The Law of Dominion teaches that God intends man to reign over this earth as His steward.

Having been explicitly stated in Scripture, these principles are God-breathed. They will change the world as we know it and prepare the way for the coming new world, even speeding its arrival. They, and they alone, can calm the crises choking the world and thwart the imminent slide into chaos and dictatorship of the right or the left. They pose a realistic alternative.

The Outlook

So on the foundation of these laws and the words of the prophets, here is what we can expect to happen in the days, months, and years ahead.

The nation of Israel is God's prophetic time clock. Having been regathered from the countries of the world, Israel, a unified nation living in relative security, will be invaded by a confederation from the north and the east. The prophet Ezekiel described this force as massive, coming like a storm, a cloud covering the land. He identified elements of it as "Gog of the land of Magog, the prince of Rosh, Meshech, and Tubal," joined by "Persia, Ethiopia, and Put," along with "Gomer," "Beth-togarmah from the remote parts of the north," and "many peoples."[4]

Various people have been viewed as Gog and Magog throughout history—the Goths, the Cretans, the Scythians—but the land described by Ezekiel would be directly to the north. Among the present-day nations that have been suggested by biblical scholars as allies to this confederation are Ethiopia, Iran (as Persia), Somalia, and Libya (as Put). The Muslim republics that formerly comprised the southern region of the old Soviet Union may possibly be included.

It is noteworthy that, at this writing, there is mounting tension and strife in all those regions. Conflicts with and between renegade Arab leaders, of course, continue to make headlines; however, there is also a dangerous rise in fierceness, fear, and famine, stretching from Somalia and Ethiopia to the northern frontiers of the Middle East.

People have asked me quite often over the past year, "What is the significance of Saddam Hussein and the 1991 Persian Gulf War?" I have to say that I have the distinct impression that the war with Iraq was the necessary prelude to that bigger confrontation yet to come.

By that I mean that there will come a time when the nations will unite to pressure Israel to conform to the dictates of the so-called new world order. In the disturbances in Iraq, Syria, Lebanon, and Turkey today we are seeing the early symptoms of that process.

In Jeremiah 23, the prophet makes it clear that instead of saying, "Blessed be the Lord God of Israel who brought His people out of the land of Egypt," the people will cry out, "Blessed be the Lord God of Israel who brought his people out of the land of the north." In sheer numbers, the current exodus from Russia is much greater than the original exodus from Egypt. That this should happen now cannot be accidental.

I believe the settlement of those Russian and European Jews is critical to the fulfillment of prophecy. Personally, I always like to cooperate with prophecy, not fight it! If God has a purpose—as He certainly does in Israel—we don't want to be seen as opposing it. Now that the United States is offering Israel loan guarantees for $10 billion, the process will be accelerated.

The Temple Restored

One of the clear signs given by Scripture that would signal the beginning of the "time of troubles" is the rebuilding of the ancient temple in Jerusalem. Until 1948, the very idea of a Jewish homeland seemed impossible; until 1967, the idea of a restored

Jerusalem seemed impossible; and until 1991, the idea of a recon-
structed temple seemed impossible. But each of these steps has
now been taken, and it is clear that the prophets were revealing
God's perfect truth, not holy metaphors.

As additional evidence, today archaeologists are unearthing
the foundations of the ancient temple in Jerusalem. They now
know that the actual site of the Hebrew temple is, in fact, the one
at the foot of the Dome of the Rock. The Muslims are not resist-
ing the excavations because the Jewish site does not immediately
affect their mosque, but the foundation stones, the pavement, and
even the massive columns of the temple are being uncovered. This
is an enormously important sign to students of biblical prophecy.

Discovery of the ancient Hebrew temple after thousands of
years is just one more indication that the march of world events is
right on schedule. And if the uncovering and rebuilding of the
temple takes place according to the Scriptures—which of course
it will—then this may be a confirmation that what is happening
today in Russia and the Confederation of Independent States is,
indeed, just a temporary stage.

It may also be that when that land is finally reunited and the
critical social issues are resolved to some degree there will be a
movement to take up arms against the nation of Israel, perhaps
through the provocation of the belligerent Arab nations surrounding her—such as Syria, Iran, and Iraq, and now the former Muslim republics of the Soviet Union.

These events have great consequence in light of Ezekiel 38.
For years, like many students of the Bible, I thought that the references in the prophetic writings to the nations of the North referred only to the Soviet Union. Now I have begun to believe it is
more likely the Muslim republics—such as Kazakhistan, Tadzikhi-
stan, Uzbekistan, and Azerbaijan. Should these nations align with
Iran and Iraq to form a coalition against Israel, and should the
Confederation somehow arm, support, finance, or even join them
in that effort, this would be a perfect fulfillment of the prophecy.

At this moment we can see that the growing number of Russian refugees inside Israel could well become a factor in some sort

of dispute. As I pointed out in chapter 15, I knew that the Soviet Union would collapse; as far-fetched as that idea seemed at the time, it proved to be true. Their destruction did not take place because they invaded Israel, but it was the first step toward breaking loose the Muslim republics who could quite possibly form an unholy alliance—and possibly a new state—against the Jews.

Imminent Struggle

The Palestinian issue continues to incite bitter strife. At issue is some sort of autonomy for the Arabs living within Israel, for which a satisfactory compromise may well be possible. However, from the United Nations to the PLO, public figures are demanding that Israel turn over the West Bank region and the Gaza Strip to Arab rule. On that volatile issue there is no room for compromise.

If the Israelis were ever forced to surrender sovereignty over the provinces of Judea and Samaria, which are very important parts of the Holy Land, that would surely set off a bitter struggle. We must not forget that the land of Palestine was given to the Jews by divine decree. America and its leaders stand against God's purpose in these matters at their peril.

Nevertheless, the globalist thrust is against Israel, has been, and always will be. When the northern forces move against Israel and its "unwalled villages"—"to capture spoil and to seize plunder"—questions will be raised by people identified as "Sheba, and Dedan, and the merchants of Tarshish, with all its villages [or young lions]."[5] Ezekiel did not say that these people would resist the invaders, but merely ask, "Why have you come here?"[6]

These questioners can probably be pinpointed as Yemen, Saudi Arabia, and the United States, which was once settled by people who could be identified as Tarshish merchants. Tarshish was probably a Phoenician settlement in Spain, near Cadiz, that sent ships to Ireland, then to England, and on to the New World— their passengers traveling all over what was to become the United States of America. *If* there is a reference in the Bible to America, that would seem to be it.

Whether these questioners will assist Israel is unclear. Regardless, God, who is even in control of the invading horde from the north, will intervene in Israel's behalf with a great shaking—earthquakes, volcanic activity, fire, confusion, and even fighting among the allied invaders. He also speaks of fire falling upon Magog, the homeland of the leaders of the force, and upon "those who inhabit the coastlands in safety." This could, of course, be a vision of a nuclear holocaust. But it may also be the direct, miraculous intervention of God, for the prophecy says the following very pointedly: "And My holy name I shall make known in the midst of My people Israel; and I shall not let My holy name be profaned anymore. And *the nations will know that I am the LORD, the Holy One in Israel.*"[7]

According to Ezekiel, this will be followed by seven years of Israeli ascendance as the nation grows strong in the Middle East and increases in knowledge of the Lord, climaxed by a nationwide outpouring of the Holy Spirit.

Words of Revelation

At the same time, the Book of Revelation appears to point to a successor kingdom to the Roman Empire that could roughly parallel the current European Community.[8] It is a ten-nation confederation that has an eleventh nation added, apparently along with a merger of two of the nations, and that league could then be a forerunner of what the apostle John called the Antichrist. Presumably this group will make a treaty with Israel and then turn on her and begin to oppress her.

The leader of this confederation will be a spiritual being who will become a counterfeit Christ and draw men's allegiance. Exploiting confused, chaotic conditions, he will turn the league into a dictatorship, thus poising two kingdoms—the kingdom of God and the counterfeit kingdom—for climactic conflict.

Revelation points to another development that will be instrumental in this period. A system of buying and selling that utilizes individual marks will make possible the economic control of the world's population. The tremendous explosions in computer technology have made this feasible. Even now in Brussels, the headquarters of the European Economic Community, a giant computer system—an interbank transfer system—makes it possible to give every person in the world a number and allocate credits and debits on the basis of that number. I understand that the technology now exists and has been successfully tested to allow an identification device of some type, including a tiny microchip, to be implanted under the skin of the hand. This is nothing short of a fulfillment of prophecy which, only a few years ago, seemed improbable if not impossible.

Banks will institute debit cards, with the capacity to debit accounts instantly, and eliminate the need for exchange of currency. Today many companies and government agencies are using so-called smart cards, which contain a remarkably powerful magnetic strip capable of adjusting debit and credit balances as the card is scanned at the point of sale. The next logical step is to control buying and selling through a similar device in one's hand, as indicated in Revelation.[9]

Whatever the technological possibilities, we should keep in mind that the "forehead" signifies volition or will, and the "hand" signifies action. People will submit their wills and their actions to the Antichrist system, with or without the implanted smart cards.

Thus, one scenario seems capable of fulfillment at almost any time: A major war erupts in the Middle East, with the armies of the northern nations leading the assault upon Israel. That force is destroyed; a catastrophic upheaval results, in which oil supplies to Europe and elsewhere are cut off. Europe is thrown into economic shambles, setting the stage for the sudden rise of a charismatic and resourceful dictator to move swiftly to establish his new economic order.

The Return of Messiah

In the meantime, the kingdom of God will move forward, its future never in doubt. Those who choose to live by its rules will do so and be continuously prepared for that time in history when Jesus Christ will return to earth. The Bible says that He will come back to destroy this new political leader and his "kingdom," setting up in its place a reign of peace and justice forever.[10] At that moment, the invisible kingdom will become a visible one. The secret kingdom will be a secret no longer. And the world—the principalities and powers and the angelic host—will see the way God intended for His universe and His society to function.

We need to understand that God will not abandon His world. He has from the beginning been concerned about the historic record and about His own justification. He does not act arbitrarily. It is as though He will send Jesus, then gather His archangels, the angels, the entire heavenly host and say, "Look, this is the way the world would have worked had man not sinned. This is what I desired." God does not have to justify Himself. He merely does it because He is a God of love and order and justice.

But that will not be the end. It might almost be called a transition period, between the earth as it has been and the ultimate plan of God, in which evil and opposition to the Lord will finally be removed and paradise established.

The Bible says this transition period will cover a thousand years, hence the name "Millennium."[11] In it Christ will reign and there will be peace. He will hold everything together and His greatness will be manifest for all the world to see. He will be revealed in the fullness of what the Scripture has been proclaiming for centuries: He is altogether righteous and perfect; there is no failing in Him; His wisdom is absolute.

Seven hundred years before the birth of Jesus Christ, the prophet Isaiah wrote:

> For a child will be born to us, a son will be given
> to us;
> And the government will rest on His shoulders;
> And His name will be called Wonderful
> Counselor, Mighty God,
> Eternal Father, Prince of Peace.

> There will be no end to the increase of His
> government or of peace,
> On the throne of David and over his kingdom,
> To establish it and to uphold it with justice and
> righteousness
> From then on and forevermore.
> The zeal of the LORD of hosts will accomplish
> this.[12]

Speculation will not be necessary. The beauty of the Lord will be evident to all, as is described in the vision of John:

> And I saw heaven opened; and behold, a white horse, and He who sat upon it is called Faithful and True; and in righteousness He judges and wages war. And His eyes are a flame of fire, and upon His head are many diadems; and He has a name written upon Him which no one knows except Himself. And He is clothed with a robe dipped in blood; and His name is called The Word of God. And the armies which are in heaven, clothed in fine linen, white and clean, were following Him on white horses. And from His mouth comes a sharp sword, so that with it He may smite the nations; and He will rule them with a rod of iron; and He treads the wine press of the fierce wrath of God, the Almighty. And on His robe and on His thigh He has a name written, "KING OF KINGS, AND LORD OF LORDS."[13]

The laws of the kingdom will prevail, and His people will govern with Him. Food, water, and energy will be ample. No longer will trillions of dollars be spent on weaponry. It will go for parks and forests, for scientific advances as yet beyond imagination.

But if His people are to govern with Him under these circumstances, they need answers to several big questions. How do you run a just government? How do you run a world? Which principles work and which do not?

That is why Jesus spoke so often about the kingdom. He let His apostles teach about the church. He, the King, spoke of the kingdom and how it works. He wants us to master these principles so we will be able to serve with Him properly.

Remember, those who are great now will become the least, and those who are least will become great.[14] He will take the little people, His kingdom saints, and exalt them to positions of power. The wealthy, the arrogant, the oppressors—they will be diminished. Their authority will go to the saints, "the fulness of Him who fills all in all."[15]

The Removal of Evil

The Bible says that at the end of the transition period, Satan will be allowed to lead a revolt of those who have still refrained from voluntarily accepting the rule of Christ. Then, after a relatively short period, the Lord will remove Satan (along with all evil and opposition) and bring forth "a new heaven and a new earth."[16] This will be the ultimate and eternal kingdom.

Jesus spoke at some length about the removal of evil in a story that has come to be known as the parable of the tares.[17] It tells of a man who sowed good wheat seed in his field, but at night someone sowed tares—false wheat, weeds—in the same field. Both the wheat and the tares grew, and when the landowner was questioned, he said, "An enemy has done this!"[18] But he wouldn't allow his workers to root up the tares for fear of what damage would be done to the wheat. "Let them both grow," he said, "and at the time of harvest I'll tell the reapers to put the wheat in the barn but to gather the tares for burning."

Later, when Jesus was alone with His disciples, they asked Him the meaning of the parable.

And He answered and said, "The one who sows the good seed is the Son of Man, and the field is the world; and as for the good seed, these are the sons of the kingdom; and the tares are the sons of the evil one; and the enemy who sowed them is the devil, and the harvest is the end of the age [the consummation]; and the reapers are angels. Therefore just as the tares are gathered up and burned with fire, so shall it be at the end of the age [the consummation]. The Son of Man will send forth His angels, and *they will gather out of His kingdom all stumbling blocks,*

261

and those who commit lawlessness, and will cast them into the furnace of fire; in that place there shall be weeping and gnashing of teeth. THEN THE RIGHTEOUS WILL SHINE FORTH AS THE SUN in the kingdom of their Father.[19]

Everything that is offensive will be removed from the kingdom of God, not by men or the church or military might, but by the angels. They will know the righteous from the evil, and they will know how to act.

At that point, the "sons of the kingdom" will be the only ones left, basking in the light of the Lord, living in ultimate reality and perfection.

Jesus reinforced this understanding for His disciples, following the parable of the tares with one about fish, for several of His close followers were fishermen. He compared the kingdom of heaven to a dragnet cast into the sea to gather fish of every kind. When it was hauled in, the good fish were sorted into containers, but the bad were thrown away. The explanation was the same as before: "So it will be at the end of the age [the consummation]; the angels shall come forth, and take out the wicked from among the righteous."[20]

At this moment, our minds cannot comprehend the perfection that will exist then. We can't even speak about it. Our ideas and words are still too limited.

But think of this: What would it be like if all the energies of men and all creation were founded 100 percent on love? Or consider it in reverse: What if there were not a single trace of hatred anywhere?

That is the world God created for us. No pride, no greed, no fear, no crime, no war, no disease, no hunger, no shortages.

The Final Step

The Bible speaks of a step in this progressive unfolding of God's perfect plan that would appear to come after all the other phases. It sets forth magnificently the unity and harmony of the

Godhead and the ultimate unity and harmony of all creation.

The apostle Paul spoke of it in a complex passage on the sequences of the resurrection of the dead. The point we should see in our context is illuminated clearly:

> For as in Adam all die, so also in Christ all shall be made alive. But each in his own order: Christ the first fruits, after that those who are Christ's at His coming, *then comes the end, when He delivers up the kingdom to the God and Father,* when He has abolished all rule and all authority and power. For He must reign until He has put all His enemies under His feet. The last enemy that will be abolished is death. FOR HE HAS PUT ALL THINGS IN SUBJECTION UNDER HIS FEET. But when He says, "All things are put in subjection," it is evident that He is excepted who put all things in subjection to Him. And when all things are subjected to Him, then the Son Himself also will be subjected to the One who subjected all things to Him, that God may be all in all.[21]

Again, these plans exceed our capacity for thought. Jesus, the Son and King, in whom all things will be summed up and united in the fullness of time,[22] will present everything to His Father for all eternity.

What Will Men Do?

So, then, here we stand. What will men do? Will they continue to ignore the principles governing the way the world works? Or will they learn from the secret kingdom?

I appeal to people everywhere to lay hold of the truths of our world—the Bible's insights into the way it works—and to put them into action. There is still time.

• Give and it will be given to you. This principle will not fail. We simply must begin to execute it—individuals, families, companies, nations. Imagine what our times would be like if we treated others the way we wanted to be treated.

- Take what you already have and put it to use. Don't wait until you have everything you want. Use what you have. Multiply it exponentially, consistently, persistently. The wonders of the world will explode into fullness.

- Do not give up. Persevere. Endure. Keep on asking, keep on seeking, keep on knocking. The world will keep on responding.

- Be diligent to fulfill the responsibility required of you. If God and men have entrusted talent, possessions, money, or fame to you, they expect a certain level of performance. Don't let them down. If you do, you may lose everything.

- Resist society's inducements to success and greatness and dare to become a servant, even childlike. True leadership and greatness will follow. The one who serves will become the leader.

- Reject the dissension and negativism of the world. Choose harmony and unity at every level of life—unity centered on the will of God. Mankind flowing in unity will accomplish marvelous results in all endeavors.

- Be humble enough, yet bold enough, to expect and to do miracles fulfilling the purpose of the Lord. Once and for all, become aware of the power of your speech as you walk humbly and obediently.

- Be faithful in the calling with which you have been entrusted; for whoever is faithful in a few things will be entrusted with even greater things.

- As a follower of the Son of God, be prepared to be an agent of change, but don't frustrate yourself trying to put new wine in old skins. Watch God create new structures to fulfill His plan for you, assume the authority, power, and dominion that God intends for men to exercise over the rest of creation. Recapture that which prevailed in the Garden of Eden before the Fall. Move with power and authority.

- Obviously, there are other laws of the kingdom that the Lord wants us to learn, and He will reveal them if we seek Him.

But we can, and should—indeed, we must—begin to adhere to those that are now plain before us.

True, "the axe is already laid at the root of the trees,"[23] as John the Baptist warned nearly two thousand years ago, and those things running contrary to God's purpose will be cut down. The process has presumably already begun. But all is not lost. God's plans will not be circumvented. Yet the movement to ultimate fulfillment need not be one of terror and agony. The crises of the world can be relieved. Just in themselves, the laws of the kingdom can accomplish that. The world can be a far better place as it moves toward fulfillment.

His laws will bring blessing by themselves, but at some point, however, the laws of the kingdom outside of the kingdom will not be enough. A choice will have to be made regarding the kingdom itself. For one day there will be a final shaking by God; then only the kingdom will survive.[24]

So, why wait? Why separate the truths contained in the laws of the kingdom from allegiance to the King? Choose Him this moment. It can all be yours right now!

"Don't fear, little flock, because your Father wants to give you the kingdom."[25]

Notes

Introduction

1. Compare Matt. 15:13 KJV.
2. Matt. 3:2.
3. Matt. 26:46.
4. Matt. 4:17.
5. Acts 1:3 NCV.
6. Luke 4:43 NCV, emphasis added.
7. Luke 17:21.

Chapter 1 • The Visible World

1. T. S. Eliot, "The Waste Land," 1932.
2. Isa. 59:10–12 NKJV.
3. Isa. 57:21 NKJV.
4. Francis A. Schaeffer, *A Christian Manifesto* (Chicago: Crossway, 1981), 24, 26.

Chapter 2 • The Invisible World

1. Mark 1:15 NKJV.
2. Matt. 10:7.
3. Matt. 6:31–34 NKJV.
4. Mark 4:22–23 NKJV.
5. Matt. 6:33.
6. Matt. 4:17.
7. 1 Sam. 10:25 KJV.

8. 2 Kings 6:16.
9. Rom. 8:19.
10. Matt. 16:28.
11. Matt. 17:2–6, 8.
12. Mark 10:27.
13. John 5:19.
14. Matt. 8:26.
15. Mark 11:14 NCV.
16. Mark 11:17 NCV.
17. Mark 11:22 NCV.
18. See Rev. 4:2.
19. Gen. 1:3.
20. Eph. 3:20.
21. Mark 11:23–24.
22. 1 Cor. 3:9.
23. Matt. 3:2.
24. Matt. 12:25.
25. Matt. 6:33.
26. See Rev. 20:4.
27. Matt. 3:3.
28. Isa. 11:9.
29. Isa. 2:4.

Chapter 3 • Seeing and Entering

1. John 1:30.
2. John 1:34.
3. See Matt. 7:29.
4. See Matt. 16:16.
5. See John 3:1–21.
6. John 3:3, emphasis added.
7. John 3:4.
8. John 3:5, emphasis added.
9. See John 4:24.
10. See Gen. 2:17.

11. See John 3:6.
12. See John 1:12–13.
13. See Genesis 1–2.
14. John 3:7–16.
15. John 19:38–42.
16. 1 Cor. 2:12–13, emphasis added.
17. Matt. 28:18–20, emphasis added.
18. See 1 Cor. 2:14.
19. Matt. 18:3.
20. Luke 12:32.
21. John 4:23–24, emphasis added.
22. John 14:6 NCV, emphasis added.
23. Matt. 7:21, emphasis added.
24. John 18:33–37 TLB, emphasis added in last two sentences.
25. John 8:26, 31–32, emphasis added.
26. Ezek. 36:26–27, emphasis added.
27. John 14:17.
28. John 8:44 NCV.
29. Rev. 21:27 KJV.
30. Rev. 21:8 KJV.
31. See Col. 1:16.

Chapter 4 • How God's Kingdom Works

1. See Matt. 13:11.
2. See Matt. 13:3–8.
3. See Matt. 14:16–21.
4. Luke 2:52, emphasis added.
5. Mark 1:10–11 NKJV; see also Luke 3:22.
6. See Eph. 2:8–18.
7. See Heb. 4:14–16.
8. Eph. 2:4–7, emphasis added.
9. See Num. 6:24–25.
10. Jer. 23:18.
11. Mark 11:23–24 NKJV.

12. Gen. 1:3.
13. See Genesis 1.
14. See John 1:3.
15. See Gen. 1:2.
16. Mark 11:24 NCV.
17. 1 Cor. 2:16.
18. 2 Tim. 1:7.
19. Ezek. 37:4.
20. Ezek. 37:7–10, emphasis added.
21. Isa. 55:11.
22. Ps. 37:4–5 NKJV.
23. Heb. 11:1–3, 6 NKJV.
24. Heb. 11:1 TLB, emphasis added.
25. Rom. 10:17 KJV.
26. James 1:6–8.
27. Prov. 3:5–6 NKJV.
28. See Matt. 17:20.
29. 1 John 5:14, 15.
30. Mark 8:36–37 NKJV.
31. Prov. 13:2.
32. Phil. 4:13.
33. See Prov. 23:7 KJV.
34. See Ps. 51:6.
35. Matt. 12:50 NCV.
36. Gal. 5:22–23.
37. Matt. 18:19–20 NCV.
38. 1 Pet. 4:1–2 NKJV.
39. 3 John 1:2 NKJV.
40. Deut. 28:11–14 NKJV.
41. Deut. 28:15 NKJV.
42. Luke 6:38 NKJV.
43. Ps. 37:23–24 KJV, emphasis added.
44. Ps. 37:33.

Chapter 5 • Progressive Happiness

1. See Exod. 3:14.
2. See Judg. 6:24.
3. See Exod. 17:15.
4. See Gen. 22:14.
5. See Matt. 5:3–12.
6. Luke 18:13–14 KJV.
7. See 2 Cor. 7:10 KJV.
8. Ps. 51:17.
9. 2 Pet. 2:6–8 KJV and NASB.
10. See Gen. 19:1–26.
11. Matt. 24:38–39.
12. Jer. 31:13.
13. See Num. 12:3 KJV.
14. 2 Tim. 1:7, emphasis added.
15. Matt. 11:12.
16. See Rom. 5:17.
17. See Gal. 4:4–7; 2 Pet. 1:3–4.
18. 1 Cor. 6:9–10.
19. Acts 1:8.
20. Matt. 5:6 KJV.
21. Luke 11:9.
22. Matt. 6:24.
23. See Rev. 19:16.
24. See Rom. 8:17.
25. See Rom. 5:1.
26. 2 Cor. 5:18–20 NCV.
27. Luke 2:14 KJV.
28. Matt. 5:10–11.
29. 1 Pet. 4:14, emphasis added.
30. See John 3:19.
31. See 2 Cor. 2:15–16.
32. See Acts 8:3.

Chapter 6 • Upside Down

1. James 4:6 KJV, emphasis added.
2. Phil. 2:8.
3. Phil. 2:9, emphasis added.
4. Prov. 22:4.
5. Prov. 16:18.
6. See Jer. 29:13–14.
7. 2 Chron. 1:7.
8. 1 Kings 3:7.
9. 2 Chron. 1:10.
10. 2 Chron. 1:11–12.
11. Matt. 6:33.
12. Prov. 9:10.
13. 1 Cor. 13:13 NCV.
14. See Eph. 2:8.
15. Rom. 5:1–4, emphasis added.
16. Rom. 5:5.
17. See Ps. 37:9.
18. See John 1:5.
19. See Rom. 12:21.
20. Matt. 5:41 NCV.
21. See Rom. 12:20.
22. 1 Cor. 13:4–8.
23. Matt. 5:14 NCV.

Chapter 7 • The Law of Reciprocity

1. Luke 6:38.
2. Luke 6:31.
3. Luke 6:36–38.
4. Matt. 22:39, see also Lev. 19:18.
5. Luke 6:38 KJV.
6. Luke 6:38.

7. Matt. 6:33 NKJV.
8. Matt. 7:1.
9. Luke 6:38 NCV.
10. Mal. 3:7–10, emphasis added.
11. Mal. 3:10 TLB.
12. 2 Cor. 9:6–8, 11.
13. 1 Chron. 29:12, 14.
14. Ps. 24:1 KJV.
15. Luke 6:38 NCV.
16. Ps. 37:25.
17. Ps. 37:10–11.
18. E.g., Exodus 21–22; Lev. 18:24, 20:1–27, 21:9.
19. James 4:7 NCV.

Chapter 8 • The Law of Use

1. Matt. 25:14–15.
2. Matt. 25:26–27, 30.
3. Matt. 25:29.
4. Matt. 13:31–32 NCV.
5. Mark 4:26–29 NCV.
6. Matt. 4:8–9.
7. See John 12:31; 14:30.
8. Deut. 23:19.
9. Deut. 15:6, emphasis added.
10. Lev. 25:4.
11. Lev. 25:8–10, emphasis added.
12. Exod. 25:9, emphasis added.

Chapter 9 • The Law of Perseverance

1. Col. 1:16 NKJV.
2. 2 Cor. 4:18 NKJV.
3. Phil. 4:13 NKJV.

4. Rom. 8:37 NKJV.
5. Phil. 4:6–7 NKJV
6. John 10:10 NKJV.
7. Matt. 7:7–11.
8. Matt. 11:12.
9. Luke 18:1–8.
10. Luke 11:5–8.
11. Acts 14:22.
12. 1 Kings 19:4.
13. See 1 Cor. 10:13 NCV.

Chapter 10 • The Law of Responsibility

1. Luke 12:48 KJV.
2. See Luke 12:46–48.
3. James 3:1.
4. 1 Tim. 3:1–7 NCV.
5. See 1 Tim. 3:10.
6. Mark 4:11.
7. Rom. 1:14.
8. John 14:6.
9. 1 Tim. 3:15.
10. Matt. 28:18–20.
11. See Matt. 16:18.
12. Euripides, *Alcymene*, c. 485–406 B.C.
13. Sophocles, *Ajax*, c. 495–405 B.C.
14. Luke 12:47.
15. George Gilder, *Wealth and Poverty* (New York: Bantam, 1982), pp. 30–31 ff.
16. Mark 11:22.
17. Isa. 58:1–11 TLB.
18. Isa. 58:1–2 TLB.
19. See James 1:22–25.
20. Isa. 58:3–4 TLB, emphasis added.

21. Isa. 58:6 TLB, emphasis added.
22. Isa. 58:7 TLB.
23. Isa. 58:8–9 TLB.
24. Isa. 58:10–11 TLB, emphasis added.

Chapter 11 • The Law of Greatness

1. Matt. 18:2–4 NCV, emphasis added.
2. Luke 22:25–27, emphasis added.
3. See Gen. 1:28.
4. Matt. 23:11 (paraphrased).
5. Matt. 23:12, emphasis added.
6. Prov. 22:4.
7. See Luke 14:28.

Chapter 12 • The Law of Unity

1. Gen. 1:26, emphasis added.
2. See Gen. 3:5.
3. Gen. 3:22–23, emphasis added.
4. Matt. 6:10, emphasis added.
5. Matt. 18:19–20, emphasis added.
6. See Deut. 32:30.
7. Acts 1:14, emphasis added.
8. See Acts 11:26.
9. Acts 13:1–3 NCV.
10. See Acts 13:1, 9.
11. See Acts 4:33, 36.
12. John 17:23.
13. Gen. 11:1.
14. See Gen. 11:4.
15. Gen. 11:6–8, emphasis added.
16. See Rev. 14:8.
17. See James 1:6–8.

18. James 1:6 NCV.

19. See Rom. 4:13–21.

20. Ps. 57:7 KJV.

21. Luke 10:38–42.

22. See Matt. 6:24.

23. See Eph. 5:25.

24. Eccles. 9:10 (paraphrased).

25. Matt. 12:25.

26. Prov. 11:29.

27. James 1:8.

28. 1 Cor. 12:4–7, emphasis added.

29. John 17:20–23.

Chapter 13 • The Law of Fidelity

1. Luke 16:10–12 NIV.

2. Rev. 22:15 NIV.

3. Luke 16:11 NCV.

4. Luke 12:47 NCV.

5. 2 Cor. 5:10; see also Rom. 14:10.

6. See Neh. 8:10.

7. Matt. 25:21 NKJV.

Chapter 14 • The Law of Change

1. Eccles. 1:9 NIV.

2. Mal. 3:6 KJV.

3. See 1 Kings 8:47.

4. Ps. 121:4.

5. Isa. 34:4.

6. See Luke 5:36–38.

7. Matt. 9:17 NIV.

8. 2 Cor. 3:17.

9. See Isa. 6:8.

10. Luke 3:3 NIV.

11. Rom. 12:2 NCV.

12. 1 Kings 19:4 KJV.

13. 1 Kings 18–19.

14. 1 Cor. 5:17.

Chapter 15 • *The Law of Miracles*

1. See John 14:12.

2. Matt. 8:10.

3. Mark 11:22.

4. See Numbers 13–14.

5. See 1 Sam. 14:1–15.

6. Rom. 4:20–21 KJV.

7. Mark 10:27 NCV.

8. See Mark 4:39.

9. See Mark 5:38–42; Luke 7:11–16; John 11:43.

10. See Mark 9:25.

11. See Matt. 8:3.

12. See Matt. 8:13.

13. Mark 9:29 NCV.

14. John 11:43.

15. See 1 Thess. 5:17.

16. Exod. 20:7.

17. See Acts 2:4.

18. See Luke 24:49.

19. Mark 11:25–26 (many manuscripts do not contain verse 26).

20. 1 John 1:7 NCV.

21. See Matt. 22:37–40.

22. Matt. 18:21–22.

23. Matt. 18:32–35.

24. See 1 Corinthians 12–14.

25. 1 Cor. 12:7.

26. 1 Cor. 12:8–10, emphasis added.

27. See John 3:8.
28. See Isa. 42:9.

Chapter 16 • The Law of Dominion

1. Gen. 1:26–27 KJV.
2. Matt. 16:18 KJV.
3. Hos. 4:6 JB.
4. Gen. 1:26 KJV.
5. Gen. 1:29.
6. John 8:31–32.
7. Heb. 2:14–15, emphasis added.
8. Mark 4:39 KJV.
9. Matt. 28:19–20 NKJV.
10. Mark 16:20, emphasis added.
11. 1 Cor. 3:9, emphasis added.
12. 2 Cor. 5:20; 6:1, emphasis added.
13. 2 Tim. 2:12, emphasis added.
14. Luke 9:1–2 NCV, emphasis added.
15. Luke 10:19 NCV, emphasis added.
16. See Gen. 3:15.
17. Matt. 28:18–19, emphasis added.
18. John 17:4.
19. 1 John 3:8.
20. See 1 Tim. 1:15.
21. Phil. 4:13.
22. 2 Tim. 1:7.
23. Matt. 24:14, emphasis added.
24. Rom. 15:19.
25. Mark 11:22.
26. Gen. 1:28, emphasis added.
27. John 12:31.
28. Eph. 6:12.
29. Eph. 6:13, 17.

Chapter 17 • The Coming King

1. Luke 8:10 NCV.
2. 1 Cor. 15:50.
3. See 2 Pet. 3:9.
4. See Ezek. 38:2, 5–6, 9.
5. Ezek. 38:11–12.
6. Ezek. 38:13 (paraphrased).
7. Ezek. 39:7, emphasis added.
8. See Rev. 17:9–14.
9. Rev. 13:16–17.
10. See Revelation 19.
11. See Rev. 20:2, 4, 7.
12. Isa. 9:6–7.
13. Rev. 19:11–16.
14. See Luke 9:48.
15. Eph. 1:23.
16. Rev. 21:1.
17. See Matt. 13:24–43.
18. Matt. 13:28.
19. Matt. 13:37–43, emphasis added.
20. Matt. 13:49.
21. 1 Cor. 15:22–28, emphasis added.
22. See Eph. 1:9–10.
23. Matt. 3:10.
24. See Heb. 12:25–29.
25. Luke 12:32 NCV.